ETHCASTE

*PanAfrican Communalism
and the Black Middleclass*

Douglas V. Davidson

University Press of America,® Inc.
Lanham · New York · Oxford

Copyright © 2001 by
University Press of America,® Inc.
4720 Boston Way
Lanham, Maryland 20706

12 Hid's Copse Rd.
Cumnor Hill, Oxford OX2 9JJ

Library of Congress Cataloging-in-Publication Data

Davidson, Douglas V.
Ethcaste : PanAfrican communalism and the Black
middleclass / Douglas V. Davidson.
p.   cm
Includes index.
1. Afro-Americans—Social conditions—1975- 2. Afro-Americans—
Race identity. 3. Afro-American families. 4. Middle class—
United States. 5. Pan-Africanism. I. Title.
E185.86 .D377   2000   305.896073—dc21   00-048909 CIP

ISBN 0-7618-1915-0 (cloth : alk. ppr.)

DEDICATION

This manuscript is dedicated to all AfricanAmerican women struggling to maintain and perpetuate AfricanAmerican peoplehood, but especially to those who have been and continue to be essential to my being:

MRS. ORA WILEY-MULLINS
Maternal Grandmother (deceased*)*

MRS. LYDIA W. MULLINS-THOMAS
Mother

MRS. JENNY R. DAVIDSON
Wife

MS. MIDORI DENISE DAVIDSON
Daughter

MS. SHARDIER L. BEARD
Step-Daughter

MRS. HARRIET STUBBS
Godmother (deceased)

MRS. VELMA MINER
Godmother (deceased)

DR. CHARLOTTE "CHARSHEE" LAWRENCE-MCINTYRE
Friend and Mentor (deceased)

TABLE OF CONTENTS

ACKNOWLEDGEMENTS

F ew works of this length are ever the result of a single individual. That statement is especially true for this effort. I have had the love, warmth and companionship of family, friends, colleagues and students. To mention all of them would be beyond the scope of these few lines. However, I would like to single out the following individuals for special thanks.

I want to thank my parents, Lydia W. Mullins-Thomas and William J. Davidson, for caring about each other enough to conceive me. I especially thank my mother and her maternal extended family for nurturance through the years. This work is a reflection of what they raised me to "see" and how they taught me to think. Thus, it is not my manuscript, but *OUR* manuscript. Indeed, the same holds true for my brothers and sisters (the Slate-Davidson-Thomas Clan) who have contributed in their own special way. We BE, therefore, I am.

I would also like to express my deep appreciation to those who have served as my mentors (and sometimes role-models) during my student life. The late Professor Ernst Borinski, of Tougaloo College, was both teacher and friend as I navigated the uncertain waters of the social sciences while an undergraduate. Professors Benjamin Shepard, John T. Braxton (coach), Marvin Hoffman, John T. Salter, and Helen B. Williams—also of Tougaloo College—contributed in their unique styles toward stimulating and directing my academic interests. Given my anti-intellectual undergraduate "head," they had their work cut out for them.

During my graduate student tenure at the Illinois Institute of Technology, I had the pleasure of working with and being influenced by several faculty friends in the Sociology Department. I am expecially indebted to Professors Howard F. Taylor, Kenji Ima, and Daisy Tagliacozzo. Their theoretical approaches and methodological techniques contributed immensely to my evolution as a sociologist. Although I have moved in intellectual and political directions different from theirs, I am certain that they will recognize the fruits of their labors.

I was also fortunate to meet and to become friends with several fellow graduate students during my stay at Illinois Tech: Andrew Gale, Thomas Hilliard, Hillary Knight, Annie Bell Williams, Walter Davis, Robert Holden, and Walter Herrs, to name a few.

When I matriculated at the University of California at Berkeley, I experienced the esteemed friendship and intellectual acumen of several politically astute and innovative social scientists. I wish to express the gratitude I feel and the debt I owe to Professors Robert Blauner, Troy Duster, Herbert Blumer, Andrew Billingsley, and Kenneth Simmons. In addition, I was blessed with the warm friendship of several AfricanAmerican graduate student peers: Albert Black, Jr., Hardy T. Frye, the late Fredricka Teer, Ken Noel, Teresa Green, William H.L. Dorsey, Howard and Jualynne Dodson, George Napper, Jr., Donald J. Davis, Carl Mack, Jr., Ida F. Rousseau, Ortiz Walton, Douglas and Doris Daniels and my good friend and fellow rent striker, Brother Horace Upshaw. I am certain that each will recognize the results of numerous animated, prolonged, intense and provocative discussions we have shared.

During my teaching career, I have had the pleasure and good fortune to engage in dialogue with several leading AfricanAmerican scholars. However none have influenced me as much as Vincent Harding, William Strickland, Lloyd Hogan, James Turner, Charshee and Ken McIntyre, and the Honorable Nana Kobina Nketsia IV. The list would be incomplete without mentioning my very good friend and former colleague, Andrea Benton Rushing, who was both a warm, nurturant supporter and critical reviewer. She and her lovely daughter, Osula Rushing endured and shared the agonies and anxieties accompanying the initial draft of this work. Jah, Love and Blessings.

I must say special thanks to Ms. Henriette Martineau for diligently typing several drafts of the manuscript and to Ms. Linda Mizzell-Taylor

Acknowledgments

for her excellent assistance as a library researcher — verifying footnotes and organizing the bibliography. Also, a note of thanks to the staff of the Amherst College library who gave generously of their time and expertise. Other friends and colleagues at Amherst who deserve special mention include Professor James Maraniss for his editorial comments and the late Dr. John W. Ward, former President of Amherst College, and Dr. Prosser Gifford, Professor of History and Dean of the Faculty, offered both critical comments and assisted with small faculty development grants to defray expenses.

Additionally, I would like to extend thanks and appreciation to my friend and colleague Dr. Elaine Nichols, Curator of the African American Exhibits at the South Carolina State Museum, for her astute remarks on the quality of the manuscript. The aforemetioned William Dorsey and his professorial colleague, Ojeda Penn were also generous enough to read and make timely comments. Further thanks go to Professor Dorsey for both his final-stage editorial contributions and computer layout and typesetting.

Last, but far from least, the manuscript benefited tremendously from the critical, integrative suggestions of my former wife, Leslie Hill. I also must acknowledge and give thanks for all of the help, guidance, and technical expertise I received over the past two years from the Director, Carl R. Blackman, and the staff, Mario Brathwaite, Marc P. Seybold, Trevor L. McKenzie, and Nancy E. Vatalaro of the State University of New York/College at Old Westbury's Educational Technology Center. This final edition owes a tremendous debt to the late Dr. Charshee Lawrence-McIntyre for both technical assistance and editorial revisions. A very special note of thanks to all of my students — past and present, graduate and undergraduate — who were both a source of constant encouragement and spiritual inspiration. If this work assists you to acquire more clarity in your lives, it will have been well worth the effort.

As with any work which takes literally years to bring to fruition, the author often goes through several life changes. That most certainly has been the case for this one. All that to say thanks to my current wife, Jenny, and our lovely daughter, Shardier, for enduring the mood swings, hyper-activity, and occasional emotional "lows" which characterized the last months as I completed this process. I know that it was difficult to share living space with a chronic "absent-minded" professor/writer. Thanks for your patience.

The work is clearly a collective effort and I hope this final product is a true reflection of the energy, thinking, and discourse which gave it birth. In the words of the great Reggae singer, Jimmy Cliff — GIVE THANKS, GIVE THANKS!!!

INTRODUCTION

When this project was initiated, the intent was to conduct a qualitative study of the Black middleclass of Atlanta, Georgia. However, as the study began to unfold, I soon discovered that the existing theoretical models for analyzing and interpreting the unique position of the Black middleclass were inadequate. The existing frameworks did not reflect nor capture the contradictions and the dialectic which are embedded in the race, class, and cultural relations between AfricanAmericans and EuropeanAmericans in the United States. The general tendency among all the models has been one of imposing a pre-existing theoretical construct on the unique situation of this somewhat controversial group. The end result has been the production of some highly simplistic, often dubious descriptions and interpretations of Black middleclass life and culture. Recognizing this pattern led me to a critical examination of these models along with an in-depth review of the historical experiences of AfricanAmericans in an attempt to expose the biases and distortions and develop a more accurate model to account for the cultural-and-class realities of this group.

The critical review of existing American sociological class theories has been a seminal interest of mine since my undergraduate studies. As many AfricanAmerican sociologists of my generation will readily attest, sociology courses were the only ones which treated the topic of "race relations" during the early Sixties. Those of us interested in making sense of the world of African Americans in this society were drawn immediately to sociology departments. Little did we know at that time that we were choosing an option which we would grow simultaneously to love and hate.

As I became increasingly comfortable with my understanding of the theories and methods of the discipline, its inadequacies for explaining and interpreting the AfricanAmerican experience were more apparent.

The discipline provided a language for describing and interpreting United States society, yet, the descriptions of AfricanAmerican life did not reflect what I had observed and experienced.

One of the first experiences with the distortions occurred during my early studies of the AfricanAmerican family. I discovered in the texts and several professional research studies that AfricanAmerican families were disproportionately headed by women. As such, they were viewed as deviant or pathological. I could not understand that conclusion. I had been raised in a female-headed family during much of my youth. I had not experienced any of the disabilities the studies described. For example, I did not suffer any gender confusion or suffer the consequences associated with the absence of a male role model. My extended family provided numerous role models ranging from the "good" to the "ugly." I had older brothers, cousins, and Godparents who filled in the space reserved for a father. Thus, I had many male roles to emulate or reject as I approached adulthood, and I knew at an early age that some males were successes in the conventional sense of the term, some were failures, and others used unorthodox means to make a living. Some had successful marriages that lasted for a lifetime; others had marriages that failed. The "scientific" literature was not reflecting any of this diversity. I actually discoverd that I could find more accurate observations of AfricanAmerican family life from novels, biographies, and short stories in the creative productions of writers such as James Baldwin, Zora Neale Hurston, Margaret Walker, Richard Wright, Toni Cade Bambara, Toni Morrison, and James A. McPherson. It was on the pages of these non-scientific explorations of AfricanAmerican life and culture that I discovered the male characters and family dynamics that informed my world.

Subsequently, I became interested in developing an alternative conceptual framework for describing and interpreting AfricanAmerican society in the United States. This desire was fueled by the political and intellectual consciousness movement of the 1960s. The winds of change were blowing through the AfricanAmerican community as those who had been perceived as docile, happy second-class citizens began to demand "Freedom Now!" and "Free in '63!" AfricanAmericans came alive on the stage of American history again as they demanded new definitions of democracy and human rights. We were touched by it, changed by it — often painfully — both physically and psychologically. The discourse which follows evolved from that awakening.

During the Sixties, many of us learned for the first time how abysmally ignorant we were about AfricanAmerican life and culture. The cultural brainwashing performed so diligently by the public school system had been quite effective and total. This painful journey into critical political consciousness resulted in a movement which began by demanding "civil rights" and changed to one demanding a separate nation (the liberation strategy of the Republic of New Africa). These demands grew out of the anger and frustration accompanying the awareness of the extent of our miseducation. One of the most simultaneously painful and enraging realizations young AfricanAmericans had to confront was that we had been willing participants in our collective brainwashing. We had believed in the lofty values espoused in the *Declaration of Independence* and *Bill of Rights*: passively repeating an open, overt lie every morning as we pledged allegiance to a Eurocentric racist government.

The Black Studies Movement emerged as an extension of the Black Liberation Movement. Its historical origins were rooted in the expanding political consciousness, heightened sense of race pride, and cultural awareness accompanying the Liberation Struggle. Black students were accepted in predominantly White institutions of higher education in record breaking numbers. Many of these students had been activists in the Liberation Struggle and were committed to creating an institutional base for sustaining and perpetuating this "new" definition of self. Militant Black undergraduates and graduates demanded the implementation of Black Studies Departments to educate present and future generations of AfricanAmericans about themselves. Many also noted that White students, indeed, all students — needed to be familiar with the history and culture of AfricanAmericans. These visionary young people quite correctly perceived that what "passed" as education in the U.S. was basically White studies with all the racist biases inherent therein. Additionally, many wanted future generations of young Black people to avoid the aforementioned brainwashing *we* had experienced.

Black Studies provided an academic forum for challenging White assumptions and assertions regarding the supposed inferior intellectual abilities of peoples of color. Black intellectuals committed to promoting the ideological and theoretical orientation inherent in the Black Studies Movement began to criticize and challenge the descriptions and interpretations of AfricanAmerican life and culture presented by their White colleagues. This challenge lead to a rather heated debate between several highly prestigious White social scientists and militant Black scholars.

This controversial debate led to what many referred to as the "outsider" vs. "insider" perspectives within American sociology. Militant Black social scientists charged their White peers with using the AfricanAmerican community as a laboratory for conducting oftimes highly dubious studies. Many of these studies had given the aura of "scientific" legitimacy to most of the prevailing racist practices and policies. Further, many White scholars had advanced their careers within academia and had become high level consultants to both public and private sector agencies which victimized the AfricanAmerican community. While a significant number of these White scholars were considered to be "liberals" on the race issue, Black scholars noted that liberals believed in the ideals of the existing political economic structure, the very same structure which was dominating and exploiting the AfricanAmerican community. Liberals wanted to reform the worst racist practices but did not want to dismantle the entire system. From a radical Black perspective, this position was a form of racism in that it supported the social Darwinistic assumptions at the core of their liberalism. In the eyes of radical Black scholars, the loyalty of White social scientists to a system which had been described as fundamentally racist by a racially mixed panel organized to study the causes of the Sixties riots (the Kerner Commission Report), made them hypocrites. Given the inherent racism which destroyed their ability to be "objective," Black intellectuals demanded that White scholars cease their research activities in the AfricanAmerican community and focus their attention on understanding the phenomenon of White racism.

I found this controversy very invigorating and stimulating. It was an exciting period for the Black intellectual community. Black students and their faculty supporters forced the dominant intellectual community to re-examine its theories and practices. The controversy also challenged Black intellectuals to create alternative paradigms which could be used to "paint" a more accurate social portrait of U.S. society and the position of AfricanAmericans in it. More importantly, the debate led to serious discourse on the role of culture and cultural conflict in academia. Several Black scholars and some revisionist White scholars correctly noted that the racial- or color-based division of sides in the debate was a reflection of the cultural differences between AfricanAmericans and EuropeanAmericans.

At that time, many scholars of both races had accepted the theory that

AfricanAmericans did not have a unique culture. This theory emanated from an earlier school of thought which asserted that AfricanAmericans had been stripped of their African culture during slavery but had *not* been allowed to participate fully in European American culture. Thus, culturally, AfricanAmericans were some form of "bastardized" European American. The Black Liberation Movement, and the Black Studies Movement which it initiated, refuted this perspective. Several White scholars became allies in illuminating and promoting the concept of AfricanAmerican culture. Their approach was perceived as a rather radical position and has gained academic legitimacy only slowly and grudgingly.

Now that the existence of an authentic AfricanAmerican culture has been accepted, the task for Black and like-minded White scholars is that of defining, describing, and interpreting this culture to the larger public. Further, Black scholars and their allies must begin discussing the political economic implications of this cultural presence for the larger society and the world. Indeed, Black scholars must take the lead in this next stage of analysis and practice. What follows is one Black social scientist's attempt to move this process forward. It is an effort to develop an alternative theoretical perspective which captures the complexities, contradictions, and dialectic *between* AfricanAmerican culture and EuropeanAmerican culture as well as those *within* AfricanAmerican culture. The framework introduced in this work is that of *PanAfrican communalism*. This model attempts to reconcile two too-often-opposing theoretical schools of thought within Black scholarship: the cultural nationalist and Marxist schools. It builds on the impressive tradition of W.E.B. DuBois, Walter Rodney, Kwame Nkrumah, C.L.R. James, and numerous others. This model is not presented as *the* model, but as a framework for critical debate and dialogue.

I have chosen PanAfrican communalism as the analytical construct because it captures the empirical reality of AfricanAmericans. During the numerous intellectual gatherings hosted by the Institute of the Black World (the now-defunct Atlanta-based independent AfricanAmerican research center), it was often stated that AfricanAmerican political activists and scholars needed a social theory which had its roots in the culture and life experiences of AfricanAmericans. As scholar-activists, we were constantly commenting on the distorted, racist theories of EuropeanAmericans. These critiques of prevailing Eurocentric theories were a valuable and necessary step in creating such a theory. Yet, this was inadequate unless and until AfricanAmerican scholar-activists accepted and successfully met the challenge. The theory should not only be true to the prevailing socioeconomic conditions of the larger AfricanAmerican community but also contain a vision for what constitutes a *liberated* AfricanAmerican community. PanAfrican communalism embraces those principles and requirements.

The historical dimension of the model includes the current scientifically based assumption that humans as we know them had their origins on the African continent. Thus, Africa contributed to all of humanity the soil on which the first humans learned to organize themselves into viable groups, develop languages, establish family systems, create sophisticated religious systems which contained their visions of how humans came to be, solve the elemental problems of feeding and clothing themselves, and developed technological artifacts to enhance their abilities to meet their economic and aesthetic needs. Indeed, PanAfrican communalism acknowledges and accepts the controversial assertion that the first advanced civilization were created by African peoples; the Kushitic/Nubian/Ethiopian/Egyptian Empires with their religious, agricultural, architectural, technological, and political organizational genius. Thus, PanAfrican communalism accepts and celebrates the historical connectedness of AfricanAmericans with these ancient civilizations.

PanAfrican communalism shares the Marxian assumption that humans are both the products and producers of culture. As such, it assumes that Africans on the continent and those in the diaspora inherited and perpetuate this basic human characteristic. Peoples of Africa were the first to experience the trauma and excitement of cultural change as it occurred through both natural and coercive means. This perception of African peoples contradicts the existing image in the Western, racist literature which depicts Africa as a "dark" mysterious continent peopled by "primitives" who maintain stagnant, unchanging ways of life for generations. African peoples have developed social formations ranging from hunting and gathering groups living in perfect harmony with their natural environment to sophisticated state formations. Thus, the image that African people did not create higher systems of social organization through peaceful, cooperative group exchanges as well as enforced consolidation is false. African peoples have been in the vanguard of demonstrating the various ways humans can organize their lives and continue to do so.

This theoretical model also embraces the cultural nationalist position with respect to the cultural unity ↔ diversity dimension of AfricanAmerican life. That is, the theory acknowledges cultural diversity in our African past as well as the current era. Yet, there is a growing body of literature which demonstrates many underlying cultural elements common to West African peoples who are the acknowledged ancestors of most AfricanAmericans in the diaspora. These common elements have survived the painful wrenching from their source and the various geopolitical environments imposed on our slave ancestors. This unity-in-diversity is accounted for both by the common cultural heritage and by the similarities in treatment inflicted on African slaves. PanAfrican communalism accepts the reality that this cultural unity includes both positive and negative aspects of African peoples' lives. As Frantz Fanon (*cf.*, *The Wretched of the Earth* and *Black Skins, White Masks*) and others have demonstrated, slavery and colonialism created deep psychological scars among African peoples. These scars are reflected in the values and practices that exist in the culture(s) around problems associated with skin-color, hair texture, lip size, desire on the part of many AfricanAmericans to integrate with their EuropeanAmerican oppressors, racial and cultural confusion on the question of identity, and so on.

The model contains what the famous AfricanAmerican musician Charles Mingus referred to as the view from "beneath the underdog." It is a theory which reflects the fact that AfricanAmericans have been systematically excluded from the mainstream of American society. As such, we have a different perspective on the so-called liberal progressive revolution; a view which illuminates the hypocrisy of the ideological superstructure of this country—its "underside." It challenges the state's assertion of its way of life as democratic and points to the country's racist, imperialistic, cultural chauvinistic origins and contemporary practices. PanAfrican communalism perceives the essential vacuousness of the democratic ideal of "rugged individualism." As a people with a cultural heritage of communalism, the notion of individuals who are largely self-centered and self-directed is incomprehensible. Humans are quintessentially group-oriented beings, both phylogenetically and—more to the point—psychologically, due to our rather long period of dependency as infants. To create a cultural system which forces children to ultimately sever their relationships with their parents, siblings, and extended kin is unconscionable. The fact that communal values and practices continue to be core cultural elements in African peoples' cultures on both the continent and in the diaspora reflects an awareness and appreciation of human nature.

The framework of PanAfrican communalism recognizes that peoples and cultures with a communalist orientation are in fundamental conflict with Western individualism. This model emphasizes the need to re-cast race relations theory in the language of cultural conflict and cultural struggle. The individualist-materialist vision of society is fundamentally incompatible with that of a communalist-spiritual based orientation. For African-cultured peoples, communalism is the highest form of social existence and there can be no peace in the world until White Westerners and their "colored" allies come to this realization. The discourse which follows further elaborates the theoretical model and discusses its implications for the sociocultural and political-economic prospects for both AfricanAmericans and EuropeanAmericans.

I urge my fellow AfricanAmerican social scientists to join the the dialogue and further clarify this model. No single authored work can be comprehensive and exhaustive. At best, it can be suggestive and invite critical comment. Let's get on with it.

CHAPTER I

THE PROBLEM

In a critique of what he termed the "strengths-of-black-families" school, Nathan Hare suggested that Black social scientists often use mainstream theories and the biases peculiar to them in their efforts to refute racist descriptions of AfricanAmerican life and culture.[1]

He observed that the "strengths" school relied on Talcott Parsons' systems theory in its efforts to combat the negative stereotypes of AfricanAmerican family life. In his article, Hare cited William Wilson extensively and both noted that Parsons essentially oriented his theory toward "order-consensus" rather than "conflict-change."[2] Hare asserted that Black intellectuals and their White counterparts had misdirected the Black movement from an attack on the racist capitalist system responsible for the deplorable conditions impinging on AfricanAmerican families to a position which glorified those families' abilities to endure and persevere. For Hare, endurance and perseverance or "survival" substituted poorly for needed radical change.

Hare's critique of the "strengths" school revealed the pitfalls inherent in applying theoretical models and concepts derived from the cultural experiences of a dominant group to that of culturally oppressed groups. He perceived this approach as using the "ruling ideas." The colonizers developed these ideas in part to rationalize and justify the oppression and to define the cultural existence of the colonized. For members of the colonized group, using this approach becomes a futile process at its best and a self-denial or negation at its worst. In her provocative article "Culture and Imperialism: Proposing a New Dialectic," Mina Caulfield noted that the ideologies of White supremacy and cultural superiority express "parts of a cultural value system and important items in the cultural self-definition of West Europeans and North Americans." She further argued that

1

In the colonial setting, and here I include the "internal colonies" of Indians and Blacks in the United States ... it is clear that they [ideologies] operate not only to partially define the dominant cultural identity, but by the same token, they define the "other"—by exclusion, negation, by opposition to all that is held in high esteem or given value.[3]

While Hare attacked the "strengths" school for being misled by liberal reformers, it is interesting to note that he accepted what has been termed the E. Franklin Frazier pathological or pejorative tradition: the "strengths" school attacked the Frazierian school of thought. These attacks and counterattacks regarding the social conditions and situations of AfricanAmerican families reflect the sensitive, ambiguous, and ambivalent reactions of both "outsiders" and some "insiders." Hare would consider himself an "insider," I'm sure, regarding the issue of AfricanAmerican culture in America.

Hare's position, however, ignored the origins of the pathological school (possibly because of his allegiance to his mentor, Frazier). In an article which antedates Hare's, John Szwed observed that the pathological model (Charles Valentine's concept) emerged out of the debate between E. Franklin Frazier and Melville Herskovits. In this debate, Frazier based his position on an ideological premise similar to that of the "strengths" school. In other words, Frazier rejected Herskovits' thesis affirming the presence of African cultural elements among AfricanAmericans because Frazier feared the data presented in Herskovits' book, *The Myth of the Negro Past,*[4] would be used by racist politicians and policy makers to justify "Jim Crow" segregation in the South (and in the North as well, quiet as it is kept).

In order to demonstrate that AfricanAmericans were the same as European Americans, Frazier, like his mentor, Robert E. Park, emphasized the fact that most AfricanAmericans had adopted EuropeanAmerican forms of institutional life and values. They believed most AfricanAmericans had become acculturated. They considered environmental factors such as poverty, lack of education, urban migration, and so on as the causes for the differences between AfricanAmericans and EuropeanAmericans. Committed liberal reformers, Frazier and Park believed these differences could not be considered as evidence of a distinct culture.

Szwed, Frazier and Park, along with their anthropological counterparts, such as Franz Boas, Ashley Montague, and Ruth Benedict believed that no racial or other biophysical differences in innate intellectual ability nor any significant cultural differences existed between AfricanAmericans and EuropeanAmericans. This position grew out of their dedication to social change. Szwed further cautioned,

> It is important to reiterate that these anthropologists arrived at their conclusions, not on the basis of ethical neutralism, but through a deep commitment to the need for social change. Indeed, it was in their very zeal to refute "generic" racism for general audiences and to demonstrate a universal capacity for culture that they argued that AfroAmericans shared essentially the same culture as White Americans.[5]

Both the "strengths" and "pathological" schools reacted or responded to the racist pressures occurring in the larger society. The earlier liberal-inspired denial of AfricanAmerican culture responded to the geneticists' theories of Black racial inferiority; whereas, the advocates who argued affirmation of AfricanAmerican culture responded to the more recent efforts of Daniel P. Moynihan, Lee Rainwater, and Nathan Glazer whose works presented pathological models of AfricanAmerican community life. Although the response to the "pathological" position affirms the presence and notes the positive dimensions of AfricanAmerican culture, it lacks a theoretical model based on the AfricanAmerican experience in the United States and the world, historically and presently. I noted earlier, agreeing with Hare, that such a model must have at its core a concept of cultural struggle and conflict rather than one of order and consensus.

As a consequence of the "outsider" versus "insider" polarization within sociology, two major theoretical and methodological issues have emerged. First, social scientists from various disciplines renewed their interest in the impact of imperialism and colonialism on subordinated peoples and cultures. Anthropologists traditionally have ignored the political-economic effects of colonial oppression upon indigenous people and their cultures. Rather, analysts maintained patterns of studying subordinated indigenous groups in isolation as a means of developing theoretical models to account for the evolution of humans and culture from their "primitive" beginnings to the more "advanced" stages of civilization.

Earlier anthropologists consistently used this approach on peoples and cultures that they deemed exotic. Once invaders subdued and/or pacified a population, anthropologists usually followed the military to gather information on the life and cultures of the indigenous groups. Colonizing nations used this information to develop their programs and policies for social control. Taking this ostensibly objective, value-free approach, anthropologists ignored the colonizer-colonized relationship and the cultural disruption wrought by colonial domination.

Caulfield defined imperialism as "a broad term covering an extremely wide range of situations, including direct political control, indirect political control, and economic control." She amplified this definition and claimed,

> The central characteristic uniting these situations is that key decisions on the disposition of resources and benefits in a community are made by members of another ethnic or cultural group, and that the purpose of such decisions is ultimately the extraction of profit from the community and its resources for the capitalistic enterprises of the dominant group. This definition, then, would include not just the "old colonialism" of the European but also the multitudinous forms of neocolonialism of the present period.[6]

To Caulfield, the traditional Marxist explanation for this form of imperialism remains inadequate and inappropriate. In her view, one cannot apply the Marxian dialectic for change in a capitalist situation to the colonial situation because of the dissimilar underlying contradiction. She argued,

> In the colonial situation, the basic contradiction, the opposing interests, the social and economic transformations, and the changes in consciousness all take different forms; in short, a qualitatively different dialectic is at work, and the nature of the ensuing synthesis is likewise different. *It is my thesis that the underlying form of exploitation under imperialism is not that of class over class but rather of culture over culture.* As expanding capitalism with its industrial base in the home country, encountered and engulfed non-industrial cultures, the dominant system developed modes for exploiting not just the labor power of these people but their entire cultural patterns.[7] [Emphasis in original.]

Caulfield's critique of the traditional Marxist position with an emphasis on cultural patterns compliments the model being developed here. Though a special enactment of the colonial dialectic, the AfricanAmerican experience in the United States encompasses all the forms of cultural exploitation and resistance existing in other colonial situations. I am attempting to demonstrate the value of a model that analyzes the AfricanAmerican experience generally and one that particularly accounts for the situation of the Black middleclass, a subsegment of the AfricanAmerican community. While developing this PanAfrican communalist model, I will be concomitantly refining and extending what Staples and others have termed PanAfrican Marxism.

I offer more detailed discussion on this model later; however, the significance of Caulfield's observation deserves a special comment. That is, when European colonizers encountered Africans and other indigenous peoples, the dialectic can be more accurately described as one thesis, "European culture," encountering a different thesis, "the Native indigenous culture"; thus, the situation is not that of the Hegelian "thesis" versus "antithesis" but one of "thesis" versus "thesis." Since the indigenous peoples had and continue to maintain their cultures — though not as cohesively as they had possessed originally and during colonial occupation and domination — these cultures cannot be said to be antithetical to European cultures. In essence, the indigenous cultures reflect more than the simple negation of the colonial regime.

Most Marxists and many neo-Marxists make the common error of assuming or implying that the cultures of conquered peoples are destroyed or eliminated due to colonial imposition. To the contrary, the colonial situation creates a situation of cultural conflict expressed on many levels in a variety of ways. I will critique Marxian and neo-Marxian theory in greater detail later in this discourse. Now, however, I will discuss the other major thrust related to the concept of cultural struggle.

The second great trend to emerge out of the "outsider" versus "insider" debate involved a renewed interest in AfricanAmerican culture. This trend includes: the increasing nationalistic tone of the 'Sixties Civil Rights Movement, especially as articulated through the high priest of Black Nationalism, Brother Malcolm X; the spurning of the revisionist analyses of AfricanAmerican culture: the publication of Cruse's timely critique of Black intellectuals; and the coerced creation and implementation of Black Studies departments and programs in America's colleges and universities. Social scientists, engaged in studies of what they termed Black lowerclass life, have carried out a re-examination of the prevailing descriptions and characterizations of AfricanAmerican culture.

As I noted above, while discussing the Hare thesis on the "strengths" school, many students of what is called Black lowerclass life viewed the behavior patterns of this group as a kind of deficit culture, a view consistent with that of Park and Frazier. Szwed observed in his critical summary of these studies, "Afro-American culture was (in Ralph Ellison's phrase) nothing more than the sum of its brutalization."[8] The highly acclaimed studies of Black *Streetcorner Men* by Elliot Liebow and

Kenneth Clark's *Dark Ghetto* represent classic examples of this school of thought.[9]

Significantly, due to their political conservatism or latent racism, none of these authors arrived at a progressive position on AfricanAmerican culture. Quite the contrary, they were all deeply committed to social change and remained very sympathetic toward many of the goals and objectives of the Black Power movement. Their positions reflected a political concern about the potential negative consequences which would occur if AfricanAmerican behavioral patterns were perceived as cultural since culture is learned and transmitted. They feared that to present the behavior of AfricanAmericans as *bona fide* cultural retentions would allow the racist, conservative, Southern dominated Congress to use the issue of AfricanAmerican culture as a rationale for blocking progressive social legislation aimed at ameliorating some of the problems confronting African Americans.

In essence, the Frazier and Park argument, appearing some twenty-plus years after Herskovits' publication, suggested something about the so-called "Black progress" which had occurred during the intervening years. And these liberal defenders and supporters of the AfricanAmericans' struggle for first-class citizenship in the United States continued the tradition of perceiving AfricanAmerican culture as a retarding agent— something to be explained away or denied rather than as a set of beliefs, values, attitudes, and norms which define and distinguish AfricanAmericans.

However, as Szwed noted, an expanding body of social-scientific and socio-literary studies has presented an alternative interpretation of Black lowerclass culture. He summarized briefly these studies' main conclusions,

> First, they all assert that from the beginning of slavery, Afro-Americans exercised the capacity to perpetuate and create the means of comprehending and dealing with the natural and social worlds surrounding them —they were cultural bearers and creators as well as receivers and learners. In other words, although slavery, poverty, and racism have severely circumscribed the exercise of this capacity, even driving it underground, these constraints can in no way be seen as the sufficient cause of Afro-American behavior. All of this is borne out by both the continuities and the discontinuities that exist between Black people in North and South America and in Africa. Nor do these studies see Afro-American culture as being exclusively negative ... or "reactive." Far from seeing Black Americans as having "no" values and culture to guard and protect, they cumulatively suggest that in some

respects Afro-Americans have guarded and protected their culture better than any other ethnic or national group in the United States. In fact they ... argue that Blacks have elaborated some cultural domains in such a rich and vital manner that they have been the source of a huge portion of unacknowledged American culture.[10]

Szwed observed further that these studies also indicate that with EuropeanAmericans forever the "norming group," one can never adequately describe or measure the alleged AfricanAmerican cultural incapacity or pathology by crudely comparing and contrasting Black and White behavior and institutions to see how closely AfricanAmericans approximate European American cultural norms. He remarked that this practice occurs often, despite a century of EuropeanAmerican criticism by Marx, Veblen, and Mills (to name a few) of the pathology of Western behaviors and institutions.

These and other dimensions of AfricanAmerican culture and the cultural struggle will be pursued in greater detail as this analysis unfolds. In addition, I will introduce something important but omitted in the usual discussion regarding AfricanAmerican culture: the Black middleclass and its position within the alternative theoretical framework designated above, PanAfrican communalism.

The Black middleclass has been the victim of a scholarly bias, but one different in many respects from the bias directed at the Black lowerclass. The lowerclass has been perceived as suffering from a deficit culture or cultural deprivation. The Black middleclass has been perceived generally as culturally assimilated, as that segment of the AfricanAmerican community that has "made it," and, thus, held as shining examples of the ability of WASP-dominated American culture to absorb and integrate a segment of the most oppressed group into its institutional life.

The social and cultural interpreters of American life use the Black middleclass as the "successful" group in the AfricanAmerican community; this group represents the examples of what all AfricanAmericans could become if they worked to achieve a mainstream lifestyle through institutional means. Until passage of the Civil Rights Bill in 1964, "institutional means" meant "through the segregated institutions created by the dominant society to socialize (civilize?) the former slaves into mainstream values and conduct." These interpreters presented the achievements of the Black middleclass as ultimate confirmation of the Horatio Alger myth. The "society" pages of *Ebony, Jet,* and occasionally even some White liberal magazines illustrate and perpetuate this myth.

The earlier scientific investigators of European life usually commended the Black middleclass and complimented it for its strict adherence to Puritan-inspired morality, its genteel social graces, its conventional public behavior, and its loyalty to the American creed. These descriptions of the Black middleclass appeared in the studies of DuBois on both the Philadelphia Negro and on the Atlanta Negro; Frazier's on the Black elite of Durham, North Carolina; Drake and Cayton's classic on Black life in Chicago; and Myrdal's classic on Southern Blacks. This tradition continues in several more recent studies of the Black middleclass; for example, Muraskin's treatment of the Black Masons, Scanzoni's study of Black middleclass families in a midwestern urban area, and Kronus's work on the Black middleclass in Chicago.[11]

Yet, while analysts described the Black middleclass as the "model-American" segment of the AfricanAmerican community, many also severely criticized this same group for its lack of racial and cultural consciousness and for its lack of concern for the social conditions which continue to bear on the lives of its lowerclass racial brethren. The works of Frazier, Allen, Hare, and Cruse include scathing critiques of this group's "shallow, imitative" adulation of White (read "WASP") cultural forms. The Black middleclass then occupies an ambiguous and contradictory position in the cultural struggle between AfricanAmericans and EuropeanAmericans in the United States.

In this work I attempt to resolve and clarify some of these ambiguities and contradictions in a more detailed in depth analysis of the role of the Black middleclass in this continuing struggle. I introduce, define, and expound the concept of *ethcaste* — a theoretical concept which I believe more accurately explains and clarifies the Black experience in the United States. I also attempt to connect this concept to PanAfrican communalist ideology and theory. The "insiders" created this PanAfrican communalism in their continuing efforts to formulate an alternative theoretical perspective which explains the race, class, and cultural dynamics of AfricanAmerican and EuropeanAmerican relations in U.S. society as well as the cultural and class dynamics within AfricanAmerican society.

While presenting my formulation of this cultural struggle, I discuss American sociology's major theories of social class. In a critical review of selected theories, I delineate the biases inherent in those theories so that AfricanAmerican sociologists (and others who share a similar orientation) will not make the mistakes that Hare and Wilson mentioned in their critiques of the "strengths" school. I also demonstrate how these theories serve as rationales for the dominant capitalist culture's oppression and repression of AfricanAmericans and other peoples of color, nationally and internationally. These theories can be perceived as analogous to what Marx called the "ruling ideas."

With a few notable exceptions, bourgeois intellectuals developed these theories to give legitimacy to the class oppression which is characteristic of capitalist culture as well as of the precapitalist cultural oppression of AfricanAmericans and other peoples of color. Several other social theoreticians developed their theories as a part of a radical, progressive critique of capitalist culture. Yet, they, too, often ignored the cultural oppression of peoples of color. Their concerns focused primarily on improving or reforming certain negative features of capitalist culture, not on altering substantially or radically the position of capitalist cultures in the world system. Marxian class theory is an excellent example of this tendency. While it proposes radical changes within the political-economic organization of capitalist states, it accepts the cultural hegemony of Western society. This acceptance is due to the fact that both capitalism and socialism as theoretical models originated in the Western world.

Another reason for my recasting of racial conflict theory into cultural conflict theory comes from a growing concern about the inherent Western bias which permeates European sociological theory. I have paid special attention to the number of sociological theories on social class that have focused on political-economic factors rather than upon other modes of organizing human group life. And, when we discuss social class, we attempt to describe the organization of human group life within a particular cultural framework.

To focus on its history of ignoring culture in intergroup relations as a critique of much of Western sociology may appear to be rather simplistic but it is, nonetheless, valid. One can read literature on social class and conclude that culture exists unrelated to politics and economics or social class except when discussed as class culture. The concept of class culture retains some relevance, but the literature permits a rather narrow discussion of culture as something specific to a distinct group in a rather large, amorphous, loosely stratified (egalitarian) nation state. We find this definition to be far from the truth. The liberal democratic egalitarian capitalist nation state represents a political, economic, social, moral, and spiritual — in other words, a *cultural* — system.

Social classes and their class cultures include variations of a common cultural heritage; that is, the normative and valuative belief system which serves as the ideological basis of that society determines the manner in which people hierarchically group other people. Thus, the class system in a capitalist culture represents the distribution of its population according to each person's ability to achieve a certain level of material comfort and his or her apparent willingness to accept the values, norms and beliefs which serve as the bases for individual, national and group identification.

The ideological superstructure houses the norms, beliefs, and values (the moral oughts) of liberal democratic capitalist America. These oughts can be found in the *Declaration of Independence,* the *Bill of Rights*, property rights, the separation of church and state, the balance of power in the branches of government, popular elections, a presidency rather than a monarchy, and the political party system. These oughts affirm the relationship between the capitalist moral superstructure and the evolution of capitalist man so brilliantly elucidated in Weber's monograph, *The Protestant Ethic and the Spirit of Capitalism.*[12]

The Protestant ethic and pseudoscientific social Darwinistic justification of superiority and inferiority help explain the origins and functions of social classes in a liberal democratic capitalist culture. I should add that the United States' variant of capitalist culture differs in many respects from that of western European capitalist nations. But few would deny the European origins of the United States' variant. This work in many ways highlights the uniqueness of the cultural system of the United States.

The cultural system of which we are a part determines what we see and how we see it. It becomes the prism through which we explain and refract the world and peoples of the world. In a capitalist culture, people view politics and economics as inherently associated with social class. Politics and economics constitute the core elements in class position, orientation, and lifestyle. Marx perceived this class orientation quite accurately; and for this reason, I will discuss Marx's theory in some detail in the forthcoming review of the literature. However, other peoples exist whose cultural superstructures emphasize different values and factors as the bases for their social organization. Since this book is concerned primarily with AfricanAmerican and EuropeanAmerican issues, I cite West African traditional beliefs as illustrative of these differences.

In many West African societies, individuals and groups organize according to their relation to their community of humans, their deities and spirits, their physical environment (their land), and their ancestors. In their moral superstructure, they ground the values guiding their behavior which contain ideal perceptions (their moral "oughts") regulating the relationship between men/women and the deities, men/women and nature, and men/women and the human community — all ages. A specific example of differences would be Africans' orientation toward property. The people in the West, especially the United States, perceive property as being owned by the individual. An individual can take h/er property and do with it as s/he pleases; that is, expand it, sell it, neglect it, bargain with it, *etc.* The property belongs to h/er personally and remains subject only to the desires of the individual.

In many West African societies, property is owned communally. Since these societies also believe ancestral spirits intervene in the daily lives of the living, they understand property as belonging to the whole community, which includes the living, the dead, and the still unborn. This ideological superstructure allows little place for the type of individuality characteristic of Western society. The community entrusts the living with maintaining and improving property not for their own individual benefit but for the well-being of the collective, and most especially, to assure that the property will provide the still unborn with the sustenance needed to perpetuate the family, clan, and village.

Significantly, people with this particular orientation toward life — an orientation which appears to be widespread throughout the "Third World"— also venerate older people. An old Chinese proverb captures most accurately the rationale for this veneration. It says, "If you want to know what awaits you on the road ahead, ask someone who's coming back." These societies perceive older people as intermediaries between the spiritual world and the material world. The elders have been here a long time; they have experienced a great deal. That they have survived for so long indicates they have something of value to say about how one survives. Of course, this veneration of the elders stands out in startling contrast to the common capitalist cultural view of older people as persons to "hide" or herd into shelters and allow to die as useless anachronisms in a youth-oriented culture. "How to stay young" programs and products constitute one of the fastest growing commercial industries in the United States. People flock to health spas, health camps, health foods, cosmetic surgeons, *et al.*, in desperate efforts to retain youthful appearances.

The perceptions of most Western social scientists of the cultures of Third World peoples manifest an emphasis on politics and economics which in itself represents a cultural bias. They characterize the cultures of people of color as primitive, animistic, ancestor worshipping and culturally inferior to the "rational," sophisticated, liturgical, impersonal, cos-

mopolitan—"seditty" (sedate, "stuck-up"), if you will—Western European cultures. Many Western social scientists consciously and uncon-
sciously claim to provide "scientific" evidence to support the notion that
if politics and economics cannot be considered as the bases of class
organization and structure, the people are primitive, underdeveloped, and
culturally backward. An examination of this cultural bias and its consequences provides the core of this discourse.

For this discourse, I present the concept of *ethcaste* which more
accurately captures the sociocultural uniqueness of AfricanAmericans as
well as their political-economic status in the United States. Through a
presentation of PanAfrican communalist interpretation of the historical
"roots" and subsequent development of AfricanAmerican culture, I
attempt to demonstrate the fallacies and inadequacies of referring to
AfricanAmericans as a racial group with no distinct cultural heritage.
First I distinguish my concept from *ethclass* introduced by Milton Gordon
in *Assimilation in American Life: The Role of Race, Religion and
National Origins*. Then I establish the relationship between *ethcaste*, a
central sociological concept which unites the previously contradictory
but equally valid theoretical approaches of PanAfricanism and Marxism.
PanAfricanism, with its stress on sociocultural unity and humanism
grounded in African and Native American cultures, has an affinity with
Marx's social humanism. As such, the concept of PanAfrican communalism represents a creative fusion of the positions of PanAfrican nationalism and nonWestern as well as Western socialist humanism.

Next, I focus on a particular variant of the international cultural
struggle — that between the AfricanAmerican and the White Anglo-
Saxon Protestant (WASP) who culturally dominates the United States. To
the extent that this WASP culture also dominates virtually all of the
Western and nonWestern world politically, economically, and militarily,
the cultural struggle between AfricanAmerican and WASP includes international dimensions. African Americans, and especially middleclass
ones, have often been accused of cultural parochialism. They have been
seen as assimilated Americans who are ignorant of and unconcerned with
the plight of their Third World (especially African) brothers and sisters.
While the apathy may to some degree exist, the PanAfrican communalist
model of cultural confrontation between AfricanAmericans and WASPs
avoids the error of ascribing that sense of disinterest to cultural parochialism.

By clarifying some critical aspects regarding capitalist cultures, this work provides other Third World peoples with valuable insights into the nature of their own struggles. More importantly, the discussion becomes valuable if it makes some small contribution toward bringing people of color into closer cultural and political unity. People of color must move toward becoming better informed about ourselves individually and collectively or we always find ourselves responding and reacting separately and sometimes divisively against each other and toward a people and culture which does not place our survival, not to mention our material and spiritual progress, as a priority on its political and economic agenda.

I turn then to a selective review of the literature on social class in capitalist culture. My focus is not on the merits or demerits of these theories and theorists. Rather, I approach each theory as a window or lens through which to view the capitalist culture. From this vantage point, even the contradictions, disagreements, modifications, and/or revisions become instructive. I am not attempting to be objective in the traditional sense of that word; therefore, my analysis reveals my theoretical biases and justifications. I consider myself to be a part of that AfricanAmerican intellectual tradition that remains outside of any established school of thought. This tradition holds that for us to achieve a more in depth understanding of the nature of the situation which constrains and controls our lives in innumerable ways, we must listen to and analyze the internal arguments of the dominant culture's intelligentsia. I begin this journey by introducing the concept of *ethcaste*.

CHAPTER II

ANALYSIS OF CONTROVERSIAL ISSUES SURROUNDING THE BLACK ETHCASTE ELITE

I begin this journey by critically assessing the tendency in the social science literature to refer to AfricanAmericans as a racial group with no distinct cultural heritage as opposed to an ethnic group, a position modified to perceiving AfricanAmerican culture and ethnicity as "emerging." I attempt to demonstrate the fallacies and inadequacies of this position through the presentation of a PanAfrican communalist interpretation of the historical "roots" and subsequent development of AfricanAmerican culture. In addition, I present a concept, ethcaste, which more accurately captures both the sociocultural uniqueness of AfricanAmericans as well as their political-economic status in the United States.

The concept of ethcaste includes the class diversity dimension of Gordon's *ethclass* while simultaneously emphasizing the caste status of AfricanAmericans in this society. I offer ethcaste as a way to explain the consequences of systematic domination, exploitation, exclusion and oppression of a group on the basis of an ascribed racial trait. In the ethcaste concept, the critical factor, racism, explains or accounts for the position of oppressed groups. Although societies that are more nearly racially homogeneous, like India, contain ethcaste subordination due to caste and cultural differences, in the United States and other so-called technologically advanced capitalist-based democratic cultures, the significance of the racial factor deeply overshadows the cultural factor.

Groups suffering under ethcaste subordination also experience cultural exclusion, repression, and assault. But the superordinate group tend to see culture as less important than race. They will generally acknowledge that groups experiencing ethcaste domination have highly developed, complex, and integrated cultures but are victimized primarily because of racial differences. Native American groups come most readily to mind. However, the dominant group most commonly perceives other groups as being racially different but cultureless, providing a type of double jeopardy to ethcaste status. AfricanAmericans prove to be the prime victims of this latter type of racist thinking and practices.

The concept of *ethclass* assumes that Whites exploited Blacks purely because of the racial differences between AfricanAmericans and WASPs or other European Americans while ignoring, thus, in effect, denying, that the AfricanAmerican community encompasses cultural (multiethnic) and political-economic diversity; that is, class stratification with a variety of political, cultural, and economic subgroups. The ethcaste concept takes into account the caste/cultural status of AfricanAmericans in the United States which resembles that of other Africans in the "New World" and, furthermore, reflects the status of African nations within the world capitalist cultural system. Therefore, the concept of ethcaste forces us to discuss the historical experiences and cultural continuities indigenous to African peoples as well as their contemporary political-economic and cultural conditions. In so doing, using the ethcaste concept provides Black social scientists a framework with which to transcend the provincialism and ahistoricism characteristic of White social scientific analyses and theory.

I further attempt to demonstrate that the concept of ethcaste remains theoretically consistent with the domestic colonial model as conceived by Robert Blauner.[1] In noting the relationship between ethcaste and the concept of domestic (and classical) colonialism, I seek to demonstrate that ethcaste as a central concept unites the heretofore contradictory but equally valid theoretical approaches of socialist humanism and PanAfricanism, which stresses sociocultural unity and humanism grounded in African and NativeAmerican cultures. As such, PanAfrican communalism represents a creative fusion of PanAfrican nationalism and socialistic humanism.

Humanism from other than the west European world differs in that it emphasizes the fundamental equality of all humans to and with each other, with nature, and with the spiritual world. This egalitarian worldview stresses economic equality, communal sharing and caring, the importance of the survival of the group as a distinct cultural unit as opposed to a preoccupation with acquiring individual wealth and private property. Indeed, as practiced by many NativeAmerican and African ethnic groups, the concept of private property has no meaning. It is a worldview encompassing behavioral practices and values which acknowledge the fact that in order for the individual to survive and prosper, s/he must be a part of and supported by the larger group. Thus, the vulgar acquisition of individual wealth for personal use and abuse is outside of their system of comprehending the world.

I contend that AfricanAmericans are the biocultural inheritors of this communalistic worldview; and to the extent that they remain "true" to that heritage, they continue to practice and value economic equality as presented in Marxian theory. I stress the importance of the origins of this fundamental sense of economic justice as an inherent dimension of AfricanAmerican culture in order to divorce it from the social Darwinist evolutionary flaws permeating Marx's theory and vision. However, as noted above, the PanAfrican communalist accepts Marx's brilliant exposure of the fundamentally exploitative nature of capitalist culture.

Ethcaste, consequently, provides a PanAfrican communalist theoretician with a conceptual tool for analyzing intercaste relations as well as intracaste relations, both nationally and internationally. *Ethcaste* both forces the analyst to recognize that man does not live for the pursuit of bread alone and to be conscious of racial and ethnic groups as more than mere aggregates of individuals hierarchically arranged according to their possession of material or nonmaterial symbols of social stratification.

The struggle to develop a framework for analyzing the Black middleclass stimulated me to create the concept of ethcaste. After citing the theoretical foundation and presenting both sociocultural and political-economic profiles of the Black ethcaste elite, I apply this PanAfrican communalist concept to the theoretical and political controversies surrounding this segment of the AfricanAmerican community. I noted in the "Introduction" that both Black and White social analysts persistently tend to discuss the Black middleclass as if it encompassed a relatively homogeneous group. However, this approach is both inaccurate and misleading. Most have willingly made the traditional distinctions using Warner's categories in a modified form, that is, the aristocratic upperclass, the bourgeoisie or *nouveau riche*, the upper middleclass professionals, the lower middleclass, the upper lowerclass, and so on.

Charles A. Valentine's article, "Deficit, Difference, and Bicultural Models of Afro-American Behavior," suggests that these categories fail to reflect the ethnic diversity characteristic of urban African American communities. The Valentine study produced evidence revealing the existence of approximately fourteen different AfricanAmerican subcultures.[2] Using language which indicated rural versus urban origins and country of origin, Valentine found the AfricanAmerican ethcaste composed of numerous subcultures and ethnic groups: Northern urban Blacks, Southern rural Blacks, Jamaicans, Haitians, Panamanians, Bahamians, Guyanese, Black Cubans and Puerto Ricans. Obviously, ethclasses which reflect the juxtaposition of a variety of Black ethnic subcultures and their socioeconomic status hierarchies exist within the *ethcaste*. This ethnic diversity in urban AfricanAmerica indicates that the numerous Black immigrants who established residence in the major cities of this country have been forced to accommodate themselves to America's domestic colonial oppression.

Other observers of the AfricanAmerican community have chronicled the presence of AfricanCaribbeans within the AfricanAmerican urban community. However, I am not presently aware of any study focusing on the cultural and class characteristics of these Black ethnics that notes their relationships with each other and with the AfricanAmerican population. Harold Cruse, in *The Crisis of the Negro Intellectual,* raised some issues regarding the impact of Caribbean intellectuals in Black leftist politics, but no other analyst offers a fairly systematic analysis of this phenomenon.[3] This omission reflects the paucity of Black sociological research on issues and problems vital to the AfricanAmerican community's consciousness of itself.

Valentine observed one consequence of Black ethnic diversity: the necessity for perceiving AfricanAmericans as bicultural or multicultural, socialized into two or more cultures simultaneously. That is, they learn the prescribed behaviors for their ethnic subculture within their homes, neighborhoods, and communities while acquiring mainstream culture through the secondary institutions like schools, courts, the police, the media, and the welfare system which intrude and impinge upon their lives. One of the major consequences of being bicultural may be that it creates the problematic DuBoisian "double-consciousness" (or triple, quadruple) for all Black ethnics, but that remains an hypothesis to be tested. If Black ethnics suffer "double consciousness," that fact reinforces the PanAfrican thesis of cultural continuities (including Fanon's observations regarding the colonized mentality), since colonial oppression and capitalist economic exploitation have victimized all the Black ethnic groups. A major point emphasized in this work involves the socioeconomic diversity of the Black middleclass in the United States as well as its sociocultural diversity as a consequence of its African cultural roots.

The emphasis on the many aspects of diversity in the AfricanAmerican community is an important prerequisite before offering the following critical sociohistorical overview of the Black middleclass (or bourgeoisie) in American capitalist culture. None of the literature discusses these complexities in the depth they demand, and that constitutes a serious omission. Therefore, while DuBois correctly criticized White social scientists and social workers for their failure to recognize the socioeconomic and cultural diversity in the AfricanAmerican community of Philadelphia, in some respects, he made the same mistake. He captured the socioeconomic diversity of Black Philadelphia but failed to document the ethnic diversity.

DuBois's omission may be seen as a consequence of the oppressed caste status of all AfricanAmericans and the rather clear differences in Philadelphia at the time between the long standing northern born urban AfricanAmerican and the newly arriving rural migrant from the south rather than Blacks arriving from outside the continental United States. But for analysts today to disregard Blacks' national origins, given the multiplicity of Black ethnics coming from throughout the diaspora to all major cities of this nation, constrains their analyses into limited "they all look alike" assumptions, and lumps them into the uninsightful and uninspired mass of rote studies.

Valentine's concept of biculturalism represents a tremendous contribution to the continuing efforts to develop theories and methods for analyzing AfricanAmerican life and its interaction, competition, and conflict with the dominant caste. Yet, as he developed it, he did not focus on the intracaste bicultural strain — the bicultural strain which Jessie Bernard referred to as the two cultural "strands," the "externally adapted" versus the "acculturated"; or, what Drake and Cayton referred to as the socially "respectables" versus the socially "non-respectables"; or, what DuBois referred to as the "genteel" tradition versus the "rowdies." [4]

In essence, Valentine neglected to include in his discussion the fact that within the AfricanAmerican ethcaste, two major competing and conflicting cultural traditions exist. These two competing traditions transcend class lines and exist in all occupational, educational, and income groups. Yet, people tend to see one strand as predominating in the upper classes and the other characteristic of the "lowerclass."

The literature asserts, explicitly or implicitly, that in the experiences of the externally adapted, disproportionately large lower and working class strand, AfricanAmericans forged a traditional Afrocentric "field hand" culture while the experiences of the more conventional, acculturated, genteel strand brought about the heritage of the house servant and "free persons of color" groups during the era of enslavement. Analysts generally assumed that the externally adapted strand with its more emotional, present-oriented, unconventional lifestyle, its "shouting" churches, soul-rending gospels and spirituals, "weary" and not-so-weary blues, "hard" drinking and loud music, sensual and energetic dancing, matrifocal extended family structure, and so forth, represented the more authentic "Black" culture as opposed to that of the conventional strand with its conservative dress, higher education, refined "Eurocentric" manners, Episcopalian, Congregationalist, United Methodist, Presbyterian religious memberships, "proper" English and white dialect, and so forth. Needless to say, the relationship between these two strands has served as the subject of much debate and scholarly research.

DuBois' early study of Philadelphia's AfricanAmerican community set the tone for much of the subsequent research on this sensitive issue of class relations within the Black ethcaste. DuBois applauded the genteel elites' refined manners (given his regional and cultural grounding in and preference for this tradition), their moral, religiously virtuous lifestyle, their respectability and industriousness, and their stable family life, but he also critiqued their tendency to isolate themselves in a narrow, restricted social world. He complimented their superior status and felt that these aristocratic, "blue blood" mulattoes represented the "finest" of the race. Yet, he criticized them for being slow to assume the proper role of an aristocracy: that of "serving the lower classes."

Rather than serving the lower classes, he saw the Philadelphia "Black" elite as consumed by activities in its own narrow circles, expending a great deal of energy to maintain the social distance between itself and the lowerclass, often darker-skinned, brethren. DuBois felt some justification for this attitude since no one wished to be associated with a race of hedonistic, lazy, ignorant, criminal, "ne'er-do-wells." He appealed to the elites' "noble" sense of paternalistic mission to lead the so-called lowerclass "riff-raff" out of its slavery-inherited immorality towards behavior which more closely approximated the conventional White cultural norm. Interestingly enough, he charged that if the Black elite did not engage in this enlightened leadership activity, the Black lowerclass masses would look to the White community for leaders. It apparently never occurred to him that members of this "lower" section — the overwhelming majority of Black Philadelphians — could capably lead themselves.

In their study, Drake and Cayton observed this tendency for members of the acculturated, genteel elite to isolate, insulate, and alienate themselves from the masses of "non-respectables." Their research on Chicago's Black community during the 1930s "Great" Depression revealed the presence of a similarly situated, disproportionately mulatto-blue blood, small aristocracy which rejected for the most part its White counterpart. This group rejected both the lowerclass, "uncouth," dark-complexioned southern migrants and the growing (and by their standards), unconventional "new" Black bourgeoisie. This "new" group comprised the "shadies" (financially successful, prominent underworld Blacks like policy bankers, hustlers, and gamblers), the more prominent and "wealthy" entertainers and professional athletes, as well as a new group of Black professionals and businessmen who derived their wealth from serving the Black population of Chicago.[5] The emergence of the "new" Black bourgeoisie constituted a major change in the occupational structure of the elite and reflected the ideological heritage of Booker T. Washington.

The flamboyant style of this new bourgeoisie repulsed and chagrined the old aristocratic mulatto elite. The new bourgeoisie's ostentatious conspicuous consumption; huge lavish parties, debutante balls, and weddings; "loose" moral standards; social crudeness as well as darker skin became obstacles or barriers to gaining acceptance in the aristocratic organizations and cliques. finding itself rebuffed by the aristocratic "set," the new bourgeoisie, because of its wealth and relatively larger size, gained ascendance in Chicago and began to redefine upperclass conventional culture.

Although the older elite never accepted many of the first generation of this new group into its circles, they accepted the children. Many of the "nouveau riche" sent their children to private, elite, predominantly Black or predominantly White colleges where they acquired the education and cultural manners befitting members of this group. Once the offspring possessed these traits, they became eligible to intermarry and structurally assimilate (to borrow Gordon's term) into the aristocratic group life. Drake and Cayton agreed that the new non-aristocratic elite's ability to successfully challenge the older elite occurred because the older group lost its economic base due to both the cultural and technological changes discussed earlier.

August Meier and David Lewis noticed a similar change in the economic base of the Black elite in their study of Atlanta's Black upperclass. However, in Atlanta, the friction between the "old" and the "new" elites appeared less intense than in Chicago. Meier and Lewis cited several factors which contributed to this more benign state of affairs. The small, "old" elite required its members to marry the upcoming, morally conventional *nouveau riche* because many of the descendants of the older group migrated and married into elite families in other cities like Washington, D.C., New York, and Durham, North Carolina. In addition, several members of the older group became business partners and associates with members of the new elite. The older elite lost its economic ascendance, somewhat, but retained much of its social ascendance because the new perceived the older elite as its most "significant other," to use Mead's and Blumer's term[6]; the older elite constituted the reference group into which the new elite sought to become integrated. Thus, those in the new group modeled their behavior, taste, and values after those of the older elite. In this sense, one could say that the old traditional upperclass in Atlanta simply expanded to accommodate the new bourgeoisie's economic ideology and practice.

The difference in the method of transition reflects in part a regional difference between the northern aristocratic elite and the southern. That is, the southern Black aristocrats, regardless of the fact that they tended to be mulattoes, related more closely to the Black working and lower classes because of Jim Crow segregation. Although "White" in their conduct, deportment, and oftentimes color, they still had to ride in the segregated section of buses, drink at "colored-only" water fountains, respond to Whites of all classes with "yes, sir" and "no, sir" (as opposed to "yassuh" and "nawssuh"), and suffered equally (if not more so) as targets of police or private White citizen brutality and insults. The existence of an overt ethcaste system muted the deleterious effects of classism in the South much more than the covert ethcaste system in the North. The "Mulatto" aristocracy in the North could isolate itself more thoroughly from the masses through its ability to own homes in recently integrated neighborhoods (usually as a consequence of "block busting" by White real estate agents). Although rejected by their White neighbors whom they in turn rejected, they could create an insulated social world which allowed them to "do their own thing," almost completely isolated from the masses.[7]

August Meier, in a later article, attributed this difference to the northern traditional elite's essentially hostile response towards Booker T. Washington's nationalistic economic program:

> By and large it was the older pre-1900 entrepreneurial and professional upper-class that, especially in the North, tended to be indifferent toward or opposed to the philosophy of racial solidarity, even though members of this group came to favor it to the extent that they were forced, or found it desirable and possible, to turn to the Negro market. ... On the other hand, the new upward mobile middle-class, composed for the most part of self-made men whose economic roots were in the newly urbanized masses, naturally found the philosophy of self-help and solidarity — and consequently the philosophy of Booker T. Washington — congenial to its experience and interests; and its members easily appropriated the symbols of American individualism and social Darwinism to explain and rationalize their social role. It was this group that was especially instrumental in the burgeoning of the philosophy of racial solidarity, self-help and group economy — rationalizations of the economic advantages and disadvantages to be found in segregation and discrimination, to use a phrase commonly employed in those days. Washington's National Negro Business League was the platform on which this group expressed its point of view.[8]

This transformation of the Black elite would appear to support Harold Cruse's thesis regarding the competition between the nationalistic strain in the Black bourgeoisie versus the integrationist strain.[9] During this period, the rising influence of Booker T. Washington and his supporters and students reflected the ascendance of the nationalistic strain. This change appeared to be politically and economically positive in that it sought to create a Black nation with a Black economic base within the White Anglo-Saxon-Protestant-dominated capitalist culture. However, from a PanAfrican communalist perspective, the latter half of the preceding Meier quote indicates a major ideological flaw; that is, Washington's desire to create a Black capitalist economy within the White capitalist economy.

Washington's major limitation resided in his refusal to acknowledge that American capitalism had become firmly established and was well on the way toward becoming monopolistic capitalism, ending the laissez-faire, "rags-to-riches" days of free enterprise capitalism. Washington's Black entrepreneurial capitalists, at best, included small businessmen retailing goods and services to the AfricanAmerican community but neither owners of the means of production nor major producers. The ownership of the means of production (the corporations and banks) remained firmly in the hands of the WASP corporate elite.

The Black capitalist class as middlemen and petty (technically, *petit*) bourgeois small businessmen provided services to the AfricanAmerican community, since Whites excluded Blacks from their entrepreneurial institutions, especially service institutions. Black entrepreneurs who internalized and practiced capitalist principles simply replaced the color of the exploiter and heightened class conflict within the AfricanAmerican community. Cruse's rather laudatory treatment of Washington's program omitted this critical dimension. Although DuBois and others severely criticized Washington for being an "Uncle Tom" accommodationist because of his stand on segregation, many often applauded Booker T. for his economic program. Many continue to praise, even today.

Oliver C. Cox's critical analysis of Washington's leadership philosophy revealed the dangers of even this aspect of Washington's program. In the earliest of two articles focusing on the leadership of Washington, Cox characterized Washington's leadership as that of a "collaborator." He noted that a collaborator differed significantly from either the passive, tame "Uncle Tom" or the grudgingly compromising protest leader whom the White upper class could never trust:

> ... [T]he collaborator is an active advocate of the purposes of the dominant group. He has to be exceedingly versed in subtleties because, although he is fundamentally antagonistic to the people's cause, he must appear to be their champion. His leadership is essentially negative .... The collaborator ... cannot be in conflict with the dominant power, for his significance as a leader depends entirely on that power. In fact, the distinguishing attribute of a collaborating leader is his peculiar influence and power — power vouchsafed him by its source. To oppose the collaborator is to oppose the dominant power itself, and for this reason those who opposed Washington ordinarily realized that their bread and butter became involved.[10]

Cox further argued that since the programs and policies essentially come from the ruling class, the collaborating leader is protected from failure, receives a great deal of publicity, becomes portrayed as the "super-star" or role model for all members of his group, and serves as an intercessor between his group and the dominant class. The masses never perceived Washington as a mass leader like Garvey, and AfricanAmerican people never granted him a leadership mandate. Cox characterized those whose interests Washington served as endowing him with leadership and the prestige and privileges associated with it. He perceived Washington's mission essentially as one to subdue the spirit of protest in AfricanAmericans and to encourage them to be satisfied with their "second-class" citizenship.

Cox argued that Washington acquired his power and prestige because the new southern business or bourgeois oligarchy which replaced the planter aristocracy following the Reconstruction period chose him. This new oligarchy openly courted northern capitalists in its efforts to industrialize the South. In order to forge this cooperative enterprise, the southern oligarchy assured the northern industrial capitalists that peace between the races or castes would prevail. Cox noted that Washington's famous "Atlanta Compromise" speech supported social separation with economic interdependence and reflected an acceptance of the philosophy of the overt racist spokesman for the new southern oligarchy, Henry Grady, the venerated editor of the Atlanta *Constitution*.

An important part of Grady's strategy for peaceful coexistence between what he considered the biologically superior, omnipotent, superordinate White caste and the biologically inferior, powerless, subordinate Black caste involved the co-optation of the small "Negro" middleclass. To Grady, this class would serve as a colonial elite (an *ethcaste* elite), mollifying and managing their less privileged colonized brethren. Cox included Grady's statement that "the new oligarchy proposed to use the *best* Negroes, the *most gifted* of them, *to forestall the political aspirations of their own people*." [My emphases.] From this perspective, Washington's economic nationalism (with its emphasis on industrial education) can be seen as a vulgarization and perversion of the AfricanAmerican community's nationalistic impulse into behaviors which would serve the interests of a neo-colonial petit bourgeoisie.

Cox's criticism of Washington's leadership and program in many ways resembles Cruse's attack on the integrationist leadership of the National Association for the Advancement of Colored People, (NAACP) and the reformist aspects of the Black Power Movement. This similarity could be due, in part, to the fact that Cruse and Washington were elitists who perceived the salvation of the Black masses as dependent upon the actions and orientations of the Black elite: Cruse's intellectuals and artists, Washington's businessmen. As such, both then suffer an anachronistic, "Victorian" intraclass paternalism very much like the New England Yankee missionaries' attitude toward enslaved Black and "free" men.

Washington's program for Black political-economic progress would have resulted in the creation of an AfricanAmerican capitalist culture with all of the exploitative and dehumanizing attributes inherent in capitalism. Black capitalists could have retained a sense of "race pride" — the most elementary level of cultural consciousness — while replicating the behavioral values, attitudes, and practices of their caste oppressors. This move would have constituted the ultimate victory for liberal capitalist culture. That is, when the oppressed racial/cultural caste attempts to reproduce the cultural system of its exploiters, it has capitulated in the struggle; it has voluntarily decided to forsake its cultural heritage and adopted that of the oppressor. In sociological terms, it would have assimilated. This dynamic represents the fundamental flaw in the Black capitalist solution to Black oppression. Washington and his ideological contemporaries failed to perceive or acknowledge the fact that one cannot adopt only a part of capitalism, that is, its economic values and practices. If the subordinate caste accepts and adopts the economic system, it must ultimately adopt the ideological, moral, and spiritual values which buttress that system. Had Washington's program succeeded on a larger scale, it most likely would have hastened the cultural disintegration of the AfricanAmerican community.

Thus, while I acknowledge Washington as a brilliant and extraordinary man, the liberal democratic capitalist myth victimized and seduced him. By criticizing his program, I am not attempting to diminish his personal stature or minimize his significant contributions to the AfricanAmerican liberation struggle. Rather, I use his leadership objectives as a means of illuminating the "crisis of the Negro intellectuals" and political-economic elites. That crisis reflects their tendency to pursue political-economic objectives which would ultimately destroy the cultural integrity of the AfricanAmerican community. The goals and objectives of the Black elites may appear to be in the best interest of the Black masses, but they often tend to benefit the elites at the expense of the masses. This situation occurs as a consequence of the Black elites' marginal immersion in and limited acceptance of AfricanAmerican culture. Washington's movement provides an excellent example of this tendency.

E. Franklin Frazier also noted this flaw in Washington's program.[11]

His critique of the Washington-inspired National Negro Business League focused on the businessmen's use of nationalist propaganda to induce the Black masses to "buy Black," that is, support AfricanAmerican businesses. Since these financially insecure businesses operated on the margins of the dominant capitalist system, they charged AfricanAmerican customers higher prices for inferior goods and performed services often inadequate, and in a discourteous manner. From a PanAfrican communalist perspective, there is no worse form of exploitation than Black-on-Black.

Frazier criticized the "new" nationalistic bourgeoisie as well for being frivolous, hedonistic, and alienated from both the Black masses and from its White middleclass counterpart (the White nationalist bourgeoisie). To him, the Black bourgeoisie existed in a social world of its own creation: a world of make-believe comprised of card parties, ostentatious conspicuous consumption, and a perverted imitation of White bourgeois life. Frazier's caricature of the Black middleclass demonstrated one of the logical outcomes of Washington's approach.

Yet, this description of the Black bourgeoisie represented a radical change in perspective for Frazier. In his earlier research on the Durham Black elite[12] and in other articles and publications,[13] he quite readily complimented this group. Like DuBois, he saw it as the more intelligent, emancipated group which reflected what AfricanAmericans could achieve if provided with the opportunity to acquire an education and equal access to upper echelon occupations and professions. These people belonged to White, "high Protestant" churches (Episcopalians, Lutherans, Congregationalist, and so on) or the Black Baptist and Methodist churches which catered to their subdued style. Members of this elite group shunned the more "primitive," emotional, fundamentalist Baptist, Methodist, and Pentecostal churches. They exhibited their refined manners in the best WASP tradition. With graphic clarity, their behavior demonstrated a degree of incorrectness in Melville Herskovits's assertions regarding the presence of African survivals.[14]

Frazier's earlier discussions of this group, therefore, reflected an awareness of the dual cultural strands in the AfricanAmerican community as well as a tendency to accept and identify positively with the culturally White "respectables." Yet, Frazier's generally positive characterization of the Black "respectable" upper classes coexisted with his admiration and appreciation of Southern rural AfricanAmerican folk culture. In his discussion of the urban "non-respectable" lowerclass culture, he lamented the demise of the southern rural folk culture.

Although he appeared to be saddened by its demise, he also felt optimistic about the assimilating process which accompanied urbanization; that is, urbanization exposed AfricanAmericans to the modern realities of the United States. This urban lifestyle compelled southern migrants to make the transition from their rural, communal, cooperative lifestyle to that of sophisticated, cosmopolitan, individualistic urbanites. They received better educational training and gained access to a more "open" opportunity structure.

Frazier used a Marxian approach in some of his research and analyses. He conceived urbanization as a means of transforming the Black peasantry into a Black Marxist proletariat that would join its White counterpart in political struggle against the capitalist ruling class. However, his later studies of urban lowerclass families indicated that he reversed his original optimistic assertions regarding the positive impact of urbanization. With this new vision, he perceived all as pathology, especially the dissolution of the AfricanAmerican family. One can see, then, that for Frazier both the Black lower and upper classes had become "pathological."

American social scientists, Black and White, widely accepted Frazier's pathological model of the AfricanAmerican community (both the middle and the lowerclass). However, as noted earlier, Black nationalist-oriented scholars and some progressive Whites (Charles Keil, Robert Blauner, Norm Whitten and John Szwed) took a radical position on the AfricanAmerican culture question and severely criticized Frazier's assertions and observations regarding the life and culture of the Black lowerclass. The criticism of Frazier's analysis of the Black lower classes emerged in large part from its association with the infamous Moynihan Report and the controversy which that report ignited.

This report appeared at the time of the ascendancy of militant Black Nationalism as the dominant ideological philosophy. At the same time, the remedying of socioeconomic problems of the Black masses moved to the forefront of the objectives of the Liberation Movement; some would even say it was a period of "romanticizing" the masses. Moynihan used Frazier's works to document a "blaming-the-victim" characterization of lowerclass Black family problems which caused Frazier to be perceived as a liberal integrationist with no appreciation of AfricanAmerican culture, especially AfricanAmerican urban culture. Yet, as noted earlier, several Black nationalist scholars accepted Frazier's essentially pathological portrait of the Black bourgeoisie. In essence, they criticized him

as an intellectual elitist lacking cultural consciousness and an appreciation of lowerclass AfricanAmerican urban culture but respected and
heralded him for his critique of the Black bourgeoisie. Members of the
bourgeois cultural nationalist movement accepted Frazier's analysis of
the Black bourgeoisie because they espoused the unifying of
AfricanAmericans and the eradicating any vestiges of classism, especially WASP classism. In addition, Frazier's work provided them a
framework for understanding some of the opposition that their political
and intellectual activism encountered from certain Black groups and
individuals.

A very intense period during the Sixties found several Black activists
and scholars grappling with the problems of identity and self-definition.
They engaged in critical discussions of who we were and where we were
going, which consumed much time and energy. Ideological differences
often led to physical confrontations as groups competed with each other
for the elusive loyalty of the masses. The results increased racial/cultural
and political consciousness and intracaste conflict. From a PanAfrican
communalist perspective, Frazier must be respected for providing a
model for understanding certain elements in the AfricanAmerican community. In so doing, his work allowed several groups and individuals to
engage in a phenomenon psychologists refer to as "opposition model-
ing." These individuals and groups used Frazier's negative image of the
upper classes to hurl insults at each other grounded in less-"Black
bougie"-than-thou arguments without realizing that such disputes actually contributed to the maintenance and perpetuation of intraethcaste
class/cultural hostilities.

As these scholars and groups became more reflective and introspec-
tive during the late Sixties and early Seventies (for a variety of reasons,
including increased repression by the F.B.I., the C.I.A., and local police),
more of the protagonists began to accept the reality that because of
education, income, and lifestyle they had become members of that much
maligned "Black middleclass" group This change proved to be a startling
revelation for many. Were we the same people Frazier described in his
study? If not, then, is it possible that Frazier had misrepresented the Black
bourgeoisie?

As scholars and activists confronted their positions within the
context of the larger AfricanAmerican community, the limitations of
Frazier's analysis became increasingly apparent even though much of
what he had written was then and continues to be undeniably true for

some segments of the Black elite (as painful as that is to accept). Indeed, given the successes of the Civil Rights Movement, the AfricanAmerican community may now have a larger number of alienated elites, lost in the illusion of "color blind" liberalism characteristic of upper middleclass suburban communities, private schools, elite New England private colleges and universities, and the accompanying upper-level positions in private companies — the "BUPPIE" (Black upwardly-mobile professionals) phenomenon.

One of the best critiques of Frazier's portrait of the Black middleclass appeared in a study by William A. Muraskin. Unlike Frazier, he did not characterize the Black middleclass as morally deficient, nor guilty of creating and perpetuating much of the "pathology" which Frazier attributed to it. Rather, he argued that the Black middleclass represented a "tragic" group marginal to both the African and EuropeanAmerican communities:

> Divided in its allegiances, forced to turn in two directions at once, wracked by its own ambivalence, it has been unable even to develop an economic base to be securely worthy of the name "bourgeoisie." The black middle-class is not a willing betrayer of itself or its race but is the victim of its own precarious economic and social position. American society's racial and economic structure conspires against it, cruelly entangling it in an impossible series of contradictions.[15]

Muraskin challenged Frazier's "blaming-the-victim" syndrome. He used the colonial analogy which emphasizes the colonized elite status of the Black middleclass as materially more comfortable than the vast majority of its racial brethren but also victims of racism and powerlessness. Its members possess what C. Wright Mills referred to as middle-level power: delegated or derived power required to keep the bureaucracies running smoothly on a day-to-day basis (in contrast to the power of elites who make the upper level decisions).[16] Often just as constrained and limited in what it can accomplish as lowerclass Blacks, the Black middleclass comprises individuals and groups marginal to or on the periphery of middle-level decision-makers and influentials. Its members' Blackness (biologically, if not culturally) limits their access to the upper echelons of power, wealth, and prestige. These interethcaste dynamics determine much of their behavior, including their politics or the lack thereof. Although some members of the Black middleclass refuse to accept or acknowledge their limitations given their cultural identification with and loyalty to WASP values and beliefs, a great deal of their ineffectiveness comes because of factors over which they have no control.

The Black ethcaste elite's limited arena for exercising power also constitutes one of the major differences between a domestically neo-colonized ethcaste group and that of the international, more traditionally neo-colonized African, Latin American, West Indian, or Asian elites. In the classical situations, the neo-colonized elite possesses political power: its members make decisions, exercise authority, and chart a course for the future evolution and development of their country. They possess property, state political machinery, an army, and a constituency which looks to them for leadership. A domestically neo-colonized ethcaste elite such as AfricanAmericans possesses no power of this type. Its power derives either from its position in a White dominated bureaucracy or from the power of influence flowing from independent Black political organizations or movements. Its members cannot impose any demands on their constituency, Mass support is voluntary, In this sense, the Black ethcaste elite confronts distinctive leadership problems which reflect its peculiar status, that of an articulate, intelligent, and often dedicated group of individuals suffering caste sanctions which circumscribe their abilities and mobility.

Most Third World nations are multiethnic and some of the groups within them suffer ethcaste oppression as a consequence of traditional cultural differences and colonizer-engineered hostilities. Within the world capitalist cultural system, this form of ethcaste oppression resembles that experienced by ethcaste groups in the United States. If one accepts Immanuel Wallerstein's thesis regarding the caste status of Third World countries on the periphery of the capitalist core, this phenomenon constitutes a form of intraethcaste oppression for subordinate groups of color in countries where the dominant group is people of color. Much more could be said on these issues, but I end this digression here and return to Muraskin's treatment of the Black middleclass.

Muraskin also challenged Frazier for rather "loosely" delineating the boundaries of the Black bourgeoisie in that Frazier's primary middleclass constituted AfricanAmericans with white collar occupations, professionals and technical workers, with most of its recent growth in clerical and kindred occupations (the lower middleclass occupations), yet Frazier claimed to focus on the lifestyle of a small Black elite, not the middleclass he so carefully delimited in his demographic data. Aside from the demographic discussions of this group, he virtually ignored them in his moral polemics against the "elite." The middleclass which Frazier formally defined differed from the people he actually discussed. More accurately, those he discussed included an elite segment of a larger group who occupy their special status by virtue of their superior wealth, education, and accompanying lifestyle. In essence, Muraskin argued that Frazier's primary concern was with the "externally adapted," or "loose living," immoral Black elite. If Frazier had concentrated on the majority of the Black bourgeoisie (whom Muraskin identified as those who are members of organizations like the Masons and their cognates), he would have found (in values, beliefs, and behavior) much greater continuity between the "old" Black bourgeoisie and the new elite.

Muraskin presented a compelling argument for accepting the cultural continuity between the old and the new elite. He observed that the ideology, values, and beliefs of Prince Hall Freemasonry coincide with those of the old elite. Members of these groups remain noted for their commitment to Black economic and social progress through the use of existing mainstream cultural institutions. Prince Hall Freemasonry is organized around the same principles as those of their White counterparts (which had their origins in the Western European crafts guilds and the rise of the Western European *petit bourgeoisie*). As such, the Prince Hall Masons and cohorts stress individual achievement in an open, competitive society. In addition, they perceive(d) themselves to be an elite group of AfricanAmericans committed to Black self-improvement as a means of counteracting White prejudice, hostility, and racism. In other words, in their interactions with each other and their White counterparts, they attempt to demonstrate the irrationality of prejudice and racism through adopting conventional Western behavior and refined manners.

Their solution to the racial/cultural struggle matched that which militant Black Nationalists criticized so vehemently during the Sixties, especially as it was manifested in the objectives and goals of organizations such as the NAACP and the [National] Urban League. Nationalists attacked these organizations for attempting to convince the Black masses that the traditional liberal formula of "learning to speak correct English," "taking a bath," "taking care to smell pleasant," "cutting and/or keeping hair proper," "buying a new suit and keeping it clean and pressed," and "shining shoes" would improve their opportunities for success because it would convince White prospective employers that "you're different" — not like the lazy, uncouth, "ne'er-do-wells" who so dominate "the race."

Muraskin succinctly captured this Black Masonic creed in the
following statement:

> The Masonic leadership's emphasis on rigidly maintaining the middle-
> class style of life has been strongly influenced by their sensitivity to the
> white charge that blacks neither practice nor are capable of practicing
> bourgeois morality and, therefore, are an immoral and inherently
> inferior race. The Masons have fervently desired by their conduct to
> disprove this charge; though by their own view of themselves as
> different from most blacks they demonstrate an acceptance of the
> white stereotype, at least as it pertains to the black masses, while
> rejecting it for the race (*i.e.,* themselves) as such.[17]

One can see that Prince Hall Freemasonry represents the institutionalization and perpetuation of Booker T. Washington's philosophy, with
the notable exception of the acceptance of segregation.

The Mason's "privileged" or respected position in the larger
AfricanAmerican community reflects the ideological success of the
traditional, refined, originally predominantly mulatto elite in creating an
organization which forces its members to adhere to its ideological creed.
As Muraskin noted, the Masons screen their initiates before they are
ultimately admitted. Masons reflect the group's class bias in its membership fees which appear somewhat expensive according to AfricanAmerican
community standards. They expect members to be able to own property
and to maintain it without tremendous financial strain. Its code of ethics
purported to exclude the externally adapted elites like the "shadies," early
sports heroes, and entertainers although this "jet-set" element of the
bourgeoisie tend to possess more wealth and property than many Masons.
Consequently, since these people could prove to be financially considerable, the exclusionary practice failed miserably.

The Masons established chapters all over the United States, in the
West Indies, and in the African countries created as colonies for former
slaves, Sierra Leone and Liberia. Masons support each other in political
activities, economic activities, and "cultural" affairs. Most of the prominent Black American and West Indian leaders have been and are Masons,
including DuBois, Washington, Delaney, and [Adam Clayton] Powell.
The various chapters hold local and regional meetings and elect representatives to attend national meetings. They, therefore, create opportunities
to interact with other Masons on a continuous basis. Muraskin also
observed that the Mason's various fraternal and sororal affiliates repre-

sent a relatively large and well-organized segment of the AfricanAmerican community determined to maintain its style of life, leadership positions, and distance—both social and, today, geographic—from the Black lower classes.

Although Masons take great pride in demonstrating their superiority over and exclusion of the masses, they still perceive themselves as the "significant other" for the masses. This attitude is due, in part, to their dependence on the masses for their livelihood. They know that without Black working- and lowerclass support, they would not hold high public office, would have no clientele for their professional practices, and would not be appointed to upper echelon public bureaucratic positions. Although Muraskin chose not to emphasize this dimension, he presented strong evidence to support the Black Marxian position regarding the variety of class consciousness of certain segments of the Black ethcaste elite: that it is a class-for-itself.

Muraskin also stressed the Masons' need to maintain its hegemony over the masses through participating in the institutional life of the AfricanAmerican community, that is, the churches, schools, politics, and recreational activities. Because of the Masons' superior organization and resources, members usually occupy leadership roles and attempt to influence the less fortunate by functioning as role models. They maintain "model" AfricanAmerican families which society encourages working- and lowerclass AfricanAmericans to emulate. The Masons represent the "rags-to-riches" success stories which can be achieved through hard work, savings, good grooming and discipline. Elementary and high school teachers urge AfricanAmerican youth to become like "Drs." Washington, Carver, Drew, and Banneker. In addition to functioning as role models, they also use charity to induce community support. They give financial gifts to churches and ministers who project a "positive" image of the community, financial contributions to the United Negro College Fund (U.N.C.F.), and college scholarships to "outstanding" Black students. However, as Muraskin correctly noted, these "gifts" and "uplift" programs function to maintain and reinforce Masonic values and leadership:

> While the Masonry has lauded charity as one of its highest ideals, it has set some very specific limits to how and when it should be dispensed. For the Masons, charity and middle-class morality go hand-in-hand; one without the other is unacceptable. Charity must go to the "deserving poor," and to no one else.[18]

One can easily detect echoes of Jane Addams and other liberal WASP dispensers of benign alms and its accompanying paternalistic dependency.

The central point to this discussion thus far is that Frazier's presentation of the Black bourgeoisie ignored this very disciplined, organized, proud, and resourceful segment of the Black ethcaste middle and upper classes. I contend that the majority of this segment are not suffering from the pathologies which Frazier attributed to them; that is, existing in a world of make-believe, inferiority complex, ostentatious conspicuous consumption, and powerlessness. While they obviously possess little of the power which accompanies the ownership of the means of production, they do possess a circumscribed (often narrowly so) amount of middle-level power—the power that determines whether budget allocations should go to sectors of public bureaucracies, whether an accused person is innocent or guilty, whether a mother and her children should receive welfare benefits, whether a student should be admitted to colleges, universities, or professional programs, and whether students should pass or fail an academic course. The Masons tend to accept the social Darwinistic premises of the American capitalist class system and become "trapped" into pursuing their class interests — often at the expense of the Black lower classes.

Yet, by capitalistic cultural definitions of wealth, this middleclass possesses very little. But, they live substantially more comfortably and securely than the majority of Blacks and a significant proportion of Whites. And, although committed to WASP values and beliefs, they also often hold anti-White feelings, preferring their own ethcaste *class'* cultural life to that of integration. Consequently, Frazier not only misrepresented the sociocultural lifestyles of the majority of this group, he also attacked it, in part, for the wrong reasons; and those who continue to attack it for these reasons perpetuate Frazier's misconceptions.

On the other hand, Muraskin's criticism of this group's ideology and practice comes closer to the PanAfrican communalist position informing this discourse. He identified the difficulties involved in defining the Black middleclass in social behavioral terms; the sociocultural terminology tends to divide AfricanAmericans into categories of "good" and "bad," "respectables" and "non-respectables." While Muraskin criticized this method of delineation, he, too, ultimately adopted a modified version that emphasized the importance of public behavior, those who conform to WASP definitions of appropriate public behavior versus those who do not.

His and others' methods also reinforced the observations that a substantial proportion of the AfricanAmerican community—like the Masons' "deserving poor" and Jessie Bernard's acculturated lowerclass families—conform to conventional codes of public behavior.

Their emphasis on AfricanAmerican cultural styles further reflects the ethcaste, political-economic status of AfricanAmericans. The Black upper middleclass, or "bourgeoisie," lacks the financial or psychological security which should accompany its status. And, in terms of income, the economic distance between the Black lower and the upper classes remains much smaller than the economic distances between these groups for Whites. Therefore, the Black upper middleclass uses public behavior as the only means it possesses to exhibit higher status. Since the group recognizes its status as very precarious, this public behavior assumes crucial importance. It magnifies deviations from the code beyond their "normal" importance. Lacking the financial security of its White counterparts, the Black upper middleclass seeks to impose its adherence to WASP behavioral ethics on those economically beneath it and those aspiring to enter its institutional life.

Muraskin accurately observed that the liberal-democratic, capitalist cultural ethos cannot be considered inherently "White" nor peculiarly WASP or European. One recognizes the cultural values of hard work, thrift, cleanliness, ownership of property, and so on in numerous other cultures, past and present; for instance, Japanese, Hindu, and various West African ethnic groups and past empires. However, the Black ethcaste middleclass's internalization of these values in a situation of oppression compares to the identification of Jewish concentration camp detainees with their German S.S. Guards. These inmates identified with and essentially attempted to become the oppressor. This internalization is especially manifest through negative elements characteristic of capitalist middleclass culture, such as individualism, competition, conspicuous consumption, and "phony" lifestyles. The Black ethcaste elite, as noted above, must become aware that these dominant caste middleclass values serve to buttress the system which relegates AfricanAmericans, individually and collectively, to an inferior, subordinate caste.

In a situation of racial/cultural conflict, the sociocultural pathology embodied in imitative behavior which Albert Memmi referred to as the "colonized mentality," is highly dysfunctional and destructive.[19] Muraskin quite perceptively discussed this dynamic:

> Built into the foundation of middle-class ethics are philosophical

assumptions that are in and of themselves destructive of black class cooperation. The bourgeois ethic is designed for dynamic economic change. It is highly functional for mobilizing and channeling individual abilities and aspirations toward sustaining social and economic change. Part of that ability comes out of its emphasis on human capacity, responsibility, and free will. The ethic assumes that a man can control his destiny, especially economic, by conscious effort. Those who adhere to the code and succeed are praiseworthy and those who do not are blameworthy. ... To the extent that black men, or any men, adhere to a doctrine of social activism such as this and emphasize personal responsibility [a term which has come to be quite politically popular in the Conservative last two decades of the Twentieth century], there is a strong tendency to be hostile and unsympathetic to those who fail to achieve. This attitude is built into the ethic, and its effect on a group with exceptionally limited freedom (such as the blacks) is bound to be destructive.[20]

When a racist, cultural chauvinistic attitude reinforces the liberal democratic laissez-faire capitalist Protestant ethic's inherent bias against the "less successful," the end results in domestic colonization and the accompanying ethcaste status of AfricanAmerican and other colored "citizens," as well as the economic and military subordination of the "colored" world (classical neocolonialism American style). Thus, the cultural identification of the Black middleclass with the WASP liberal democratic ethos places it in the unenviable position of being *racist* against AfricanAmericans. But White liberals usually use the term "Black racist" to describe Black Nationalists who hate White people — witness the definitional game they play on us.

Muraskin, Cruse, Turner, and Mumford[21] recognized the Black ethcaste elite's political diversity which includes Nationalists, Democrats, Republicans, and Independents. Many prominent Black nationalists belonged to the Masons which becomes somewhat contradictory if one accepts Cruse's observations regarding the importance of Nationalism in the AfricanAmerican liberation struggle. Cruse correctly observed that most prominent Black Nationalists were members of the Black intellectual elite, the Black bourgeoisie. As Nationalists, their commitment to perpetuating and politically organizing around the concept of racial/cultural consciousness should have prevented them from accepting membership in an organization which ideologically committed itself to the eradication and negation of such consciousness.

Robert Allen's provocative critique of bourgeois cultural nationalism explained this apparent contradiction. Allen presented strong evidence to support his thesis regarding the relationship between the domestically neo-colonized Black elite and the American corporate elite, asserting that as a consequence of the potent Black political thrusts of the Sixties, the American corporate elite adopted a policy of co-optation. He argued further that the corporate elite decided to fund programs, organizations, and individuals whom it perceived as "militant but responsible." Although the corporate elite's involvement with the traditional Civil Rights organizations became generally known and accepted, the corporate elite (especially the Ford Foundation) also began to fund non-mainstream cultural nationalist leaders and organizations such as Maulana Karenga and US; the Newark Black Power conference; the Black capitalist, Black power segment of C.O.R.E. (Congress on Racial Equality) — especially floyd McKissick; Leroi Jones(Amiri Baraka)'s United Black Brothers of Newark; and Kenneth Clark's original M.A.R.C. program for radical Black leaders.[22]

The result of this approach changed several previously militant and radical organizations into increasingly conservative groups. The members of the more privileged sector of the Black bourgeoisie usually replaced the radical nationalistic leadership. These foundation-funded groups often invited the heretofore radical groups to participate in their activities as a "show of unity," the "Black United Front" era of the late Sixties and early Seventies. The bourgeois cultural nationalist elites gained ascendance and forced the more radical Black Nationalist leaders to the outer fringes of the Movement. An illustration of this trend would be Kenneth Gibson's election in Newark and the decline of Baraka's influence.

Martin Kilson's observation regarding the new Black bourgeois political leadership accurately captured this process.[23] These new elites, generally first-generation middleclass, had participated in some aspects of the Civil Rights Movement but still managed to acquire the necessary "credentials" (advanced degrees and/or professional training) to move into the new political-economic niches generated by the capitalist corporate elite's concessions. In this process we perceive a classical example of the "sponge effect" of America's corporate capitalism, its ability to buy-off and "soak-up" disruptive, dissatisfied elements in its constituency. However, as Allen clearly revealed, several militant bourgeois cultural nationalists proved readily "available" for co-optation, bearing witness to the often-heard accusation among militants that no bourgeoisie in the world "sells out" as cheaply as the Black American bourgeoisie.

Of those who make up the nationalist strain in the Black bourgeoisie, we generally find them elitist, whether members of the conservative Masons or leaders of radical groups or organizations. The Nation of Islam organization (perhaps better known as the Black Muslims), under the direction of the Honorable Elijah Muhammed (and, after his death, revitalized under the leadership of Minister Louis Farrakhan), represented one notable exception to this elitist trend. The Nation of Islam combined Washington's economic nationalism with a Black Nationalist theology that emphasizes AfricanAmerican cultural superiority. Analysts labelled the Muslims a middleclass movement because of its (Booker T.) Washingtonian oriented emphasis on moral purity, cleanliness, order, submission to authority, rigid disciplinary code, sacrifice, and the subordination of womens' to mens' roles. But its approach proved to be very effective in attracting and maintaining the support of a significant segment of the Black lowerclass and underclasses, especially males; and it quite successfully recruited, cured, and politically activated drug addicts.

Although perceived as one which reinforced mainstream middleclass values by imposing them on its constituents, it received very little support from the Black ethcaste elites and suffered denunciation from the dominant White liberal middleclass. Local police and Federal law enforcement agencies subjected its leaders to constant surveillance and harassment. Both Black and White liberals charged the Muslims with "Black racism"— a rather ludicrous charge, given their ethcaste status.

From a PanAfrican communalist perspective, the Muslims represented a creative and innovative alternative political-economic model. They combined religious thought and practice with an economic infrastructure, laying the foundation for protracted cultural struggle. In addition, their approach conformed to the cultural values characteristic of the AfricanAmerican community. The Muslims, a highly integrated organization, maintained an extended family or clan-type bureaucracy, It functioned on principles grounded in AfricanAmerican extended family relations: all members addressed each other as "brother" or "sister"; elder members received appropriate respect for their age and experience; an elderly patriarchal figure respected for his wisdom and vision presided over this organization; if anyone attacked one member of the "family," all felt attacked and responded accordingly.

However, while much of the style, organization, and interpersonal relations within the Nation of Islam seemed grounded in the AfricanAmerican cultural tradition, Elijah, their leader, also attacked several important elements in AfricanAmerican lifestyle; like eating pork and other "soul" food and supporting the traditional Black Christian church, Black ministers, and Black popular music — especially gospel, blues, and rhythm and blues. In attacking these core cultural patterns and institutions, the Nation alienated a large segment of the AfricanAmerican community, many sympathetic believers and potential recruits.

Many AfricanAmericans agreed with certain aspects of the Nation's philosophy, but they could not accept it *in toto*. Consequently, the majority of AfricanAmericans in all socioeconomic groups perceived this non-elitist, cultural nationalist movement to be opposed to AfricanAmerican culture because it did not demonstrate appropriate respect for important dimensions and elements in AfricanAmerican values and practices. Yet, much can be gained from a critical analysis of the strengths and limitations of the Nation of Islam. Like Garvey's Movement, it touched the lives of millions of AfricanAmericans, and I am convinced that the Muslims' (and Garvey's) strategies and tactics, with appropriate changes, represent viable models that could launch the AfricanAmerican community into the next stage of mass struggle. These movements could be the basis for an organization and philosophy whose time has arrived.

According to Will D. Tate, a new, university-trained group of Black urban managerial elites occupy positions today because of their "competence" rather than their color.[24] But these folk figure as racial/cultural "neuters" oblivious to the fact that their positions were gained from lowerclass struggle. One could hypothesize that if these "neuters" are not now so conscious of the reasons for that struggle, they will be in the near future as the number of professional AfricanAmericans are "laid off" because of "temporary" fiscal difficulties. The consciousness of its precarious class position (dependent on both its White masters and reference group, and its less appreciated lowerclass racial brothers and sisters) cements the traditional ethcaste elite. Biologically and geographically diverse, they need class consciousness, or a concept of "consciousness of kind," for their survival, although a purely Marxian analysis would designate this group's consciousness as a severe case of sociocultural and political-economic false consciousness, much like the

White middle, working, and lower classes.

Frazier, Cruse, and Allen presented detailed criticisms of the Black bourgeoisie's (upper middleclass's) rejection of the Black masses and AfricanAmerican culture, but none of them discussed or attempted to define AfricanAmerican culture. Cruse evaded the issue by concentrating on aesthetic culture and artists; Frazier constantly vacillated on the issue of urban AfricanAmerican culture but apparently found rural AfricanAmerican culture admirable; Allen's Marxist approach, *i.e.*, ignoring culture, reflected many of the biases characteristic of that position on the cultural issue. Cruse's position, while being quite consistent with that of PanAfrican communalism, suffers from a failure to acknowledge and appreciate the cultural and political significance of the African heritage. Undeniably, the cultural base of AfricanAmericans resides in the South, and it has become increasingly difficult to challenge the African roots thesis of southern AfricanAmerican culture. Simple logic, then, leads one to conclude that Africa as the source of much of urban AfricanAmerican culture exists in all parts of the country. This African-derived rural southern base has been and continues to be perceived as the cultural origins of those who have been designated the "externally adapted," "non-respectables" who must be ignored and/or "escaped from." Yet, the lifestyles of Black ethcaste middle and elite classes contain many cultural elements in common with these rejected lower classes.

Robert Staples noted that the Black middleclass has retained many African values such as brotherhood, communalism, and cooperation, values supposedly more extensive among the externally adapted lower classes.[25] These values were both reinforced during our enslavement and, arguably, were a main reason for the "success" of African slavery. In addition, a growing body of revisionist history, like that of Eugene Genovese and John Blassingame, seriously challenges the often-cited assertion of a division between "house niggers" and "field niggers."[26] From an AfricanAmerican cultural perspective, these works suggest a much closer relationship between the two groups along the lines reflected in Alex Haley's *Roots*. Staples also argued that after the period of enslavement, African communal values survived in the forms of Black fraternal organizations like the Masons and its affiliates, and other benefit associations. The Black middleclass, including the bourgeois segment, use AfricanAmerican cultural values to pursue their interests yet criticize and ostracize lowerclass Blacks for maintaining in a less demure and acceptable manner the very same cultural values. In their culturally nonconscious efforts to impress their White superiors and maintain their precarious distance from the Black masses, the Black middleclass ignores the positive elements in its African heritage although its members continue to practice them in modified forms.

There are other areas of cultural overlap between the two "strands" (the respectables and the externally adapted), so many that some PanAfrican nationalists in the Sixties rejected the notion of class division in the AfricanAmerican community. Carol B. Stack's study of underclass extended family functioning revealed that the lowerclass AfricanAmerican family still practices African communal values extensively.[27] Robert Hill's analysis of the *Strengths of Black Families* also documents the extent to which communal values (especially the informal adoption practices of Black families) prevails in all classes in the AfricanAmerican community. Andrew Billingsley's analysis of the "screens of opportunity" for middle and upper middle-class AfricanAmerican families further documents the importance of the extended family (which is often composed of relatives both biological and non-biological) in Black upward mobility and survival.[28]

Another area of overlap between the supposedly "divergent strands" occurs in the area of politics. Staples cited evidence indicating that AfricanAmericans of all social classes stay closer to one another in their political orientations than to Whites of comparable education and income. He cited Charles Hamilton's study which suggested that class collaboration in politics result from most middleclass Blacks being salaried employees in the public sector. Consequently, their job interests match those of lowerclass Blacks. The racial/cultural hostility directed towards Whites reveals still another obvious area of cultural overlap between the strands. Lowerclass Blacks tend to be more overt in their expression of their anger and frustration, probably because structurally they serve much more often as the victims of overt racist practices than middleclass Blacks. Yet, as noted above, a substantial proportion of the Black middleclass and elite harbor hostile attitudes towards Whites of all classes. Individuals may conceal their hostility when in the actual presence of Whites, but once within the safe and comfortable confines of their ethcaste *class'* social milieu, they openly express their antagonism.

AfricanAmerican culture is a culture of struggle forged in the fiery furnace of the middle passage, slavery, peonage, Jim Crow, urban migration and its accompanying exploitation, isolation, and economic strangulation. Both cultural "strands" participated in and supported the movements, organizations, and individuals that emerged during various eras in AfricanAmerican history to challenge racial injustice. Although a certain amount of friction and hostility between the various groups and their leaders surfaced, this friction played an important role in increasing the political consciousness of AfricanAmericans at all levels. In this sense, the existence of a culturally schizophrenic segment of the Black middleclass constitutes a cultural and political problem. Members of this group who accept WASP values, ethics, and beliefs lose their appreciation of the positive elements within their own culture.

With the possible exception of Cruse, the critics discussed in this review failed to clarify the cultural position of this segment of the AfricanAmerican community. And although Cruse correctly noted the importance of culture as an organizing principle in Black politics and economics, he failed to delineate the cultural elements which should be perpetuated. His program for implementing his concept of African-American culture represents a valuable contribution, but he does not include the "meat" or content to use as guiding principles for the AfricanAmerican liberation struggle. In other words, he does not present the AfricanAmerican cultural values which should serve as the basis for political objectives, a Black political-economic vision of America, or a definition of AfricanAmerican freedom. He argues that Black artists and intellectuals should take the leading role in creating this type cultural and political consciousness at the same time he demonstrates why they found it impossible to accomplish this charge.

I contend that AfricanAmerican cultural values exist which have unified the AfricanAmerican community since our arrival in this Babylon; and that, at times, certain segments of the Black elite (as well as all other segments of the AfricanAmerican community which identify with them) have been guilty of both denying their cultural roots and leading the masses down a similar culturally destructive path. These groups and individuals accomplish this destruction through their acceptance of the negative stereotypes of AfricanAmerican culture and by their political alliances with Whites (be they Marxists or liberal Democrats) who share these same negative attitudes. In another of his numerous vacillations on AfricanAmerican culture, Frazier claimed that the "new" Black middleclass has given a new content to the Washington-Masonic-WASP creed of piety, thrift, and respectability:

> The new content is partly of a negative type and it involves a

rejection of everything represented by the Negro folk. The Negro literary and artistic renaissance which turned to the Negro folk for inspiration is rejected by the emerging new middle-class and it is completely forgotten today. Nevertheless, the new middle-class cannot escape from its folk background and this background mixed with some elements of the genteel tradition explains the fact that the middle-class Negro is often a mixture of a gentleman and a peasant.[29]

It appears that Frazier was truly prophetic when one thinks about that segment of the contemporary Black middleclass which resides in affluent, predominantly White suburbs and raises its children in an atmosphere of total isolation physically and culturally from the Black masses. The fact that most young Black adults and students know little or nothing about AfricanAmerican history or culture attests to the eroding effect that desegregation has had on the larger AfricanAmerican community. While this middleclass segment remains rather small—which limits the damage it can do to the larger community—desegregation has practically eliminated young African Americans' knowledge and consciousness of their culture. This latter situation constitutes the greatest challenge confronting the AfricanAmerican community in that if the next generations do not know their culture, they will not know what to protect or how to use its strengths to sustain them in the continuing, protracted struggle. If that happens, the AfricanAmerican community as a biocultural community will not survive in a recognizable form. We may finally succumb to White domination and actually become only colored White people.

CHAPTER III

CRITICAL REVIEW OF SELECTED SOCIOLOGICAL CLASS THEORIES 1: KARL MARX AND RACIAL CULTURAL STRUGGLE

In this chapter I will analyze and interpret the works of Marxist theoreticians from an evolving PanAfrican communalism perspective. In so doing, Marx's theoretical approach will be discussed in terms of what it illuminates as well as what it conceals when applied to the AfricanAmerican community's experiences in the capitalist cultural system of the United States. Marxist social thought has had and continues to have a profound impact on AfricanAmerican academicians and political activists. Harold Cruse noted that the "Marxist" versus "cultural nationalist" visions of the strategies, tactics, and objectives of the AfricanAmerican liberation struggle have been and continue to be a major source of tension, debate, and division within the intellectual, political, and cultural elites.[1] This discussion develops a framework which brings together these apparently contradictory ideologies.

A number of areas in Marxian theory coincide with the sociological perspective informing this analysis. One of these areas, Marx's central assumption, is the concept of man as an active, creative being as opposed to a passive or routinized being. This central assumption also stands as the basic, core premise of symbolic interactionism, another school of sociological thought most clearly presented in Herbert Blumer's excellent book.[2] Several scholars[3] have alluded to the theoretical similarities of these two schools, but Richard Lichtman subjected them to a systematic, critical analysis. He presented the symbolic interactionist characteristics which are implicit in Marxian theory: (a) the emphasis on the social nature of humanity and human activity; (b) the view of the person as a subject-agent who acts on the world and is not merely reacting to its pressure or stimuli; (c) an approach to the study of humanity which highlights the uniqueness of the human enterprise, the construction of a meaningfully interpreted, reciprocal, and ongoing project; (d) the advance over Weber's conception of social action which requires that one explicitly direct h/er activity toward the interpreted meaning of others — for "social idealism" (symbolic interactionism), every person is intrinsically social regardless of how solitary or isolated s/he appears; (e) the emphasis on methodology as coextensive with the entire scientific enterprise (Herbert Blumer); and, (f) the insistence of direct acquaintance with the social world of human activity.[4]

These elements in symbolic interactionism and Marxism emphasize humans as creative, innovative beings whose behavior is not "determined" by external social facts which "control and constrain [them]." To the contrary, humans can choose to obey cultural norms of behavior or to disobey, subvert, or pervert them and even develop new norms through their ability to imaginatively construct situations and responses to situations before encountering them. These assumptions regarding humans and culture provide important insights into the nature of the relationship between people from different cultures, especially when one race or cultural group is considered subordinate to another racial or cultural group. This conception of "active," self-objectifying humans helps one to understand how oppressed racial or cultural groups can maintain their dignity, self-respect, and identity in the face of racial or cultural assault under colonialism, slavery, or indenture.

For example, although Europeans brought Africans to the Americas and enslaved and treated them as property, the Africans did not lose their sense of humanity. If one accepted the theory that external or culturally imposed definitions determined an individual's or group's identity or self-definition, one would have expected enslaved Africans to perceive themselves as some lower form of animal life rather than as culturally different human beings. Improvisation, a cultural feature most obvious in Black music, amplified and facilitated Africans' ability to modify, transform, and shape their past cultural heritage and use it as a basis for survival as well as weapons in their struggles for liberation; a manifest achievement which classically confirms the Marxian and symbolic interactionist principles and coincides with the PanAfrican communalism perspective guiding this analysis.

Further, these underlying assumptions and descriptive processes constitute the most objective, "value-free" theoretical approach to the study of human society extant in EuropeanAmerican sociology. They do not rest on the culturally and racially chauvinist premises inherent in most sociological theories such as structural-functionalism, systems theory, or social Darwinism.

Marvin Harris's analysis of the origins of anthropological theory noted that most early theoretical explanations of the rise of "civilization" were culture-bound and racist.[5] Earlier "theorists" excluded nine-tenths of the world's sociocultural systems from consideration:

> The argument that only "progressive" societies can yield an understanding of "progressive change" is totally specious, probably little more than a rationalization for the lack of knowledge about primitive and non-western systems so conspicuous in the writings of Saint-Simon, Comte, Hegel, Marx, Engels, and many other early nineteenth-century figures who are reckoned among the founders of academic sociology.[6]

Harris observed further that these earlier theoreticians' preoccupation with "progress," or the evolving urban industrial civilization, along with their increasing racial arrogance, led to the development of theories of racial determinism. While most scholars usually associate these theories with social Darwinism, Harris presented compelling evidence to document the racism present in Eighteenth century enlightenment philosophy, despite the fact that the doctrine of "perfectibility" complicated the simplicity of that racism by conceding the possibility for less "enlightened" peoples to be guided to the "sacred" state of EuropeanAmerican civilization. In the years leading up to Darwin, more and more men of "science" rejected this egalitarian principle, and "it came to be accepted that the White race had an innate and almost permanent advantage over all the rest." He continues,

> The *prima facie* case for these beliefs seemed overwhelming. Since the fifteenth century, Euro-Americans had met with countless peoples in Africa, America, Asia, and the Pacific Islands, not one of whom had

been able effectively to ward off or retaliate against the advance of European military, economic, political, and religious institutions.[7]

Most contemporary sociological and anthropological theories have their roots in these earlier formulations and rest on a racist, cultural chauvinist foundation.

As Harris noted, this assessment holds true for the Marxist theory of social change in capitalist culture as well. Yet, the Marxian and symbolic interactionist conceptions of the human capacity for socialization and resocialization (that is, one's ability to be both a product and producer of culture) provide a general principle applicable to all human groups. While racist and chauvinist, some of the underlying assumptions regarding human nature can be applied across racial and cultural boundaries. Consistent with the aforementioned purpose of this critical analysis of selected social class theories, I will elucidate the useful dimensions of these theories to the development of an AfricanAmerican sociological perspective while noting the racist aspects.

As Nathan Hare wrote in his critique of the "strengths" school's reliance on systems theory, we must be ever alert to the underlying assumptions of these social theories and theoreticians as well as to the historical forces which shaped or influenced them. From an AfricanAmerican sociological perspective on cultural struggle, Marx's theory stands as an alternative or radical model within the dominant or culturally superordinate body of ideas. His exposure of capitalist culture as an inherently exploitive system challenged the liberal universalistic myths which his contemporaries had constructed. However, Harold Cruse observed that the Marxian position with respect to AfricanAmerican culture and the cultures of other peoples of color held essentially the same attitudes as that of the progressive liberals. These EuropeanAmerican would-be "superiors" perceived AfricanAmerican culture as an oppressive condition which should be destroyed or transformed. Marx differed in that he preferred to have this process administered and directed by supposedly more humanistic proletarian socialists.

The authentic and central aspects of Marxian theory however have not been as popular as those in what Robert Blauner termed "vulgar Marxism."[8] In his examination of Marxian theory's position on the question of race, nationality, and colonialism, Blauner noted this deviation. He wrote,

> "Every theorist working in the Marxist tradition is confronted with the problem of distinguishing between the essential and creative principles of Marx's thought and the simplified, mechanistic schema that

are commonly referred to as "vulgar Marxism." [9]

I agree with Blauner's position regarding the usefulness of the creative principles within Marxism (and, I would add, symbolic interactionism) as part of a universal theoretical model for the comparative analysis of cultural groups within capitalist state formations. However, I also agree with Cruse's assertion that the blind acceptance of a Marxist orientation amongst Black and White scholars causes negative cultural implications; for, as Blauner states (and Cruse implies), many American Marxist interpreters have been vulgar, mechanistic, dogmatic, and deterministic.

This strand of Marxist thought offers the same position on the question of race, ethnicity, nationality, and colonialism as that of the social Darwinists and structural-functionalists: that race, nationality (or nationalism, such as Black nationalism), and ethnicity serve as cultural anachronisms which impede the global march to establish advanced, progressive, modern systems. Cruse's perceptive observation that the acceptance of either "vulgar Marxism" or "liberalism" results in racial/cultural negation because both approaches share what many sociologists perceive as the essence of the sociological tradition: the liberal-universalistic orientation toward race, nationality, and colonialism. For liberal universalists, traditional or "primitive" sentiments and the institutional life structured around these values and beliefs are "cultural lags" to be discarded, or cast-off in humanity's pursuit of the "enlightened," "progressive," socialist or liberal democratic system.

From a Black sociological perspective, Marxist theory makes a valuable conceptual contribution through its penetrating insights into the nature of capitalist culture. However, as Hare and William Wilson noted, Black social theoreticians must maintain the critical distance necessary to expose and resist the cultural chauvinist ideas Marx inherited from his predecessors; that is, we must expose the underlying assumptions of any theoretical model and note the implications these assumptions contain when the models are used to study the AfricanAmerican experience.

In this summary discussion of Marxian theory, I rely heavily on Charles Anderson's text, *The Political Economy of Social Classes*.[10] This work presents an excellent neo-Marxian interpretation and application of Marxist theory to contemporary capitalist culture, especially that of the United States. With the exception of his treatment of the relationship between the White workingclass and racial minority groups (especially AfricanAmericans), his treatment represents a model of what Blauner alluded to with his terms "creative" or "open" Marxism.

According to Anderson, Marx perceived capitalism as a political-economic and sociocultural system which radically transforms human beings' relationship to labor or productive work and the product resulting from that labor; that is, capitalism as a cultural system perverts humans' ability to creatively express their humanity through labor. Humans are forced to surrender this ability in order to meet the rational, efficient production needs of capitalism. The specialization and routinization of tasks require that humans use less and less of their creative ability (both mental and physical), thereby retarding human growth and development as productive beings. Humans as workers no longer control the pace of their work nor the quality of the finished product. Laborers cannot identify with the finished product since their contribution is so slight and essentially mechanical. Pride and a sense of personal accomplishment are lost as workers increasingly become an appendage of the machine, organized to work with machine-like precision and efficiency. Anderson noted an intriguing implication in the concept of the alienation of labor:

> The alienation of labor... implies that in the act of labor itself the worker is fragmented and shredded, has been stripped of a sense of purpose, and has lost sight of even the product of his labors; his work leaves him emasculated, frustrated, and often desperate, meaning his leisure will take on many of the same traits.[11]

To Anderson, such alienation profoundly affects the humanity of a capitalist cultural society:

> Because man is alienated in practical labor creativity, he is also alienated from his "species-life," that is, from all potentialities that mark man off from the animal world. This includes the important dimensions of relating cooperatively with the people, particularly in the labor process. Man is thus alienated from other men and from human life as such. And through all this, people have alienated themselves from nature, and have reduced it as well to the status of a commodity to be exploited and standing externally to human life. On all fronts, capitalism has transformed the world into a selling process, a cash-nexus relationship.[12]

While this characterization of laborers in capitalist cultures may today appear to be unduly harsh, Marx derived his observations from the social conditions of the workingclass in Western Europe during the middle of the nineteenth century. Yet, George Orwell's mid-twentieth century descriptions of the social conditions of the workingclass in London and Paris corroborated Marx's perspective.[13] Needless to say, many considered the social conditions of the workers in the early stages of the United

States capitalist cultural evolution equally harsh, exploitive, and dehumanizing. Although numerous studies have demonstrated that, at least in some enterprises, these alienating factors and consequences not only exist today but in many industrial settings the situation remains essentially as Marx described it. [14]

However, the Black Marxian scholar Lloyd Hogan noted that Marx's genius resided in his ability to expose the fundamental contradiction in the progressive liberals' definition of freedom for the laboring masses inherent in capitalist culture.[15] While the capitalist "revolution" freed the masses to become property owners and participate in the bourgeois political process, it forced them to leave the land (their basis of economic survival) and enter the labor market. This change had the effect of forcing the "free" laboring masses to sell their human energy (labor power or ability to work) to the capitalist owners of the means of production. The capitalists purchased the laboring masses' human energy under conditions which the capitalists determined and controlled. Thus, in order to survive, the laborers had to accept the conditions and terms of employment as dictated by the owners. Marx noted that "freedom" for the laboring masses, operationally defined, meant freedom to become a slave to wages. For without wages, the laborers could not procure the goods and services required to sustain themselves and their families. Viewed in this perspective, one can see that capitalist culture and mode of economic organization is, indeed, brutal and vicious.

If one accepts W.E.B. DuBois's assertion that the quality of life of the masses of a society reflects its moral and ideological priorities and commitments, obviously the *laissez-faire* free enterprise, liberal democratic practice of capitalism (*vis-a-vis* the masses) diametrically opposes its lofty humanistic rhetoric. As the brilliant Black poet and musician Gil Scott-Heron cogently observed, under capitalist cultural organization, "'freedom' ain't nothin' but a word"— a "con" or "hustle"— to dupe the masses into believing that life under bourgeois rule and domination is better or superior to life under an oppressive feudal regime. Illuminating the nature and character of the class structure in liberal bourgeois capitalist culture led Marx to challenge and expose the theoretical biases and *status quo*-affirming character of much of his contemporaries' academic research and writing. The fact that capitalist social formations contain essentially two social classes—the owners of the means of the production and those who work for them—destroyed the egalitarian myth created and perpetuated by liberal universalist humanists. For, as the preceding discussion clearly indicates, the power of the owners greatly exceeds the power of the workers. Thus, inequality remains an inherent component of capitalism. Power remains concentrated in the hands of a relatively small capitalist elite who make decisions which determine the life chances of the laboring masses.

The logical question for a Marxian analysis and interpretation of capitalist cultures becomes, "How do the masses remain intact? That is, how does it (the working class) reproduce itself over time and remain relatively stable?" As a PanAfrican communalist attempting to combine an understanding of the significance of culture with the method of historical materialism, I would contend that Marx (and the various schools of thought which take their direction from him) underestimated the power of culture and the ability of the bourgeoisie to manipulate its meaning or content. If one defines culture as the socially shared beliefs, attitudes, values, norms, and language transmitted from generation to generation, one can see that culture constitutes the cement which binds people together. It is the source of their identity, that which distinguishes them from others.

The method of historical materialism tends to place this vital component of organized human group life into a residual category. While humans are both products and producers of culture, these processes occur within established cultural parameters. For without a cultural context, humans could not be truly human. It should also be remembered that culture (contrary to the static portraits often presented by anthropologists) is constantly in change, and institutional practices may be in conflict or may change at different rates. Thus, the fact that capitalist ideological rhetoric contradicts its institutional practices will not necessarily lead to massive social disruptions. Culture, then, endures simultaneously as rigid and flexible, static and changing, and more importantly, tenacious.

It appears that Marx (and many of his contemporary followers) failed to appreciate the cultural impact of the liberal bourgeois revolution, just as they fail today to fully appreciate the magnitude of cultural change required to establish a socialist society, especially in an ethnically heterogeneous state. Anderson noted this tendency of the bourgeoisie to "con" the masses when it convinced feudal serfs that they had mutual interests. As the middle "class" in the feudal caste system, the bourgeoisie understandably developed as a class for itself under the feudal system and absolute monarchy, eventually "sanctifying" its interests in the Protestant

Reformation. As a class for itself, it played an important role in the overthrowing feudalism and monarchy in order to transform that society into a bourgeois society. The overturning of the old order opened up the class structure of society in a way that made it seem to all classes that the bourgeoisie was representative of the interests of the entire society as compared to the old ruling class. Individuals consigned to lowly life stations by birth were led to believe that they had been set free to climb into the ranks of the bourgeoisie or at least the middleclass, a process which may continue throughout the capitalist period.

The bourgeois revolution was eventually codified in lofty, liberal egalitarian language, as in the slogan, *"Liberté! Fraternité! Egalité!"* which galvanized the French masses, and in the public documents written to usher in the new social order, such as the *Magna Carta* in England and later the *Declaration of Independence* and *Bill of Rights* in the United States. The revolutionary leaders used the principles espoused within these documents to awaken the consciousness of the peasantry and convert them to the bourgeois cause. At this initial juncture, the proletariat became integrated into capitalist culture. And, critiquing from the perspective of PanAfrican communalism, *both* the bourgeoisie *and* the proletariat came to believe that they possess a vested interest in maintaining and perpetuating capitalist culture.

The inadequate attention to this point exposes the Achilles heel of Marx's theory in terms of its vision of an internal dialectic leading to social revolution with the workers taking over and controlling the means of production. This reason that this revolution has not occurred is because the workers have been socialized to accept and believe in the values, beliefs, norms, and ideological justifications of capitalist culture. Marx apparently underestimated the essentially conservative but flexible nature of culture and the persuasiveness of the bourgeois intelligentsia, whom Anderson characterized as the rationalizers, justifiers, and systemizers of the bourgeois political status quo.

Marx's theory presents an excellent analysis and description of capitalist evolution and the social processes accompanying its emergence. Most importantly, Marx noted the impact that these evolutionary processes had on human behavior, especially upon the laborers at the bottom, the "have-nots," whom Anderson described as being "as both indispensable to the existence of the system and readily dispensable should another warm body be standing behind them."[16] The fact that Marx's vision of social change and the new socialist system which would correct what he perceived as the fundamental flaw in capitalism has not occurred does not alter the essential validity of his analysis. Instead, the failure of his predictions confirms his overemphasis on the economic and material dimension of culture and his failure to demonstrate how the connections between the various dimensions of a culture coalesce. Many of Marx's critics observed this flaw. This theoretical flaw lends credence to the old adage that "man does not live by bread alone."

It is my contention that the workers' revolution has not occurred in Western European and American capitalist societies, particularly the United States, because the workers have been to a greater or lesser degree integrated into and both enculturated and socialized to accept the legitimacy of capitalist culture. To the detriment of his vision, Marx chose to de-emphasize what Weber demonstrated in his monograph, *The Protestant Ethic and The Spirit of Capitalism*: European peasants became captivated by and organized around the ethos of liberal democracy, which is the moral and superstructural ideology for capitalist culture. Weber traced the evolution of the Protestant ethic's emphasis on radically altering the nature of the relationship between humans and God, humans and nature, and humans and other humans; and he demonstrated how these new ideas or perceptions (revolutionary for the time) captured the imagination and loyalty of the Western European peasantry. Liberal ideology—with its emphasis on achievement, individualism, and equality—became the spiritual "cement" which united the bourgeoisie and the peasantry in their successful struggle against the landed aristocracy. The emergence of a union between the old financial/commercial (mercantilist) aristocracy and new industrial bourgeoisie as the Marxian ruling class (the owners of the means of production) developed simultaneously. Anderson's summary noted this cleavage and new synthesis of Marx's analysis of the bourgeoisie:

> The most important cleavage within the ruling class ... is that between the financial aristocracy and the industrial bourgeoisie ... the financial aristocracy is not interested in producing wealth but only in confiscating it — they are essentially unproductive and usurious in orientation and behavior. ... Momentarily, the bourgeoisie of industry and the proletariat had a common cause against the waste, parasitism, and extravagance of the idle rich. Yet the immense success of industrial capital itself called into being an alliance of financial and industrial interests which became increasingly two sides of the same ruling class. There remain, however, certain conflicts of interest which wax and wane through the business cycle.[17]

To account for the relative stability or instability of capitalist societies (depending on which viewpoint one chooses to emphasize), Marx introduced the concept of "false consciousness." For Marx, the class which ruled or controlled the material forces of a society also ruled the intellectual life. In noting this, he emphasized that the ruling ideas in ascendance (that is, accepted as legitimate) do not exist because of self-evident correctness or a detached or independent existence in history; on the contrary, "ruling ideas hold sway because their exponents made them *appear* as naturally right and autonomous by those who wield institutional powers."[18] Anderson further noted, "to take an epoch at its own word, to accept as given the ruling ideas, is to engage in reification and to fetishize the world." He continues,

> It is to be in a position of alienation. To persist in the bourgeois worldview at a time when the contradictions between the forces and relations of production are growing is to have a distorted mental picture of reality, to have false consciousness. False consciousness is not an all-or-nothing phenomenon; it is a matter of degree of reality and unreality. The opposite mental picture of the world under developed capital is class consciousness. Class consciousness is simultaneously revolutionary consciousness, for it understands the source of alienation and material bondage to be in the capitalist mode of production, and that capitalist relations must be replaced by socially organized, controlled and utilized production.[19]

Thus, in Marxian terms, the stability or persistence of capitalist culture rests on its ability to prevent the development of proletarian class consciousness. I accept this and acknowledge its relevance in accounting for the capitalist cultural patriotism of the workingclass, but Marx does not say why it should be so or how it came to be that way. If the contradictions are so great (and I agree that they are), why has the workingclass in capitalist culture remained loyal to the rulingclass and its ruling ideas when they are obviously antithetical to interests of the workingclass? To answer this question, I will examine Max Weber, another visionary social observer of capitalist culture often presented as Marx's intellectual opponent.

However, before entering into an analysis of Weber's social class theory, I will briefly discuss Marx's perspective on the middleclass and the implications it holds for the AfricanAmerican middleclass. The Marxian framework argues that the middleclass is composed of highly trained, skilled workers (including professionals) whose politics exemplify the concept of false consciousness. These workers do not own the means of production, at least not to any significant degree; and they sell their skills, talents, and abilities to the ruling class. The ruling class created the middleclass — the managers, administrators, intellectual rationalizers and justifiers of the ideology and institutions — to serve its interests. Culturally, the middleclass emulates, imitates, and strives for acceptance into the bourgeoisie. In return for this loyalty, the middleclass receives higher salaries, relatively prestigious positions, and socioeconomic conditions qualitatively and quantitatively superior to those of the proletariat. The middleclass interprets, as opposed to "defines," bourgeois capitalist culture, the sociocultural base for liberal democratic capitalism. Thus, the middleclass serves as both a buffer between the proletariat and the ruling class, and as the "colonial elite administrators" of the proletariat, to use Dorsey's reformulated application of the term (personal communication).

Marxian theory suggests that the middleclass is potentially revolutionary. If it were to become conscious of itself (a class-for-itself) and perceive its class interests as the same as those of the proletariat, this group has the organizational and intellectual resources essential to execute a successful revolution. Many—perhaps most—revolutionary leaders have been members of the middleclass. Some of the more optimistic neo-Marxian theoreticians have introduced the concept of the "new workingclass" in their efforts to refine traditional Marxian theory to accommodate the liberal democratic capitalist cultural phenomenon, middleclass society; that is, the United States. The diamond-shaped class structure characteristic of the United States became an unforeseen phenomenon in traditional Marxian theory, or an "unanticipated consequence" (perhaps even a latent dysfunction?) of liberal democratic capitalist cultural evolution. This new development forced American Marxists to modify Marxian theory with respect to the middleclass, given that most of America's labor force now comes from the middleclass. During Marx's lifetime a quite different situation existed as the workingclass far exceeded the middleclass in size.

Apologists for liberal democratic capitalist culture quickly indicate that the evolution of the middleclass with its ruling class aspirations and limited, but still considerable, accumulation of what it perceives as bourgeois material goods represents something of a revolution in itself. This "embourgeoisment" of the workingclass has also contributed immensely to the stability of capitalist culture, despite the rather large and widening gap between the "haves" and "have-nots."

Peter Schrag noted in his critique of American popular culture that American capitalist production has produced "plastic" versions of the expensive material goods appearing in the homes and offices of the bourgeoisie (and has brought them to the consuming public "live and in living color" on the omnipresent television), at a price range that most Americans can afford. This ability reinforces the middle- and workingclasses' illusion that they possess everything that the higher status classes have and, furthermore, acquired it for less! This false sense of egalitarian consumption also contributed to the stability and perpetuation of an inherently exploitive political-economic system.[20] Thus, the evolution and expansion of middleclass society, especially in the United States, prevented or delayed the proletarian revolution which Marx anticipated. Liberal democratic capitalist culture's ability to absorb and satisfy the discontented elements among the working- and middleclasses practically eliminated Marxism as a serious theoretical critique of capitalist cultural dynamics. Lewis Corey observed:

> The failure of socialism to grow among the American people, which always puzzled and irritated Marxists, becomes understandable in part as changes in class relations are considered. Much of the socialist agitation was based on the argument that "opportunity has come to an end." But the emphasis always was on the opportunity to become independent businessmen. In this connection the socialist argument was largely true after 1910, although up until that year opportunity, while diminishing, was still there. But a whole field for "opportunity to rise in the world" was opened up by the astonishing expansion of technical-managerial and professional employment .... The form was new but it was opportunity and it offered "careers open to the talented." This, along with other factors—no American feudalism, the measurable completion in the 1820's–30's of the struggle for political democracy, the unparalleled economic expansion which brought to the American people the highest living standards in the world—distinguished this country from Europe and explains the failure of socialism.[21]

While Corey's factors accounting for the failure of socialism in the United States appear true for Whites, they ignore or overlook the AfricanAmerican experience which virtually remains the opposite of the EuropeanAmerican experience. Jim Crow segregation in the South forced AfricanAmericans to become physically marginal to the political struggles of EuropeanAmericans, and caused AfricanAmericans to experience minimal economic expansion, while making them America's feudal peasants. A tendency to ignore the Black middleclass or to draw special attention to the insignificance of this relatively small segment of the population characterized the Marxist approach. AfricanAmericans (historically and contemporarily) are minimally represented among the bourgeoisie as owners of the means of production.

Most AfricanAmericans in business, with few notable exceptions, own small businesses ("mom and pop" shops) catering to the cultural needs of the local AfricanAmerican community: barbershops, beauty parlors, "soul food" restaurants, bars, liquor stores, neighborhood "grocery" stores, and so on. These businesses tend to employ few people and serve primarily as means of support for a family, allowing its members the freedom to earn a living independent of the low-skilled, low-paying, menial work which this society forces most AfricanAmericans to accept. These businesses usually seem somewhat inefficient by the standards of rationally organized American small businesses. They usually carry a small range of merchandise which reflects the cultural tastes and desires of the local AfricanAmerican community. (An excellent description of such a store is found in Maya Angelou's *I Know Why the Caged Bird Sings*).

Located in AfricanAmerican communities known for their poverty and depression-level economies, these "business" establishments exist on a low profit margin and their continuation over time generally reflects the creative genius and tenacity of the owners. In the United States, most successful Black capitalist institutions include life insurance companies, Johnson Publishing Company, Johnson Beauty Products, and professional athletes and artists. A few Black-owned banks and real estate companies have achieved moderate success. I say moderate because, if one combined all their profits, they would equal a minute fraction of General Motor's profits. Only one Black-headed company, Beatrice, has appeared in Fortune's annual list of the top 500 American businesses. Thus, the Black entrepreneurial bourgeoisie is most conspicuous by its comparatively limited size.

The neo-Marxian characterization of the middleclass as the new workingclass composed mostly of highly trained white-collar and professional workers and salaried employees accurately describes the Black middleclass. The Black community divides along sociocultural lines as opposed to political-economic ones due to the relatively small (as compared to that of Whites) gap between the elite wage earners and the non-elite working and underclasses. Several AfricanAmerican community studies from DuBois's *Philadelphia Negro* to Drake and Cayton's *Black Metropolis* to Frazier's *Black Bourgoisie* and *The Negro Family in the United States* to Allen's *Black Awakening in Capitalist America* have documented the persistence of this phenomenon over time.

As a consequence of the AfricanAmerican population's disproportionate representation within the proletariat, American Marxists (both Black and White) have emphasized the similarity in political-economic interests and have attempted to organize AfricanAmerican and EuropeanAmerican workers around these interests. These efforts have been only minimally successful, primarily because of the Marxists' tendency to de-emphasize the significance of race. In so doing, they also ignore the existence and significance of AfricanAmerican culture and the continuing cultural struggle. As noted earlier, this element in Marxian theory and practice reflects its EuropeanAmerican cultural chauvinistic and racist biases, thus limiting its usefulness as a paradigm for AfricanAmerican liberation.

Despite this limitation, Marx's incisive exposure of the fundamentally exploitive and dehumanizing character of capitalist culture remains important to the development of a PanAfrican communalist perspective which describes, defines, and defends the AfricanAmerican liberation struggle. As for those members of the Black middleclass (and the larger AfricanAmerican community) who support a capitalist solution to the political-economic conditions plaguing the AfricanAmerican community, they should remember that the aforementioned elements must accompany that solution.

CHAPTER IV

CRITICAL REVIEW OF SELECTED SOCIOLOGICAL CLASS THEORIES 2: MAX WEBER

Weber's analysis of capitalist culture focuses precisely on the areas Marx chose to de-emphasize: the moral, ideological, and spiritual beliefs (the "ruling ideas") which represent the "ideal" state of society. Although their approach to the study of capitalist culture differs in some fundamental ways, Weber and Marx agree on the basic character of capitalist culture. Let me emphasize that the Black sociological perspective considers the debate about whether Marx or Weber formulated a superior theory of social class formation in a capitalist system as essentially irrelevant. Both theoretical models remain valuable because of what they reveal about the evolution, maintenance, and perpetuation of capitalist culture. This knowledge proves essential for AfricanAmericans because at this moment we have become susceptible both to seduction into acceptance of as well as integration into a system which stands fundamentally in opposition to our legitimate aspirations for freedom and liberation, not only nationally but internationally.

Weber's theoretical approach to the study and analysis of social classes in capitalist culture shows a striking consistency of vision and methodological approach. His definition and characterization of social classes appear to emanate from his earlier works on social movements, especially his observations regarding the role of charismatic leaders; the problems of replacement; of group size and magnitude; of the necessity for the routinization or rationalization of charisma; and, finally, of bureaucracy and legitimization of authority.[1] If one merges his approach to the study of social movements with the methodological principles inherent in his concept of the "ideal type," one arrives at a deeper, more refined comprehension of his theory and acquires a clearer understanding of the processes involved in the evolution, maintenance, and perpetuation of capitalist culture.

Weber, like his antagonist Marx, also assumed that man was both a product and producer of culture. However, he did not focus exclusively on the economic or material basis of society but included its ideological and spiritual evolution as well. Although many people often referred to Marx as the "humanist" sociologist, Weber remained much more consistently at the *human* level of analysis. Weber did not make the "great leap" from the day-to-day symbolic interaction inherent in human society to a sophisticated, complex analysis of its economic base and concomitant organization of the relations of production. When compared to the Marxian formulation, Weber's focus on the sequential stages of a social movement as it evolves from the ideas, beliefs, practices, exhortations of a "special," charismatic leader to its fruition in the form of a bureaucratically organized nation state presents a much clearer, more vivid portrait of how such a process occurs. He also provides insights into what "holds it together," meaning the cultural cement which unites a society and keeps it together in times of internal and external crisis; the cement which keeps a system from destroying itself as a consequence of its inherent contradictions.

He helps to explain why an exploited, expropriated, and powerless workingclass continues to accept the rulingclass's ideas of and relationship to production. Thus, if one connects the various concepts in Weber's general sociology rather than focuses narrowly on his ideas on classes in capitalist culture, one can add a great deal of "meat" to Marx's skeleton. One can more fully answer the questions of how capitalist culture came to be and why it persists over time despite what Marx accurately perceived as its essential flaw.

In analyzing social movements, Weber emphasized the importance of a special, visionary individual with the ability to attract a large number of loyal followers—followers who would be willing to die for "the cause." He termed this special personality characteristic "charisma." [2]

Charismatic leaders, whether the founders of a given movement or simply persons elevated to leadership positions because others perceived them as having these special qualities, usually become the physical embodiment of a movement. People become attracted to the movement because of that person. Obviously, the leader's mortality poses several sticky problems if the movement is to remain stable after his death.

In order to maintain the momentum of the movement, then, the charismatic leader and loyal disciples must "carve out" or create ritual procedures and objects to replace or serve as substitutes for the deceased leader. The rituals confirm the followers' commitment to the beliefs, values, norms, attitudes, and way of life advocated by and embodied in the leader. In the leader's "absence" or death, these rituals also reunite the followers symbolically. Thus, in the process of routinizing "charisma," there evolves a hierarchy of authority. The followers' voluntary acceptance of and obedience to this authority structure are rooted in their commitment to and belief in the now deceased charismatic leader. Once the charisma has been routinized or bureaucratized, it becomes a self-perpetuating institution which functions in the rational, efficient manner Weber discussed.

Weber applied his social movement-derived model to the evolution of capitalist culture in his classic study of the relationship between Protestant theological beliefs and practices and the evolution of capitalism. In this seminal work, he set out to explain how and why Western Europe, and particularly the United States, became distinctive capitalist cultural formations. He saw this phenomenon as unique, given that capitalism as a mode of economic exchange was not new to human history. Adventurer capitalists had engaged in exploitative capitalistic or profit-oriented economic transactions far back in human history. What, then, accounted for the peculiar form of Western capitalism with its emphasis on the acquisition of wealth as an end in and of itself? Western European capitalism, especially the United States' variant, elevated the accumulation of capital to a moral and spiritual level. Thus capital accumulation became the fundamental purpose for living for all classes.

Weber observed further that this disciplined, rational accumulation of capital distinctly did not allow its practitioners or "true believers" the pleasures usually associated with wealth. One made money for the sake of making money. One did not spend one's money on frivolous, ostentatious displays of material goods. One did not flaunt one's wealth. If one had been able to subsist on a certain salary or a certain amount of money, one did not change one's living conditions as one accumulated capital. The capital should be saved and invested to generate more and more capital. It is not difficult to envision these austere, bearded, Puritan, God-fearing Calvinists as the "true believers," accumulating money with the efficiency of a beaver building a dam, living in their original log cabins, eating on self-made tables, sleeping in self-constructed beds, continuing to raise and prepare their own food, making and mending their own clothes as they acquired, invested, and re-invested the fruits of their labor so as to create the financial assets which sufficed to "bankroll" the "development" of rest of the world.

Weber accounted for this "spiritual," transcendent attitude of the then modern capitalist by analyzing the theology and ideology of a particular Protestant sect and its charismatic leader, John Calvin. However, it is important to note that in focusing on Calvin and Calvinism, he dealt with what Régis Debray has called the "revolution within the revolution," [3] for Calvin represented a reformation of the Reformation. He wanted even more freedom from liturgy and dogma than that achieved through the success of the Reformation. Weber demonstrated the convergence of routinized Calvinism with what he termed the "spirit of capitalism." He charted the changes that occurred in the interpretation of one of the key concepts of Calvinism, the notion of the "calling," during the routinization process. In the original Calvinist theology, a person's "calling" was revealed to h/er in the course of a prolonged communion with God.

While Calvin was alive, he converted people to his view because of the charismatic quality of his personality. Once he expired, conversion became a "sticky" problem for his followers and proselytizers in their efforts to gain more converts and maintain peace and stability in the "fold." Therefore, according to Weber, the followers reinterpreted the notion of the "calling" to mean that a person's "calling" is revealed in the material success s/he achieved in performing h/er occupation or career. If one were a farmer, one would know that this was h/er "calling" because s/he did it well and prospered as a consequence. If one were a business-man, one knew this was h/er "calling" because h/er profits increased continuously, and as one re-invested h/er profits, they continued to rise. Thus, no one had to actually *seek* a "calling," one simply had to earn it.

However, as noted above, one could not change one's original living conditions to reflect this additional wealth. The expanded wealth was used to generate more wealth. The more wealth one accumulated, the more certain one could be that s/he was pursuing the correct "calling." In this manner, wealth became a symbol which represented the fulfillment of one's divine purpose or mission in life on earth. Thus, the accumulation of wealth became an end in and of itself.[4]

In his analysis, Weber presented the moral, ideological, and spiritual dimensions which united the bourgeoisie and the proletariat. He also demonstrated that the industrial bourgeoisie represented only one element of a larger movement agitating for cultural change in Western Europe. In fact, Weber's analysis suggests that the bourgeoisie may not have been the "prime movers" at all. Rather, the analysis implies the visionary, charismatic, radical clergy of the period served as leaders who captured the imagination, commitment, and loyalty of the peasantry. As William Muraskin suggests, the industrial bourgeois opportunists realized their objectives within the context of this revolutionary religious movement.[5]

I want to emphasize here that I am not contending that the industrial proletariat were instantly converted to the Protestant Ethic's definition of "calling." A persecuted and repressed religious sect, the Calvinists cum Puritans, immigrated to the colonies in order to pursue their religious practices in peace, without the fear of state harassment. They settled in New England and are generally referred to as the "founding fathers" in the romanticized versions of American history which includes the Plymouth Rock colony, the first winter's difficulties, the invaluable assistance of the local indigenous groups, and so forth.

One of the interesting contradictions in the manner in which the establishment teaches American history involves this emphasis on the Puritans as the "good guys" and presents their experiences as those groups which exemplify the "best" in this country's cultural heritage. At the same time, the Jamestown settlement (which was established prior to Plymouth Rock) receives less attention, with the notable exception of the Pocohontas affair. One cannot help wondering if this bias in favor of the Plymouth Rock and Puritan settlements represents the ruling class's efforts to glamorize the past through an emphasis on Christian, moralistic, industrious perseverance in the face of immense difficulties which they say characterized the Puritan group's experience. Needless to say, this image or portrait of the "founding" of America more consistently holds with the liberal democratic ideology than that of the Jamestown colony, that cadre of voluntary and coerced indentured servants and their masters (the prelude to slavery).

However, the central point here focuses on how the morals, values, norms and attitudes of this Puritan group became the "ruling ideas" for America's *laissez-faire* free enterprise capitalist culture. The colonies revolted and obtained their independence from Britain, and integrated these values into the *Declaration of Independence* and the *Constitution of the United States*. Once so concretized, the new nation's leaders forced all other immigrant groups to adapt or accommodate their behavior and values to the Puritan ethic. Since this new independent country perceived itself as more democratic than its Western European ancestors and provided both the immigrant European peasantry and bourgeoisie with a nearly equal opportunity to acquire property and the prestige and status which accompanied that acquisition, both groups had a vested interest in its political-economic development.

Each European peasant, skilled worker, laborer, or entrepreneur who migrated to America dreamed of becoming a member of the bourgeoisie, that is, to own h/er "piece of the rock." The commitment of both the entrepreneurs and the proletariat to America's imperialistic pursuit of its "Manifest Destiny" (which can be readily translated as the land grab), reflects this mutuality of interests. All White immigrant and emerging class groups united in their belief in America's right to dominate, control, and own the geographical land mass which constitutes the continental United States. The greater the amount of land the United States controlled, the greater became the possibility of realizing the bourgeois dream of owning a piece of property, or acquiring more property, of expanding one's assets.

Thus, the cultural cement which bound the various immigrant groups as well as socioeconomic groups together in the United States emerged as the desire to possess private property within the liberal, *laissez-faire* free enterprise context outlined in the nation's legal and moral superstructure. All "Americans" shared a commitment to America's sociocultural and political-economic domination, subjugation, and exploitation of peoples of color. Americans had (and continue to have) interest in maintaining and perpetuating the cultural hegemony of White people over people of color, for that power yielded skin color privileges to all Whites.

In focusing on the Protestant ethic as the spiritual and moral superstructure, or Freudian "super-ego," or Mead's "generalized other," Weber demonstrated the holistic organization of capitalist culture. He accounted for the loyalty of the "have-nots" (Marx's proletariat) to the capitalist system. Capitalist cultural "imperatives" (Calverton's term as quoted by Cruse [6]) replaced medieval cultural imperatives. The bourgeoisie and its intelligentsia created and successfully implemented a new cultural system. The evolution of capitalist culture was in this sense a revolutionary achievement. It replaced "medieval man" with "capitalist man."

Weber's approach also accounted for the cultural stability of capitalism in that it connects the spiritual or ideological superstructure to the hierarchical organization of capitalist culture, its class system. While loudly proclaiming the equality of man, individual and religious freedom, the brotherhood of man, and so forth, this ideology also places the burden of man's success or failure on the individual. If a given individual (or group of individuals) fails to achieve a comfortable lifestyle, the cause becomes h/er "unGodliness," h/er inability or lack of initiative in pursuing a "calling," or h/er pursuit of an incorrect "calling." Therefore, successful people who acquired capital as an end in itself necessarily proved themselves to be more Godly, more vigilant, more disciplined, more "saintly" in the pursuit of their "calling."

The notion that one's "calling" could be evidenced in the success one achieves in work or profession also implies that God will doom those who fail to hellfire: His punishment for their not being zealous and disciplined enough in doing His work. From this perspective, poverty represents "proof" of "sin," therefore, poverty is a condition characteristic of the unGodly, unfaithful, nonbelievers. Social Darwinism became the social "scientific" justification or rationalization of this ideological superstructure. This moral superstructure manifests in and validates the class structure in capitalist culture. Those who have both superior faith and superior ability (superior biological endowment) constitute the ruling or upperclass; those who have great faith but less ability (lower biological endowment) exist in the middleclasses; while those who have neither faith nor adequate biological endowment occupy the sinful, despicable lowerclass, the "dregs" of society.

I will return to this perception of class culture as a reflection of the material, physical, and spiritual abilities of an individual or group to realize the goals or cultural imperatives as set forth in the ideological superstructure, versus the ability to achieve the ideal lifestyle and the culturally "pure" existence ("pure" in the sense of living the ideal continuously). Now, however, I will explore the convergencies between Marx and Weber's analyses of social classes per se. Comparing Marx's and Weber's positions on the importance of the concept of property in class formations, I see them essentially agreeing that the "ideal" liberal democratic ethos as reflected in Weber's treatment stood far from the reality which Marx so accurately delineated. However, their particular approaches reflect their personal interests. Marx, an intellectual activist committed to the overthrow of the capitalist system, differed from the more "intellectually pure" Weber, a social theoretician committed to what Veblen called "the disinterested pursuit of knowledge."

My discussion of the convergencies and congruities between Marx and Weber will draw largely from Charles Anderson,[7] although Anthony Giddens[8] made several similar observations. The basic difference which tends to be overemphasized in comparisons of Marxian and Weberian approaches can be briefly characterized by the terms multidimensional as opposed to unidimensional. American sociologists, heretofore, favored Weber's theory because of its supposed complexity, meaning its inclusion of several interrelated concepts. In addition, scholars considered Weber's work more politically "neutral," therefore more "objective" and "scientific" than Marx's theories. These attributes proved highly desirable and commendable for the generally conservative apologists of the American status quo. However, as I shall attempt to demonstrate, Weber located the foundation of the class system within the nature of property relations also. Thus, as Anderson observed, his theory converges significantly with that of Marx.

Weber's perspective is reflected in his discourse on three interdependent concepts: class, status, and power. He noted that "class" refers to any group of people who exist in essentially the same situation of "life chances," that is, those groups who have the ability to obtain a similar or equal quantity of material goods and services in a society. Obviously, Weber perceived class as being determined by the ownership or non-ownership of property in a capitalist culture; a culture which elevates the acquisition of property to the status of a religious or spiritual pursuit.

Weber further refined his concept of class by positing the existence of three types of classes: property class (the determinative one), acquisition or commercial class, and social class. He then subdivided these class categories into dichotomous "haves" and "have-nots." The "positively privileged" property classes contrasted with the "negatively privileged" property classes (Marx's bourgeoisie versus proletariat). The positively privileged acquisition classes contrasted with the negatively privileged acquisition classes; again, basically Marx's bourgeoisie versus proletariat. For Weber there is no assumption of overlap or collusion between the positively privileged propertied classes and the positively privileged acquisition classes. In reality, however, they may be closely associated.

Weber approached the concept of power similarly. He defined power as the "chance of a man or number of men to realize their own will in a communal action even against the resistance of others who are participating in the action." [9] He then proceeded to explore the various dimensions of power and noted the possible range of interrelationships between them. He focused primarily on the distinction between what he termed "naked" or merely economic power and "power with honor." He noted that the possession of one need not imply the possession of the other. Thus, a person who possesses naked economic power is not always accorded the honor and prestige which normally accrue to such individuals or groups.

In cumbersome and ambiguously qualified prose (at least as translated), Weber presented categories that describe the hierarchical arrangement of sociocultural groups or social classes. As the neo-Marxist critics noted, Weber perceived that the positively privileged propertied classes tended also to be the positively privileged social classes and exercised positively privileged honorific power: legitimate, sanctioned power which was often abused, especially in America, by its possessors.

One can easily see how Weber's categories would be considered more accurate or scientific than Marx's fundamentally single-factor theory. Weber's approach remained consistent with the propaganda of capitalist culture. If one delineated the various combinations and permutations possible within Weber's model, one could place an entire population in one of his categories. The existence of diverse sources of power, the constraints and limitations imposed on the exercise of power, the qualified, questionable hegemony of one form or type of power over another, all contributed toward reinforcing as well as exposing liberal democratic capitalist culture. Therefore, Weber's pluralistic multivariate model supports the notion that individualistic, competitive liberal democratic culture encompasses a fluid and open class system with a balanced distribution of power. A Marxist would counter this argument by indicating that this perception of capitalist culture merely obfuscates its essential character.

Weber demonstrated his awareness of the essential nature of the capitalist cultural class structure in his definition of another major concept, status. As in his analysis of power, Weber here emphasized the importance of honor as an essential component of status. Individuals may possess power without honor, but a person's status usually includes the society's definition of honor: specifically, the prestige, respect, and influence associated with a given status. He observed further that while property does not always signify a status qualification, the two tend to coexist with extraordinary regularity.[10] Looking at these emphases, one can easily recognize Weber's essential agreement with Marx's theory. "Need I say more?" as Aretha Franklin so eloquently asked in a classic AfricanAmerican cultural understatement for an obvious and easily recognized characterization of a situation.

Still, one can also see why his theory could be used by bourgeois intellectuals to support their ideological and theoretical commitment to describing America as a "classless society"— the so-called pure, modern capitalist democratic image which informs so much of America's social scientific class analysis or propaganda. While he accepts the basic premises of Marx's theory of social class, Weber's language, style, and method also contain theoretical categories which can be used by bourgeois intellectual defenders and interpreters of capitalist culture to distort its true nature. In elevating his "status" dimension of class to that equal to the ownership of the power of propertied classes, Weber elucidated an alternative set of concepts which could be used to "defuse" the inherently volatile relationship between the classes as described in Marx's theory.

This "ammunition-for-the-defense-of-the-status-quo" factor of Weber's theory is also reflected in other theoretically related areas, especially his insights into the evolution of bureaucracies. As noted above, the "routinization of charisma," essentially the creation of a bureaucratic social organization, perpetuates the divine, spiritual, and philosophical beliefs and practices of the deceased leader. The creation of symbols and the rituals associated with these symbols required increasingly rational bureaucratic organization; that is, the creation of positions of authority, a chain-of-command, rules and regulations governing the conduct of the incumbent's position, rewards for each position, requirements for promotion and demotion, impersonal performance of the functions of the position, the bureaucratic personality, and so forth. Consequently, as the institution which serves to perpetuate the spiritual and ideological beliefs, values, and norms becomes bureaucratized, the other dimensions of the movement must become bureaucratized, must be made more rational and more efficient.

Although Weber did not say so explicitly, one must remember that the moral premises supporting the proliferation of bureaucracies in EuropeanAmerican capitalist culture involves the spiritual belief that one is also fulfilling the requirements of one's "calling." In other words, the better one performs h/er calling, the higher s/he moves up the bureaucratic hierarchy. These moves "up" the bureaucratic hierarchy accompany moves "up" the social class groupings with which one is affiliated or identified. In this manner, s/he achieves greater prestige, property, and power. When viewed holistically, Weber's theory presents the crucial intervening variable in Marx's polemical class struggle: the bureaucracy.

The principles governing the functioning of bureaucracies make real and tangible the more abstract, illusory, or spiritual values of a cultural system. In a very real sense, then, the uniqueness of the capitalist cultural system has been its ability to create a network of bureaucratic organizations to maintain and perpetuate a way of life based on the rational accumulation of money as an end in itself. Wealth becomes the concrete sign of the successful fulfillment of one's divine "calling."

The cultural apparatus the leaders or ruling class decision-makers have created to control the conflicts between the myriad of competing interest groups (political parties, corporations, environmentalists, minority groups, women, and so forth) represents the classic example of how effective and, in a sense, how visionary they have been in perpetuating their interpretations and definitions. Weber's analysis of the nature and actions of political parties emphasized their functions as legitimate means for containing and channeling social conflict. In this regard, Weber anticipated Lewis Coser's functionalist treatment of the importance of social conflict: the creative and innovative changes which can evolve from competing groups within controlled conflict when the conflict does not result in armed revolt or collapse of a given sociocultural system.[11]

Weber, therefore, demonstrated how capitalist culture maintained its stability and longevity despite Marx's perception of its fundamental contradiction. Cultural elites or ruling classes create the institutional apparatus which reinforces the ideological superstructure of capitalist culture. In order to maintain social order and reduce or control the tensions among a variety of potentially disruptive competing interest groups, there must exist some agreed upon means which are acceptable to the masses, rich and poor, privileged and unprivileged, "Godly" and "unGodly." The stability of capitalist cultures attests to the effectiveness of this means of legitimately resolving or channeling inevitable conflicts of interest.

Rational, efficient, bureaucratically organized parties (modeled after the social organization of the state in both its private and public sectors) competing for social power, *i.e.*, the opportunity to impose their vision of how the modern capitalist state should be "run" represent other intervening variables which Marx underestimated. Weber perceived quite accurately that the existence of parties composed of various combinations of class, status, and power groups convinces the vast majority of the masses that their interests can be articulated and realized; that they can influence the political and economic directions of the nation-state in ways beneficial to the masses. Where Marx focused on religion as an "opiate" of the masses and the downtrodden, Weber examined bureaucracy and political parties as means of controlling the proletariat.

Weber's analysis presents capitalist cultural imperatives in a more detailed manner than does Marx's. Weber not only reaffirms Marx's vision of capitalism, he also provides us with insight into how the Marxian prediction of class struggle was and continues to be reduced or "cooled out." The masses' commitment to charismatic leaders, the routinization of "charisma," with its inherent authority structure, and the acceptance of that authority structure as a legitimate reflection of the ideological beliefs and practices of the deceased leader result in the masses accepting, defending, and transmitting the way of life contained therein. Thus, all individuals committed to the leader's vision, or the interpretation of that vision by legitimate, accepted descendants, have a vested interest in maintaining and perpetuating that way of life. Humans become products of their own creation.

I suggest that this summary of Weber's theories proves he contributed immensely to the pluralist model of modern democratic capitalist culture; that is, the notion that in the industrial society a number of competing interest groups co-exist whose hegemonies wax and wane according to the extent to which they garner the support of the electorate for their programs. This perception of democratic capitalism is generally rampant in the investigations of American (and sometimes non-American) liberal and conservative social scientists. They present this model usually as a more accurate characterization of American society than the Marxist-oriented elitist depiction of capitalist society. I will discuss these theories in greater detail later when the focus shifts to studies of the American class system. However, before that, I offer a few critical observations on Weber's contribution to our understanding of capitalist culture.

Although Weber addressed the problems of ethnicity and class in some very interesting ways, his theoretical scheme suffers from the same cultural chauvinistic and racist assumptions as Marx. Implicitly an evolutionist, Weber reflected this stance in his admiration of rational bureaucracies: those "efficient" organizations or institutions which meet the needs of the state and its constituents. Robert Nisbet's summary of Weber's lasting contribution to the study of society captured this basic assumption quite cogently:

> Bureaucracy is simply the structuring of authority in terms of impersonal positions and offices rather than specific identifiable individuals. The ideal type of bureaucracy is the system in which all reliance upon the traditional, the ritualistic, the charismatic, or the personal is terminated; considerations of emotion or sentiment are excluded; and values alien to efficiency of operation are abolished. Weber did not, of course, suppose that so "perfect" a system of bureaucracy ever had or ever could be brought into actual existence .... *He nevertheless saw in the development of the modern West the gradual triumph, not merely in government but in industry, education, religion, the military, and other spheres, a vision of of the bureaucratic, of the rationalistic.* [Emphasis added.] [12]

I infer from this statement that Weber perceived the non-Western world as less rationalistic or non-rationalistic and needing to evolve toward rationality and rational bureaucracy. To the extent the non-Western world (or non-Western peoples) maintained non-rational, personal, traditional, emotional forms of organization, they lagged "behind the West," culturally "lagging," in Vilfredo Pareto's terms. Thus, at their theoretical core, Weber and Marx converge. One sees this convergence in Robert Blauner's statement: "... Marx seems to have viewed sources of identification such as race and nationality as transitory residues of the old feudal order, provincialisms doomed to extinction with the logic of capitalist development." [13]

This important point must be remembered because, once again, it confirms Harold Cruse's thesis regarding the inherent racial cultural biases of either radical "Marxist" liberal theory or less radical, more scientifically "pure" liberal theory. To accept the historical, contemporary, or future visions for the world contained therein can only result in the cultural negation of peoples of color, particularly people of African descent. Blauner's point, above, characterizes Weber as being as much a social Darwinist as Marx. It is at this crucial juncture with respect to cultural struggle that these supposed antagonists converge and thereby relegate the cultural realities and experiences of peoples of color to the status of residual categories. In addition, I agree with Anderson's and

Gordon's[14] observations that while Weber does present, in an exhaustive and distinct manner, the various dimension of stratification, his model proves too cumbersome to apply to the "real" world. Furthermore, many analysts have used his model as theoretical rationale for some very dubious efforts in class research. According to Anderson,

> While in all likelihood not Weber's intentions, his elevation of social status to an "equal" of class and power has provided an excuse for approximately forty years of increasingly sophisticated and arid methodological exercises in "discovering" the status structure of communities and sample populations. [15]

Certain researchers have used Weber's elevation of prestige to being on a par with power and class as the theoretical support or rationale for separating economic power from political power. In this view, these researchers perceived and described the economic and political sectors as groups and/or institutions in conflict. Ralf Dahrendorf's theory reflects this dimension of Weber's thought quite clearly although Dahrendorf does not explicitly admit to Weber's influence until focusing on the nature of authority in capitalist culture.[16] Essentially, then, Weber's theory has been used as the theoretical rationale for the notion that America is a "pluralist, not elitist" society. One prevailing controversy within sociology and political science involves the continuing debate about the distribution of power in America's liberal democracy. One school of thought argues that power in America is distributed across a wide variety of competing political and economic interest groups.[17] The existence of these groups presents an empirical indication of the non-elitist character of liberal democratic America since any one group or combinations of groups may control and dominate for short periods of time or it or they may dominate on certain issues or policies and be less effective or passive on others.

The elitist school which asserts that pluralism exists only in the middle-range sector of decision-making and power challenges this wide-distribution-of-power argument.[18] The political, economic and military elite who are invisible to most Americans and whose power and influence transcend that of local and nationally elected officials, however, make the "big" decisions. This argument suggests that what Americans perceive as the democratic process is nothing but an illusion, a charade which serves as an opiate to the masses and reinforces the liberal democratic façade. Further, this elite group is an invisible, amorphous entity which maintains its power (or control) over the mass media as well as its distance from the middleclass social scientists engaged in research and writing on the issues. The elitist theoreticians clearly reflect a Marxian orientation.

Weber's theory has also been used to support the contention that the existence of the middleclass in America constitutes a triumph of the progressive liberal democratic revolution. Charles Page noted in his discussion on the "founding fathers" of American sociology that many perceived the middleclass as the most anticlass segment of the population and, therefore, the repository of the socioeconomic and sociopsychological virtues of American-style liberal democracy. The middleclass constitutes the largest, most cohesive social group with shared values, attitudes, and aspirations.[19] However, Thorsten Veblen, in his analysis of the middle class's mindless preoccupation with "keeping up with the Joneses," or conspicuous consumption, challenged this optimistic faith in the middleclass.[20] Later, C. Wright Mills, greatly influenced by Veblen, also emphasized the alienated, politically inactive, conformist character of this segment of the population.[21] These critical treatments of the American middleclass suggest that while the middleclass as a group may manifest the virtues of liberal democratic capitalist culture, it also reflects the social pathology of that culture and remains as vulnerable to Orwellian manipulation as the workingclass or proletariat. Indeed, William Kornhauser's critique of "mass society" noted this dimension of capitalist middleclass culture.[22]

Weber's influence on American sociologists' treatment of the concept of social class has been and continues to be immense. Therefore, I have more to say about his model (and biases contained therein) in the discussion of American sociologists' approaches to class analyses.

CHAPTER V

AMERICAN SOCIOLOGICAL CLASS THEORY AND DEMOCRATIC CAPITALIST CULTURE

I will now turn to American sociological theories of social class as another set of "windows" or "lenses" through which one can observe the nature and functioning of American capitalist culture. In so doing, I assume again that the major theories present some pertinent and important information and insights into the cultural system which dominates and oppresses the "rest of us," to use the words of Brother Chinweizu in the title of his book. That some of these theories contradict others is a relatively minor concern for this discussion, for I assume that even those theories which contradict each other present valuable perceptions of American capitalist culture, perceptions which need to be understood if we seek to prepare our students and future generations for the challenges before them and to formulate programs and strategies for liberation. That American sociological theoreticians disagree and often contradict each other must be accepted as "normal" since those contradictions embody another way of maintaining the status quo in that they often contribute to the confusion among oppressed groups. As we analyze these arguments, we find the "no easy solution" smoke screen conveying the impression that the complexity of the issues leaves them unresolvable. Consequently, we become apathetic, lethargic, and suffer from political inertia.

American sociologists would have Americans believe that we are at one and the same time members of both an "elitist" and a "pluralist" society; that "social" classes exist but they do not necessarily have political or economic power; that "social" classes exist which do wield considerable political and economic power; that the American class structure remains open and "fluid" as well as rigidly stratified with little or no upward mobility; and so forth. I will attempt to demonstrate that in some respects these seemingly mutually exclusive positions are not incompatible since they are valid perceptions of American capitalist culture although one may be more "ideal" and the other more "real." The review of selected theorists undertaken for this discourse confirms Gerald McWhorter's observation regarding the nature of the relationship between science and ideology: "Science is the handservant of ideology."[1] In no other area of American sociology is this axiom more true than in the literature on social class.

The cavalier, "loose," arrogantly subjective, armchair philosophical utterances I found in the literature profoundly disturbed and angered me because no Black social scientist who used such subjective language would be published. Many "theories" of social class merely offered the analysts' personal reflections on the issues associated with the concept, relegating their work as dubious for scientific value. I attribute this dismal state of affairs to what Howard Jensen called the retarded emergence of social class analysis in American sociology. He emphasized that the "sociocultural context within which American sociology emerged was distinctly unfavorable to all basic conceptions of such research." He continued:

> The dominant ideology was too firmly grounded in the great intellectual traditions of seventeenth century English liberalism and eighteenth century French rationalism. The inalienable natural rights of man, his essential dignity and equality, and the indefinite perfectibility of man and his institutions were written into the Declaration of Independence and given legal status in the Preamble of the Constitutions of several states. The liberal interpretations of these documents as formulated by Thomas Jefferson and popularized in the Horatio Alger myth found constant reinforcement in the rise of frontier democracy and its national repercussions upon American political and social

thought and policy.[2]

The old W. I. Thomas axiom, "If men define situations as real, they are real in their consequences," apparently victimized social class research in America. These writers obviously believed that if you proclaim American culture as one that is liberal democratic and progressive, these values will come to be reflected in the institutional life of the nation-state. American sociological thought on these issues justified the assertions of many young militant Black intellectuals during the mid- and late 1960s regarding the cultural chauvinistic biases inherent in American social theory. We argued that American sociologists had internalized the values, beliefs, attitudes, and norms of the prevailing liberal democratic, *laissez-faire* free enterprise capitalist cultural ethos and that their analytical concepts and methods evolved from their acceptance of or belief in the inherent superiority of this culture. Their writings supported the idea that the United States represented a "revolution in the revolution," the characterization used by Régis Debray. It was more democratic, more liberal, more egalitarian than any of its Western European predecessors. It had transcended the need for a monarchy, if only in "title" rather than in substance. It had granted individual rights, guaranteed by the state. It had transcended the traditional inegalitarian caste system characteristic of the European past.

The liberal universalistic cultural ethos that directed the thought of early European American sociologists is the qualified acceptance of social Darwinism as the dominant theoretical model accounting for the evolution of man and civilization. Ascendant liberal democracy in particular reflected this early influence. Both Thomas F. Gossett and Floyd House observed that the humanitarian, philanthropic, and social reform movements which occurred during the nineteenth century strongly influenced American sociological thought. As such, several prominent American sociologists, especially Lester Ward, the "father" of American sociology, criticized the *laissez-faire* free enterprise, and social Darwinistic approaches of classical economists.[3] However, Gossett's analysis indicated an apparent contradiction between American sociologists' opposition to social Darwinistic individualism and their acceptance of social Darwinistic racism:

> Their racism was ... the result of the methods they chose in their war with Social Darwinist individualism. When they began to think of means by which the immense power of *laissez-faire*, based upon the pure gospel of Darwin himself, could be used to justify gross economic inequality, they attempted to prove that his theories had been misinter-

preted. They argued that co-operation and state intervention were just as logical conclusions from the theory of evolution as was the doctrine of *laissez-faire*. They attempted to reconcile biological law with the preconceptions of democracy.[4]

Sociologists struggled to reconcile these two "warring souls" (to use DuBois' terminology for this type of paradox) as reflected in House's discussion of the sociological thought of Lester Ward. He observed that human achievement served as the essential subject matter of scientific sociology, which he defined as the accumulation of knowledge rather than the accumulation of material goods. Humans accomplished this achievement through a continuous series of inventions, in the broadest sense of the term:

> Achievement implies social continuity or social inheritance, which is something quite distinct from biological inheritance and has not been characteristic of all races and peoples but only of what may be termed the "historic races," *i.e.*, the peoples that have a history.[5]

One can see that Ward challenged the biological determinism characteristic of social Darwinism with its Hobbsian implications for certain peoples and cultures. Yet, he accepted the Darwinistic explanation for human cultures, especially its explanation for the apparent superiority of EuropeanAmerican "historic races" over those of peoples of color that "had no history." Thus Ward and his colleagues simultaneously opposed and supported social Darwinism. They opposed its emphasis on individualistic competition; its equating superior power, prestige, and wealth with biological superiority; its pro-business biases; and so forth. They saw these dimensions of social Darwinist thought as antithetical to liberal, humanitarian democracy. However, they found social Darwinism as acceptable on the issue of race or racial cultural struggle. The different races of men, in the views of such theorists, maintained relationships to one another similar to the way different species among lower animals maintained them. As Gossett put it,

> Struggle among the species in the lower animal world became, when applied to men, a struggle among races. Thus, while they attacked theories of society based upon conflict among individuals, they actually encouraged theories of society based upon conflict among the races.[6]

As noted above, early American sociologists believed that liberal democratic America had transcended its Western European predecessors, that the new freedoms and rights guaranteed each American surpassed all the liberal reforms implemented in Western Europe. They perceived themselves as the guardians, interpreters, and defenders of this state of cultural evolution. Howard Jensen also commented on this trend in early American sociological thought:

> The pioneers of American sociology ... assumed that American society had left behind it all hereditarily determined and traditionally defined caste, rank, estate, and class categories, and that it presented no permanent hierarchical social structure.... To many... such social gradations as existed were interpreted as due to social factors such as inequality in the opportunity for education and for the development and exercise of motivational factors essential to achievement. To them social progress was the socialization of achievement which was the function of a universal and compulsory public school system to promote. They would have regarded as a repudiation of the American Credo the current sociological doctrines that stratification is a fundamental phenomenon of all social systems, and that differential rewards in terms of income and capital accumulation, with their resultant rank and status relationships, perform essential functions in motivating behavior....[7]

From a Marxian perspective, early American sociologists reinforced or corroborated the ruling class's image and definitions of American culture. Their scholarship reflected what Marx characterized as the role or function of bourgeois intellectuals—to rationalize, justify, interpret, and legitimize the cultural ethos and the institutional structure created and implemented to transmit that ethos. The liberal cultural ideas and imagery espoused by Locke, Rousseau, and [Adam] Smith intoxicated and bewitched early American sociologists. America to them epitomized the liberal democratic, *laissez-faire*, free enterprise, capitalist cultural "Garden of Eden." They maintained this image as long as the frontier remained "out there."

However, after the successful annexation of the Western frontier and the end of World War I, the economic inequalities inherent in capitalist culture became more apparent. The successful westward expansion concluded the era of cheap land. Acquiring property became more difficult for small, independent farmers. The economy was transformed from a base in agriculture to one based on industrial manufacturing. The frontier had served as an "escape" for individuals who wanted to avoid urban factory labor. With the successful annexation of the Western territories and subsequent expansion of industry, industrial jobs replaced subsistence farming.

This trend began shortly after the Reconstruction period and intensified after World War I. Most small farmers lost their land during the
recession of the 1880s and 1890s and never regained the ability to support
themselves in the same manner. The trend toward the development of
large agribusiness and the accompanying centralization of land ownership signaled the end of the subsistence farmer and the beginning of the
proletarianization of EuropeanAmerican workers.

This new state of political-economic affairs necessitated the development of a new social theory to account for the change and to remain
consistent with the liberal democratic cultural ethos. Warner's anthropological approach and structural-functional analysis provided excellent
rationales for this social reality. Jensen also noted this trend in American
social theory:

> The result has been the rise of a new school of stratification theorists
> whose view of social classes as objectively observable and clearly
> delineated entities is probably as remote from the actualities of the
> American scene as was that of their predecessors. There seems to be
> emerging out of the conflict a new conception of the American class
> structure which avoids both of these polarities, and which views this
> situation as consisting of an informal hierarchy of groups with ill-
> defined and highly permeable boundaries, obliquely recognized, and
> spontaneously functioning in the dynamics of social interaction rather
> than maintained by various institutionalized rituals and procedures.[8]

This trend in American social class theory became apparent in the
work of W. Lloyd Warner and his students. Warner, trained as a social
anthropologist (a student of Radcliffe-Brown), is noted for his anthropological approach to the study of social class in American communities. He
approached the social organization of a community through an analysis
of its subgroupings or social structures such as the family, cliques,
voluntary associations, classes, castes, schools, churches, economic
institutions, political organizations, and so forth.

As a consequence of his anthropological training, he assumed that all
societies organize around a single structure which determines the shape
and form of the total society and integrates the other structures into a
codified whole. For some primitive societies, he suggested that kinship,
age-grade, or religious systems served as the integrative structure; but for
America, he initially perceived the economic order as the determining or
integrative structure. His research on several small and middle-sized
American cities led him to modify this position. He observed in his
interviews that his respondents used occupation and income in ranking

individuals in the community, but they also used *other* factors. The presence of these additional factors forced him to depart from his original Marxist-oriented approach and to embrace a more Weberian approach. Kornhauser claimed that Warner finally decided on a definition of class which encompassed the effects of "whatever" factors (Kornhauser's term) the members of a society used to rank each other in an overall prestige hierarchy. (Note also the change from economic factors to prestige hierarchy).

> Class, then, refers to "two or more orders of people who are believed to be, and are accordingly ranked by all the members of the community, in socially superior and inferior positions." The layer of equally ranked statuses which comprises a class cross-cuts the entire society; that is, in contrast to segmental hierarchies, like, ... a church hierarchy, which ranks only some of the members of a society, a class hierarchy is an inclusive hierarchy which ranks all the members of a society into a vertical series of horizontal layers.[9]

Warner's methodological procedures of Evaluated Participation (E.P.) and the Index of Status Characteristics (I.S.C.) made his essentially subjective approach to the study of class scientifically objective.

Warner's definition of social class proves consistent with the cultural struggle perspective informing this analysis. His delineation of social classes as a hierarchical distribution or ranking of culturally prescribed values, behaviors, and material acquisitions supports the thesis presented earlier. All class groups maintain and perpetuate a cultural ethos which bonds social classes in America together. Warner uncovered this social class bonding in studies of "well integrated" American communities where individuals would on some occasions voice hostility, envy, or jealousy toward other individuals whom they ranked above or below themselves, but rarely voiced any criticism toward the "system," that is the liberal democratic, *laissez-faire*, free enterprise capitalist culture. Those on the top expressed satisfaction and expectations of remaining there while those in the lowerclasses expressed less satisfaction but expected to "move up" in the first or second generation to a higher class. This "Babbitt" portrayal of mainstream America provoked a great deal of criticism of Warner and his associates. Some criticism came from rather unexpected quarters, considering American sociologists' general diffidence — if not full-blown hostility—towards Marxist analysis.

As Ruth Kornhauser noted in her review of Warner's approach, among his critics, several perceived Warner's model as complementary to a Marxian analysis, not an alternative perspective. Warner's neo-Marxist critics argued further that his results could not be considered a refutation of the Marxist perspective for several additional reasons:

> First, the "social" classes with which Warner is concerned are not necessarily the same phenomena with which Mosca, or Marx, or Veblen...were concerned. Therefore, the data which indicate that non-economic factors are important in prestige stratification do not necessarily discount the importance of economic factors in the political sphere, in conflicts of interest, of in social change—in short, in the areas which the Marxian approach postulates the primacy of economic factors.[10]

These neo-Marxist critics also challenged Warner's narrow economic definition and interpretation as well as his tendency to de-emphasize the importance of economic factors.

The contradiction in their use of Marxist analysis to challenge the legitimacy and validity of Warner's theory and methods becomes apparent when one remembers that this school later rejected Marxian interpretations of the American class structure. While some attacked Warner for placing too much emphasis on prestige and not enough on economic factors, others criticized Marxists for placing too much emphasis on economic factors and not enough on prestige or status. The theoretical inconsistencies, contradictions, and ambiguities characteristic of American sociologists' attempt to explain class inequality in a so-called liberal, open-class system become even more apparent when one critically examines Warner's theoretical heir: structural-functionalism.

Structural-functionalists adopted a unique position which rejects Warner's approach as too anthropological, inadequate for large urban metropolitan areas, subjective, and Marxian. Their rejection of Warner's approach is surprising when one remembers that Warner was a student of Radcliffe-Brown, the "father" of structural-functional analysis. The obvious questions surface: *To what extent does contemporary or "orthodox" structural-functional analysis differ from Warner's?* and *What mistakes did Warner make?* Since most observers willingly accept his portrayal of the class structure of many American communities as accurate, what did his approach imply about the nature of American society which his sociologist colleagues found objectionable, unacceptable, or invalid? I contend that Warner's anthropological approach identified class structures and processes which evoked images of the traditional, more rigid, Western European class system which liberal democratic America supposedly had transcended.

Thus, for American sociologists (and the cultural ethos they defended), Warner's conception of the American class structure evoked an unacceptable image of American society as similar to its European antecedent. Theorists of a structural-functional persuasion found Warner's characterization with its emphasis on the sociocultural dimensions of class (church affiliation, friendship networks, ancestry, moral behavior, membership in certain social clubs, and so forth) as opposed to the political-economic (Marxian) dimension unacceptable primarily because it acknowledged the existence of discrete, distinct, recognizable social classes, contradicting the liberal egalitarian ethos. These theorists criticized Warner for imposing an inadequate theoretical and methodological procedure on the analysis of the American "class" system and charged that his use of the anthropological approach was biased and anachronistic. This position is captured in Gordon's comments on Warner and his critics:

> Briefly stated, Warner's value position, as he had presented it throughout his writings, is that social inequality is functionally necessary in complex societies, but that the channels of social mobility should be kept open. In effect, it is an endorsement of a fluid free enterprise society with open classes wherein valid individual mobility strivings will be rewarded and those who fail to climb will learn to "adjust" to the "social reality" of the status system. The major criticisms, as far as implications for his methods are concerned, appear to be that such a value system causes him to ignore economic and power issues and collective efforts to advance in the economic and power hierarchies and to concentrate on forces of tradition (social status) rather than factors making for social change.[11]

Although Warner admitted to being a "true believer" in liberal democratic *laissez faire,* free enterprise capitalistic culture, his structural-functional colleagues rejected his approach because of its evocation of prestigious, stagnant class groupings as opposed to the more acceptable view of American culture as competitive or conflictual in character, represented in the various groups and individuals maneuvering for political and economic power. They wished not to view America as caste stratified as England. Structural-functionalist theorists could accept the functionality of inequality and the basic value premises in Warner's theory, but they could not accept the structural image it evoked. Walter Goldschmidt observed an inherent bias in Warner's use of the tribal analogy for studying class realities in American communities and in the assumption that small communities existed as microcosms of the larger society:

> One cannot view a community as a microcosm, however uniform smaller communities might appear or however universally their social classes extend, because a community is but a part of a total culture with a generalized organization. And the upper and socially most significant strata are not represented on the local level, but in urban centers particularly in New York and Washington.[12]

It is important to note here that in criticizing the biases and assumptions of Warner and his students, Walter Goldschmidt (and others) illuminated important dimensions of American capitalist culture. In his opposition to the notion of a local community representing a microcosm of the whole, Goldschmidt refutes the pluralists' school of thought which perceives the existence of local elites as an indication of the egalitarian, socially leveling nature of American capitalist culture. The existence of local elites (according to one strain of pluralist thought) supposedly reflects the distribution of power, prestige, and wealth "equally" throughout the political-economic system. That the upper strata (the most socially and politically-economically significant (or powerful) groups) exist in the major urban centers attests to the validity of the elite theories of Mills and Veblen (among others) on social class relations in the United States. Goldschmidt also criticized the anthropological technique of using informants as a chief source of data:

> The use of informants is a valid technique, but the heterogeneous composition and variegated cultural values of the American community present severe limitations and one must be on guard against its inherent dangers ... whether informants are presenting a social reality or whether the method selects that pattern of thought which coincides with the predilection of the investigator. In the final analysis the method is without control, and there is no spokesmen for those not oriented to the dominant pattern of values.... In short, the informant technique is selective and restrictive; it can yield only that which has been introduced; it can deny the heterogeneity of American life by its selectivity.[13]

These critiques of the Warner school demonstrate how important it was for American sociologists to dispel any idea of stagnant, static, or traditional social classes. That his value system was essentially the same as theirs was insufficient. Warner accepted the ideological ethos of American capitalist culture. They still had to destroy any notion that people had to "adjust" to class realities because to structural-functionalists the idea of "adjusting to class realities" suggested a certain amount of rigidity in the class structure. Leftists attacked Warner for his subjective and biased approach; that is, his attack on Marx's emphasis on social mobility (*i.e.*, the lack thereof) and his championing of the "American Way." Structural-functionalists focused on the underlying implications of Warner's theory. To them hierarchically arranged social classes according to the distribution of certain normative cultural characteristics in America meant the Revolution had failed or was a failure.

Hierarchical arrangements suggest that the American class structure resembles its Western European antecedents which Americans have been led to believe they have transcended. From the structural-functionalist perspective, the earlier leftist criticism had been only partially accurate. It had ignored an important dimension of an anthropological approach: the conservative, exclusive, restrictive characteristics of culture. If one accepted Warner's descriptions of the various class cultures, one would be forced to accept the existence of a rapidly emerging rigid class system, Warner's boosterism and emphasis on social mobility notwithstanding. This latent theme in Warner and his associates' work had to be "scientifically" challenged and refuted.

Kurt Mayer, while agreeing with Goldschmidt's critique of Warner (which charcterized Warner's method as a "trained incapacity" to deal with social change), also noted this essentially jingoistic predisposition in Warner's approach.

> One cannot quite help suspect that Warner's approach owes its great popularity less to whatever intrinsic merits its theory may possess than to the deceptive ease with which it can be applied empirically, and also to the appeal which it exercises upon many scholars imbued, consciously or unconsciously, with traditional American beliefs. While not denying the existence of said classes — on the contrary, his writings strongly suggest that he conceives it as one of his duties to make Americans aware of the existence of class distinctions — Warner's theory seems to provide a convenient "refutation" of Marx. Its static concept of the social structure neatly by-passes the possibility of clashing economic interests which, under given circumstances, may lead to organized class action and fundamental changes of the class structure. Limiting its attention to social status, this theory substitutes the pleasant picture of a stable status hierarchy where the only problem concerns the adjustment of individuals to the existing arrangements and their chances to improve their personal position. The danger of this narrow view lies not only in the fact that it presents an unrealistic and

inadequate picture of the class structure but also in its use as a possible ideological prop for an uncritical defense of the status quo.[14]

While Warner's theory refuted the existence of the Marxian political-economic struggle, his analysis did not emphasize the open, competitive, fluid, dynamic nature of urban American class structures (at least not to his structural-functional critics). His portrait of the American class structure presented an "over-stabilized" image, a sense of permanence. As I noted above, many perceived this sense of permanence in the American class structure as a contradiction to what Gunnar Myrdal referred to as the "American Creed": individual achievement in an open, fluid, egalitarian social structure.[15] Many sociologists willingly conceded that Warner's portrait held true in small New England and Southern towns and villages but proved inadequate for analyzing the diversity and mobility of urban America.

Although I agree with the aforementioned theoretical and methodological criticisms of Warner for different reasons (namely that ideologically, like his critics, he was a committed liberal), I must add that his contribution to the cultural struggle perspective informing this discourse has been substantial. The major difficulty with Warner's liberalism rests in his formulations which rationalize the status quo. However, his use of the caste concept to characterize the relations between the races in the slavery and Jim Crow eras (the pre-1954 South) laid the groundwork for my concept of the *ethcaste* model (which I introduced and defined in Chapter II) to capture contemporary race and ethnic relations in America. Presently, I would like to focus more specifically on Warner and his students' use of the caste concept to capture Southern Black-White relations.

The Warner school of thought took the position that although the American Creed or ethos (its ideological superstructure) did not justify or legitimize the Southern racial caste system, the apartheid-like racial subjugation and discrimination had the essential characteristics of a caste system, meaning "ascribed status": prohibitions against intercaste sexual and marital relations; expectations that Blacks as the subordinated "untouchables" should behave in a deferential, docile, subservient manner to all members of the "superior" White caste; and separate public facilities, bathrooms, drinking fountains, motels, seats on trains and buses, and so forth. While acknowledging the differences between the Southern racial cultural caste system and the religious cultural caste system of India, the caste school of American race relations argued that they could not ignore the numerous similarities. They took the position that race can also be a criterion for caste domination. Needless to say, this school received severe criticism for its position. However, their critics based their points on questionable theoretical arguments which I will elaborate later in this discussion.

In addition to the use of the caste concept, the Warner school focused on the existence of an intracaste class structure and on the distinct subcultures characteristic of each class. Without specifying or elaborating this theme, the caste school essentially acknowledged the existence of a unique, distinct AfricanAmerican culture, dominated, constrained, circumscribed, and kept subordinated by the uppercaste White culture. While the caste school emphasized neither intracaste class conflict nor intercaste cultural struggle or conflict, it did stress the illegitimacy of racial caste domination, a violation of the American Creed, a "black" mark on "our" democratic heritage, an international embarrassment. Thus, the caste school made a substantial contribution toward increasing the public's consciousness of this type of oppression.

One can acknowledge and appreciate the contribution of this school, while perceiving and assessing its limitations; one major limitation, when seen from the cultural struggle perspective, being its inheritance of Warner's boosterism of the American Way. Warner's belief in individualistic, open competition in the marketplace led him and his students to support the destruction of Jim Crow segregation in order to "free" AfricanAmericans to become integrated into this liberal democratic "Wonderland." Their research revealed and documented the presence of a viable, functioning, and autonomous AfricanAmerican culture. Yet, they perceived nothing of value in that culture worth maintaining in the face of the "wonders" of Americanism. The chains of Jim Crow should be removed to allow AfricanAmericans, as individuals, an equal opportunity to join the frantic race up the social mobility ladder in order to arrive at their niche in the appropriate subcultural class segment.

From this perspective, AfricanAmerican culture simply functions within, and merely as a function of, caste discrimination. Its unique values, behaviors, and norms indicate mere "adjustments" (often pathological) to an oppressive situation. If the situation or oppression changed, AfricanAmericans could or would become like all other Americans in given social classes. Of course, such a process assumes that African American culture exists as a social hindrance, as unnecessary baggage in liberal democratic, universal America. Commitment to liberalism, then, remained the major flaw in Warner's otherwise substantial contribution.

In the preceding discussion of Marx, I noted that liberalism dialectically opposes the core elements of AfricanAmerican culture, such as extended and expanded families, emotional and mass participation in religious services, reciprocal obligations in communal exchange networks, unique African-based poly- and crossrhythms and syncopations in African and AfricanAmerican music, and so forth. Warner and his students, then, represent another form of "ruling class ideas" which, if pursued as a viable alternative or solution to the Black-White racial cultural struggle, would result in the loss of awareness and disappearance of AfricanAmerican culture. This aspect of his theory also places Warner in a category with some of his critics, especially the structural-functionalists. In order to demonstrate this observation, a critical analysis of the latter's position on the American class structure is in order.

THE STRUCTURAL-FUNCTIONAL MODEL

In a controversial article, Davis and Moore most clearly articulated the structural functional position on social stratification (as opposed to social class—note the difference). In this article, they emphasized the universal necessity of stratification and the fact that it was universally functional. They claimed that classless societies do not exist. Social stratification proved functionally necessary to assure the continuation and perpetuation of a cultural system. To them, cultures have to develop an institutional mechanism to make sure that the "best people" arrive in the most important positions:

> If the duties associated with the various positions were all equally pleasant to the human organism, all equally important to societal survival, and all equally in need of the same ability or talent, it would make no difference who gets into which positions and the problem of social placement would be greatly reduced. But actually it does make a great deal of difference who gets into which positions, not only because some positions are inherently more agreeable than others, but also because some require special talents or training and some are functionally more important than others. Also, it is essential that the duties of the positions be performed with the diligence that their importance requires. Inevitably, then, a society must have, first, some kinds of rewards that it can use as inducements, and, second, some way of distributing these rewards differentially according to positions. The

rewards and their distribution become a part of the social order and thus give rise to stratification.[16]

One can conclude that for Davis and Moore, social stratification universally, naturally, and normally occur in human societies. This "Adam and Eve" image of people being distributed into various positions in society through the induced desire to acquire highly valued rewards coincides with the social Darwinistic orientation of American capitalist culture. Liberal democratic, *laissez-faire*, free enterprise capitalist American culture, the democratic revolution within the democratic revolution, came closest to realizing this Darwinian ideal. For here one could ascend to the pinnacles of power and prestige through open competition with one's fellow citizens. The shackles or constraints of tradition had been broken: those of caste, kin, and religion. America's stratification system hierarchically distributes people according to their abilities to compete successfully for the various, differentially rewarded, functionally necessary (some more functionally necessary than others) positions in the American political-economic order. In this framework, social classes are analogous to positions in a large bureaucracy. It should also be noted that they have characteristics similar to those of bureaucracies; that is, the society (read *the corporation*) dispenses certain kinds of rewards.

> It has, first of all, the things that contribute to sustenance and comfort. It has, second, the things that contribute to humor and diversion. And it has, finally, the things that contribute to self-respect and ego-expansion. The last, because of the peculiarly social character of the self, is largely a function of the opinion of others, but it nonetheless ranks in importance with the first two. In any social system all three kinds of rewards must be dispensed differentially according to positions.[17]

Davis and Moore noted further that the rewards are "built into" the position as the rights and privileges associated with the position. Although some of the accoutrements are not functionally related to the position, they are essential to induce or motivate people to seek the positions and fulfill their duties and responsibilities. Of course, this assessment assumes a "natural" scarcity of human personnel to fill these essential positions, especially the more important or essential ones requiring "special" skills and talents such as medical doctor, CEOs of U.S. corporations, federal government officials, college professors and so forth. It also assumes that some positions are superior to others. Both are questionable assumptions. The importance of the social Darwinistic cultural ideology undergirding this approach assumes that humanity can be naturally subdivided into those who are superior and those who are inferior.

In order for a cultural system to maintain and perpetuate itself over time, not to mention expand or impose its hegemony over other cultures and peoples, it must make sure that the "superior" individuals occupy the "superior" positions. The special "rewards" of the privileged become their natural rights because of the important contribution they make to the culture. Consequently, a corporate executive should have a mansion, chauffeured limousine, private plane and pilot, expense accounts, personally tailored clothes, private secretary and so on. The theory assumes that the distribution of a population reflects the "natural" distribution of people in a hierarchically structured set of positions of varying importance to the society or cultural system. Society, therefore, arrives at a perfect, natural balance. People occupy positions in this system of stratification according to the level or degree of native intelligence.

As mentioned in the discussion on Marx and Weber, religion as a moral, valuative superstructure serves as an essential dimension of social class organization. It cements elements which bind a cultural system together. Davis and Moore also stressed its importance in providing human societies with certain ultimate values and common ends or objectives:

> Although these values and ends are subjective, they influence behavior, and their integration enables the society to operate as a system. Derived neither from inherited nor from external nature, they have evolved as a part of culture by communication and moral pressure. They must, however, appear to the members of the society to have some reality, and it is the role of religious belief and ritual to supply and reinforce this appearance of reality. Through belief and ritual the common ends and values are connected with an imaginary world symbolized by concrete sacred objects, which world in turn is related in a meaningful way to the facts and trials of the individual's life. Through the worship of the sacred objects and the beings they symbolize and the acceptance of supernatural prescriptions that are at the same time codes of behavior, a powerful control over human conduct is exercised, guiding it along lines sustaining the institutional structure and conforming to the ultimate ends and values.[18]

The rather cynical, passive perception of man as "determined" by the external controls and constraints of institutions (culture) reflects the impact of Durkheim's thought on American theoreticians. This combination of Durkheiman functionalist-empiricism and the social Darwinistic, Weberian-inspired mode of class or stratification analysis became the prevailing mode of explaining, justifying, and interpreting America's liberal democratic inequality.

Structural-functionalism offers but another alternative to the Marxian approach; and unlike Warner's, it does so without acknowledging the existence of clearly delineated classes. Structural-functionalists can be divided into those who describe America's social inequality or class structure as a "status-continuum" and those who describe the class structure as a mere (or convenient) ranking of individuals according to socioeconomic status (SES) indicators. The latter group I call the occupation, education, and income school who engage in various methodological and statistical debates. I should add that this distinction is merely analytical, for they actually reinforce and complement each other.

Robert Nisbet, a rather optimistic "true believer" in liberal America, produced an article in which he considered structural-functional theory ideal for explaining liberal democratic inequality. He took a position which celebrated a declining interest in social class as a viable concept for describing American cultural inequality or class system. He further asserted that the term social class now only proved useful for doing comparative or folk sociology and historical sociology but that for clarifying or interpreting the data on wealth, power, and social status in the contemporary United States and much of Western society in general, the term social class had become nearly useless.[19]

Nisbet arrived at his position through asserting that America as a society had transcended the European class system. He argued that as recently as 1910, social classes (in the European sense) were an understood accepted reality. However, as a consequence of national democracy, economic and social pluralism, ethical individualism, and the creation and implementation of public educational systems, new patterns of social power and status had emerged. These new patterns made class (as the concept was traditionally used) an obsolete term in describing the constantly expanding sectors of Western society. Conversely, Nisbet stated, in the non-Western underdeveloped world, classes still existed.

> There is a striking convergence of attributes of wealth, power, and status in such areas as the Middle-East and Latin America. But, so far as Western Europe and the United States are concerned, this convergence, this assimilation of economic and political influence within the differentiated social classes exists scarcely at all except to a small degree in those areas which have been least touched by the processes

of modern democratic industrial society.[20]

Nisbet attributed the existence of classes to "lesser developed," "backward" societies or cultures, claiming that modern, democratic, *laissez-faire,* free enterprise, industrialized capitalist cultures have eradicated traditional class distinctions. For Nisbet, social classes represented political-economic groupings necessary for the early stages of democratic, capitalist development but absent from and inappropriate for modern democratic industrial society. To him, classes served as transitional phenomena in western cultures' evolution toward the liberal democratic "paradise." Arnold Rose also observed the supposed transcendent nature of modern, liberal, capitalist culture. However, while Nisbet included much of Western Europe in his analysis, Rose contended that only the United States had achieved this stage of development (the revolution in the revolution):

> There's a great deal of evidence that the concept of class as used by European intellectuals has a different empirical reference from that in the class concept as used by American sociologists. Europeans follow the legitimate procedure of consistently using the concept of class to refer to a power group with a certain group consciousness and characteristic "life chances"; this definition is realistic because it reflects the heritage from medieval estates. There is little empirical evidence that class differences have increased over the past generation in the United States, or have affected basic behaviors that they did not previously affect. Yet there has been a sharp increase in the use of the class concept by American sociologists, as a substitute for such simpler concepts as education, occupation, and income.[21]

Rose believed that the American "class" system encompassed more flexibility or openness than that of continental Europe because of the American educational system and the "pushing up" phenomenon created by the influx of European immigrant groups as they struggled to establish themselves in the status hierarchy. The combination of these two factors supposedly prevented the formation of a permanent, stable, indigenous White lowerclass. In addition, he saw the rapid increase in productivity as a consequence of technological innovations, the presence of an abundance of resources, and the emphasis on the value of efficiency as contributing to the open, fluid quality of the United States' class hierarchy.

Finally, Rose mentioned the presence of an expansion-minded business community as a major deterrent to permanent class formations. He contended that the competitive vitality of the American economic order precluded the emergence of "upperclass" families in the United States and "gentlemen of leisure" (in the European sense), simply because they would have been scorned in this society. This state of affairs Rose considered "superior" to that of Europe's which still had established classes and the arrogant elitist tradition of "men of leisure." Moreover, he found disdainful the fact that wealth and prestige in Europe still involved matters of kinship and lineage. Rose insisted that the United States had transcended these tradition-bound obstacles to wealth and property and in so doing had freed the individual to compete and achieve at the highest level according to abilities and regardless of class origins.

Talcott Parsons' analysis of American capitalist culture also presents the idea of an American superiority over other democracies or liberal democratic, capitalist industrial societies. In a 1970 article on equality and inequality, Parsons discussed this concept of the American class structure:

> If my interpretation is correct, the concept of "elitism" in the modern, especially American setting, refers primarily to what has been called the "achievement" complex — which as a focus of inequality has tended to replace aristocracy and other ascriptive bases during the last few generations.[22]

Like those of other structural-functionalists, the Parsonian model of American capitalist culture rests on a social Darwinistic evolutionary conception of human society; that is, as societies or human groups become increasingly "modern" or "civilized," the new, more "liberating" achievement-oriented values and norms replace the old traditionally ascribed values and norms. Thus, the feudal period characterized "particularistic" (read "closed," "permanent" or "inherited") norms and values; and the more "advanced" societies or nation-states characterized "universalistic" (read open, competitive, and achieved) norms and values. For Parsons, the Marxian concept of class, and class struggle, describes simply a transitional stage between feudalism and the post-industrial revolution.

The Marxian "stratification system" with its traditional emphasis on the ownership of property as the means of accumulating status and power has been replaced by a more "democratic," universalistic set of criteria: the "ascription" of superior status to those who own property has largely broken down in favor of a highly diversified occupational structure which no longer displays a clear division between the "controllers" and the subordinate class. This occupational structure is characterized by fine gradations of prestige statuses associated with particular authorityor power relations which have emerged as one among several possible rationales for status-differentiation. Moreover, there is, especially perhaps through education, a far looser connection between adult position in the occupational world and their status by birth than was assumed by the Marxian analysis. There has, however, remained an important component of ascribed status via family origin, though substantially reduced by the "isolation" of the nuclear family and by the other factors of mobilization just discussed.[23]

One would be very hard put to find a better theoretical defense and justification of American liberal democratic capitalist culture: America possesses no permanent social classes, only "fine gradations of prestige statuses"; there is no clear division between the "controller" and the "subordinate" classes. Authority and power relations are dispersed and decentralized. Again, one receives the image of U.S. society as a huge, rationally organized, democratic, contented, harmonious bureaucratic organization coolly and efficiently processing and placing people according to Weberianly rational principles. It rather vividly coincides with, reinforces, and compliments the dominant and prevailing liberal democratic ethos which cements this particular capitalist cultural "apparatus" (to borrow a term from Cruse). However, Parsons did acknowledge the presence of a "cultural lag" in this otherwise liberal democratic cultural utopia. One such "lag" included the rather persistent problem of families or kinship networks which confer ascribed wealth, status, and prestige. But as noted above, he remained a functionalist to the core:

> The institutionalization of stratification, or more precisely the relations of inequality of status, constitutes an essential aspect in the solution of the problem of order in social systems through the legitimation of essential inequalities; but, the same holds for the institutionalization of patterns of equality .... Alternatively put, all societies institutionalize some balance between equality and inequality.[24]

One is tempted to ask, "Ah well, when all else fails, why not try a little doublespeak or tautological reasoning?" In order to account for the presence of ascribed status within the "post-industrial" liberal democratic "superstar" (U.S. society), Parsons fell back on the Darwinistic-functionalist connection. Therefore, although modern society isolated the family unit (nuclear family), the problem remains in a more tormented vein. Parsons argued that it would be possible to drastically reduce the number of families perpetuating this "residual cultural lag" without virtually eliminating the family itself. Of course, he recognized that we cannot do this but suggested developing some institutional means to encourage all nuclear isolated families to raise their children in the same manner as these successful families. He meant that all families in the various status "grades" should emphasize independence training in rearing their children. He proposed independence training as the critical factor which differentiated the socialization of the "privileged" children from that of the non- or less privileged:

> From one point of view, even though the recent increase in the emphasis on independence-training and participation weakens the hold of ascriptive features of identification with parental status from another, it may increase the status-differentiating influence of family in that children of higher status parents derive special competitive advantages from their socialization, precisely in the form of capacities for more independent and more responsible action, so that their chances of maintaining or improving the parental level of status actually improved relative to the children of less "advantaged" homes. This need not be a matter of family income level or access to the "best" schools and colleges, though it is rather highly correlated with such factors.[25]

Here we see Parsons tortuously, reluctantly acknowledging and justifying the existence of self-perpetuating class groupings as if they signified aberrations within an otherwise liberal democratic utopia. We also see him offering an excellent description of how the dominant culture maintains its hegemony through its ability to impose its definition of civilization. Of course, the fact that lowerclass or "less advantaged" peoples cannot overcome the cultural and material gap between themselves and those above them reflects the fundamental contradiction in the nature of liberal democratic capitalist culture.

Laissez-faire free enterprise capitalism and "liberty, equality, and fraternity" stand in irreconcilable opposition. The people who arrive at the top have a vested interest in remaining at the top. One important method for perpetuating their position inheres in their ability to determine the criteria for entrance or acceptance into the "inner circle." Consequently, while Parsons lamented the persistence of these "aberrations," these residual traditional phenomena, thirteen percent of the population continues to control eighty-seven per cent of the nation's wealth.[26]

Parsons perceived the existence of social classes in America as a temporary, transitional phenomenon which is reflected in his proposed definition of social class:

> We must divorce the "concept of social class" from its historic relation
> to both kinship and property as such; to define class status for a unit of
> social structure, as the position on the societal system; and to consider
> social class as an aggregate of such units, individual and/or collective,
> that in their own estimation and those of others in the society who
> occupy positions of approximately equal status in this respect.[27]

The relationship between the "ideal" and "real" is clearly revealed in this passage. For here, Parsons tells us that social class "should be" socially pure, divorced from the corrupting influences of property and biology or kinship. He also asserts that this separation could be achieved through adopting a rather subjective consensus-based definition of social class. In others words, if the "ideal" and the "real" differ, we will "make" them become the same through the manner in which we define them. Here again a social theoretician produced another scientific theory of society which exemplifies the Marxian observation regarding the role of bourgeois intellectuals.

It is interesting to note that, despite their criticism of Warner's theory and method, the functionalists, notably Parsons, essentially adopted Warner's position. In their inability to intellectually eradicate (read "rationalize") the "lag effect" of kinship ties and social class positions, they chose to emphasize the sociocultural dimension of class. So Parsons prescribed that analysts should emphasize the impersonal, social aspects of class behavior when performing class cultural analyses. Emphasizing the sociocultural allows the researcher to demonstrate the "openness" of the "loose," "amorphous," vaguely defined status groups. Parsons defined class status as the extent to which "others" similarly located would concur with an individual's self-evaluation. This definition resembles Warner's Evaluated Participation and Index of Status Characteristics. In essence, both grudgingly accept "social classes" in a complicated, highly qualified, muted language conveying the impression that classes are essentially cliques and friendship groups with, through implication, little or no political or economic importance.

Gordon's model for conducting class-oriented research revealed that structural-functionalist theoreticians have opted for a "diluted" Weberian-Warner solution to the contradictions of political-economic class groupings rather than accept the Marxian model. Gordon began by noting the importance of economic factors in determining "status differentiation":

> In modern capitalist, competitive society, it is quite obviously economic power which provides the means by which through successive generations' patterns may be enjoyed, occupational positions may be

pre-empted, politico-community power may be appropriated, and status differences may be crystallized. There is thus considerable point to the insistence of those investigators who demand that the economic factors be kept in the forefront in class analysis.[28]

Despite his clear acknowledgement of the correctness of the Marxian concept of social class in modern capitalist society, Gordon chose to emphasize the old Weberian-Warnerian concept of the sociocultural prestige dimension of social class:

> ... it is the social status structure rather than the economic or political power dimensions which plays the largest immediate role in producing those social divisions, shifting and amorphous as they may be, of American communities which center around the intimate friendship, clique life, association membership and participation, and intermarriage.[29]

Again, we confront the social scientific "doublespeak": classes exist but they don't exist; economic and political power remain crucial determinants of class position but are not as important as "status," the "subjective" dimension of class. Thus America becomes simultaneously a class and a classless society.

Methodological empiricists represent the other trend in structural-functional analysis in the United States. This school, which has been aptly dubbed the [August B.] Hollingshead school of thought, has been focused on developing increasingly sophisticated statistical and methodological procedures to "measure" social class using social economic status (SES), or occupation, education, and income.[30] This group tends to engage in various debates concerning the relative importance of one indicator over another; the adequacy of the statistical procedures used; the invention of new, and even more refined, measurable "indicators" of occupation, education, and income; ad infinitum. C. Wright Mills disapproved of this preoccupation of the empirical functionalist:

> Of late the conception of social science I hold has not been ascendant. My conception stands opposed to social science as a set of bureaucratic techniques which inhibit social inquiry by "methodological" pretensions, which congest such work by obscurantist conceptions, or which trivialize it by concern with minor problems unconnected with publicly relevant issues. These inhibitions, obscurities, and trivialities have created a crisis in the social studies today without suggesting, in the least, a way out of that crisis.[31]

One admires the cogent, perceptive manner in which Mills penetrated the various rationales (couched in terms of the necessity for "scientific objectivity") presented by this school to justify its immersion in "middle-range" theoretical concerns or problems. This trend in functionalist thought achieved the ultimate level of scientific absurdity in that the manner in which the proponents approached the theoretical problem — that is, the gathering and manipulation of data — became more important than the theoretical or social problem under discussion. If one attempted to obtain or gain some insight, one found oneself immersed in chi-squares, scaling techniques, verification and validation of procedures, coefficients of correlations, principal axis-factor analysis, and so on. In order merely to acquire the germ of insight contained in a particular work, one waded through pages of tables, charts, graphs statistical symbols, and so on, trying to extricate the socially, politically, or theoretically useful information.

In a manner one might consider more "scholarly," Gordon also noted the inadequacies of this variety of functionalist thought:

> To put together variables such as income, education, occupation and status into a conceptual whole and apply the term "class" to this construct would mean that the construct has social reality in the life of the community. If it does, then it will reveal itself empirically in the actual social divisions of the community. If it does not delineate such divisions, then the construct is an artificial one. Such being the case, it might be of considerably greater value to search for the social divisions in the first place. Indices, and the combinations of factors put together in the researcher's mind, might then be presumed to have predictive value rather than to stand for the social reality itself.[32]

Or, in the words of Lerone Bennett, an AfricanAmerican historian and journalist, "a social class symbolizes more than an SES salad." While essential to the concept, these ingredients cannot capture the nuances, subtleties, or cultural "taste" of a social class nor can they reflect its political economic significance. Gordon criticized the empiricists in terms of their potential for reification, substituting the "imagined" for the "real" and treating it as if it *were* "real." Further, Mayer charged functionalist thought in general with perpetuating a different type of "reification" regarding the nature of the class structure in American capitalist culture:

> Although structural-functional analysis need not necessarily involve any intrinsic ideological commitments…, the fact is that its practitioners are often tempted to confuse the functional necessity of social inequality in general with indispensability of a particular system of

social stratification, overlooking the possibility of alternative arrangements. Despite some explicit disclaimers regarding any such tendency,
functionalist writers have so far always confined themselves to explaining why different positions in the social structure carry different
degrees of prestige, and how certain individuals get into those positions. They have not presented any systematic account of changes in
the class structure. [33]

Mayer's analysis supports the general thesis stated at the outset of this
discourse: Much of so-called "scientific" sociological theory actually
constitutes an intellectual defense, justification, and legitimation of the
status quo with respect to both the class structure and the racial structure
in the United States. However, simply to present the liberal's theoretical
analyses and descriptions of the American social class or cultural system
without acknowledging the presence of the Marxian tradition would be to
present a very biased, inaccurate portrait of American sociology.

I will now discuss briefly the contributions that certain Marxist-oriented
American sociologists have made toward clarifying the nature of this
liberal democratic capitalist culture. Mills and Veblen stand as the two
most prominent American Marxist-oriented sociologists. Their analyses
of American capitalist culture differ radically from those of their contemporaries. Their "looser," more creative approaches and styles stimulate
reading when compared to the boring scientific "doublespeak" of their
functionalist critics and opponents. Both possessed the imaginative
vision to penetrate the layers of liberal democratic hypocrisy and expose
the cancerous innards of American capitalist culture.

Veblen's analysis of the predatory leisure class's frantic efforts at
"keeping up with the Joneses," its wasteful, frivolous, imitative pursuit of
conspicuous consumption, and its own vested interest taking precedence
over those of the "common man" revealed the actual nature of American
capitalist culture rather than justifying or legitimizing the status quo.
Veblen's dissection of American culture demonstrated the absurdity of
the liberal functionalist assertion that no upperclass in the European sense
existed in the United States.[34] His analysis preempted and nullified
Rose's assertion that the "gentleman of leisure" needs to be scorned in the
United States.[35]
Mills's observations on the nature and composition of America's

"elite" shattered the liberal functionalist "cover-up" of the existence of the American upperclass and revealed liberal democracy's potential for becoming the "living" embodiment of Orwell's *1984* society. Utilizing imaginative, innovative methods, Mills constructed a portrait of the institutional life of the elite segment of the American population which made the "big decisions" such as when to wage war, which countries to give aid to, which corporations should receive the lucrative government and military contracts, and so forth. He exposed its network of private social clubs, educational institutions, charity organizations, kinship ties, overlapping interests in corporate, political and military affairs. His image of the elite as an extended family, sitting on top, managing and manipulating the affairs of the richest, most powerful nation in the world sent shock waves through the liberal functionalist establishment — not to mention the more conservative defenders of the status quo. In essence, Mills destroyed the liberal democratic utopian image which American social scientists had struggled arduously to justify and defend.

Not satisfied with just exposing the upperclass, the "power elite," Mills also demonstrated the validity of Marx's sociopsychological insights into humans "correctly socialized" into capitalist culture. Furthermore, his portraits of the fragmented, alienated, apathetic, apolitical "white collar organization man" shattered the functionalist myth of the socially responsible stable middleclass, the image presented to American children in the old *Dick and Jane* readers, and in television series such as "Ozzie and Harriet," and "Father Knows Best." Mills presented his image of the American middleclass as that group of people whose lives revolved around essentially boring, repetitive, and unchallenging to their intellects, job skills, or bureaucratic positions. He presented white collar professionals as emotionally stunted with rather shallow leisure lives centered around office parties, swapping wives and cultivating the attention of their superiors in order to get promotions. The bored wives and children rarely spent time with the fathers. Thus, middleclass Americans lived not as the relaxed, warm, loving families portrayed in *Dick and Jane* but in reality were a striving, tense group, fervently attempting to imitate the style and taste of those perceived to be their class superiors. Moreover, they often experienced a sense of emptiness once having achieved the longed-for success.[36]

While the theories of Mills and Veblen remained characterized by what "scientific" functionalist theoreticians would deem "subjective" or "soft" methodology, other social scientists using "harder," more rigorous or scientific methods validated Mills's, and Veblen's image of capitalist culture. Edward Digby Baltzell's study of the Protestant establishment presented a similar analysis of the cultural life of the elite and noted its ethnic exclusiveness.[37] Floyd Hunter's investigation of the power structure of a southern city revealed the presence of a political economic cultural elite who made the major decisions for the city.[38] The relationship observed by Mills and Veblen (and usually grudgingly admitted in a qualified manner by functionalists) between political economic and so-called "status elites," that is ministers, heads of social agencies, doctors, and so forth, found verification in the Hunter study. The economic or business elite continued to be the most powerful group locally and nationally in the United States. Others whose research confirmed the accuracy and validity of Veblen's, Mills's[39] and Marx's conceptions of American capitalist culture include the works of the Lynds,[40] Presthus,[41] and Domhoff.[42]

THE FUNCTIONALIST SCHOOL AND AFRICANAMERICAN CULTURE

The functionalists held a position on AfricanAmerican culture quite similar to both the Marxian and Warner schools. They argued that AfricanAmericans have no distinct culture and that their behavioral and value differences developed due to their low economic position (disproportionately represented among the poor and unemployed) and their historical legacy of slavery and racial discrimination. As noted in the "Introduction," functionalists select a variety of so-called "value-free" concepts to describe and explain the peculiar political-economic and sociocultural characteristics of the AfricanAmerican community such as the cultural deprivation approach, the socially disorganized or disadvantaged model, the relative deprivation model, and the tangle-of-pathology/vicious-circle school.

These approaches share the assumption that racism and economic discrimination have produced "deviant" lifestyles and social problems in AfricanAmerican communities. To them, the dominant society could correct or reform the institutions which maintain and perpetuate these conditions and the behavioral differences between Blacks and Whites would disappear. AfricanAmericans would finally melt into the pot; that is, become integrated into mainstream America. This basic assumption undergirds the so-called "War on Poverty," the 1954 School Desegregation decision, and the 1964 Civil Rights Act.

The belief in and commitment to liberal democratic America's ability to correct its major aberration, racism, led to the publication of *The Negro American,* readings edited by Parsons and Clark. It is interesting that the volume appeared during the period in the Civil Rights Movement when AfricanAmerican activists advocated nationalism as the dominant ideology. The volume contains several articles by prominent Black and White social scientists delineating the progress or changes occurring in the status of AfricanAmericans. While acknowledging that racism had been a problem, the underlying theme emphasized the Civil Rights Movement's removal of the last barriers or obstacles to AfricanAmericans' access to the American opportunity structure. At last, AfricanAmericans, *en masse,* would be able to escape into mainstream middleclass culture where race would cease to be a factor in an individual's success (or lack thereof). The text virtually ignored the existence of a distinct AfricanAmerican culture as well as Black people's commitment to maintaining and perpetuating their cultural traditions. After having defined AfricanAmerican culture as pathological, they could only ask themselves what Black individual or group would *want* to identify with poverty, segregation, and oppression? By denying the existence of AfricanAmerican culture, structural-functionalists again demonstrated their differences with Warner and his associates.

The preceding discussion indicates that the caste school of race relations focused on both the superiority of the dominant caste and its system of class-determined subcultures. The caste school delineated the system of class-determined subcultures within the subordinate caste. The functionalists, on the other hand, asserted that once the system removed the legal basis of the caste system, the distinct class cultures of both castes would disappear, replaced by "loose" informal, and temporary associations of individuals of a similar status. Thus, structural-functionalists deny the existence of stable, exclusive, hierarchically arranged class cultures in the dominant society as well as the existence of a unique AfricanAmerican culture. For them, the Civil Rights Movement's successful attack on racial discrimination removed the final "cultural lag" impeding progress toward the creation of the liberal democratic utopia envisioned by the "founding fathers." In essence, for them the American Revolution had realized its ultimate objective: the "ideal" and "real" had become one (albeit unreal for anyone else).

From the perspective of racial-cultural struggle, structural-function-alists personify the Marxian dictum regarding the role of bourgeois intellectuals. Their reduction of the Marxian model of class struggle (as well as the sociocultural or anthropological model of class relations) to a system of techno-bureaucratic processes and relations serves the ruling class's interests in the same manner as Soviet intellectuals serve the Communist Party. In each case, the intellectuals analyze and interpret social phenomena in ways which remain consistent with the ruling ideology. Structural functionalists' cultural analyses of the United States generally reinforce and support the egalitarian, open-class myth embedded in this society's moral and ideological superstructure.

The model essentially rationalizes and legitimizes a system which relegates the cultures of AfricanAmericans and other peoples of color to subordinate, constrained, oppressed statuses. As a Black social scientist committed to the recognition, redemption, and regeneration of AfricanAmerican culture here and elsewhere in the Diaspora, I can only conclude that this school of thought inadequately (indeed, detrimentally) describes and explains the AfricanAmerican experience. Its basic assumptions include the social Darwinistic belief in the racial-cultural superiority of Western Europeans and EuropeanAmericans.

I began this chapter with a discussion of the major American social theoreticians' conceptions of the nature of capitalist culture as reflected in the hierarchical distribution of the United States' population. I noted how these social scientists have attempted to resolve the fundamental contradictions in this society, the problem of inequality in an egalitarian culture. I have demonstrated that the "challenge" yielded a variety of explanatory models, most of which deny the existence of structural inequality or discuss that inequality as a transitional stage characteristic of the industrial capitalist era. We now live in what many refer to as the post-capitalist or post-industrial society epoch, the era of multinational corporations.[43] According to these theorists, the distribution of power, prestige, and wealth supposedly balances as all classes or "status differentiation units" in society acquire and achieve equal access to the material means of higher social status and power.

This portrait of liberal democratic America, unfortunately, does not coincide with the actual social divisions in the society. Herbert Blumer noted in his symbolic interactionist critique of sociological theory that scientific concepts must be "grounded" in the "real world." We should be able to observe these phenomena in the day-to-day activities of the population. On the basis of this social scientific "bottom line" requirement for theoretical concepts, I am forced to conclude that most American sociological thought has been guilty of a gross reification of American society. It has treated the "ideal" as the "real." In so doing, the sociologists have been the ideological handservants of the liberal democratic ethos (with its Calvinist WASP moral/spiritual core) which functions as the cement holding the entire system together.

The preceding analysis of American social theories demonstrates the extent to which culture determines what one sees, how one interprets what one sees, and the inherent chauvinistic and ethnocentric biases characteristic of any individual socialized in a particular cultural milieu. As Malcolm X said, "White America's belief in its superiority over others is nothing but White nationalism." Thus, the fact that most American sociologists present an image of America which coincides with that espoused by the founding fathers appears perfectly natural and normal. The only unnatural and abnormal attribute of their work involves their insistence that others accept their interpretations as "objectively" accurate, scientifically determined, universal truths.

I have attempted to demonstrate the biases and distortions inherent in their description of their own culture. Therefore, for them to suggest or arrogantly assume that their "notions" regarding other people and cultures are true, accurate, or valid merely reflects the extent to which they have been brainwashed by their own rhetoric and deception. No other sphere of liberal democratic capitalist cultural life reveals the bankruptcy of American sociological theory more than its own efforts to account for the position, experiences and social conditions of the cultural groups of AfricanAmericans and other peoples of color here in the so-called "land of the free and the home of the brave."

CHAPTER VI

CLASS, CASTE, AND RACE: TOWARD AN ALTERNATIVE PERSPECTIVE

As the preceding discussion indicates, much of America's sociological theory regarding the nature of the system of inequality presents an image of United States society which confirmed or coincided with the ideology of its ruling class. The following represents my attempt to develop an alternative approach which one can use for analyzing and discussing America's race, class, and ethnic relations. I have attempted to demonstrate the accuracy of Marx's assertions regarding the role and function of bourgeois intellectuals and their "scientific" theories. In so doing, I exposed the Social Darwinism inherent in the cultural assumptions underlying those theories.

I concluded by noting the relationship between the culture and the social scientists, demonstrating that much of the material they present as "social fact" is often determined by and biased in favor of the ruling cultural ethos. Consequently, if the prevailing cultural ethos holds that America is a liberal democratic, *laissez-faire,* free enterprise capitalist cultural system with "liberty and justice for all," with an open and fluid class system providing each individual with the opportunity to achieve Horatio Alger-type success and fortune and guaranteeing every citizen certain "inalienable rights," then American social science theory will espouse and confirm this image in its efforts to "explain and predict" human group behavior. I take the position that inevitably the individual theoreticians, as products of this cultural ethos, indulge in this reification of the "ideal" as the "real." More importantly, their socialization induces them to believe that the "ideal" *is* real. Some groups' experiences contradict this image — perhaps as much as half of the nation — but the brainwashed (*i.e.*, correctly socialized into their profession) social scientists expect those situations to change in the direction of the ideal.

When confronted with the realities of class privileges and power, sociologists choose to minimize the importance, considering these realities temporary, transitory phenomena characteristic of the early capitalist era. They assert that we have now moved beyond that capitalist stage into the post-industrial society where freedom, equality, and negotiated, rational, bureaucratic justice prevail. The works of some social critics, particularly the "muckrakers" and pro-populist intellectuals, challenge this prevailing trend. However, the general trend overwhelms such challenges, and in the more recent period, has intensified both its reification of the ideal and its counterattacks on the critics.

In their efforts to account for the position of AfricanAmericans in United States society, American social scientists most vividly reflected the strength of their commitment to (and immersion in) the liberal democratic ethos. For here is where they confront the most blatant contradiction in the liberal democratic ethos: the "American Dilemma." I will now discuss in greater depth the theories that have been presented to explain or account for this "troubling presence" ("troubling" if one is liberal, White and male) in an otherwise liberal democratic utopia. This discussion includes a more refined formulation of the PanAfrican communalism paradigm.

Darwin's theory, especially as Spencer developed it, had a profound influence on American sociologists. Gossett noted in his critical discourse on race and Social Darwinism that Spencer's theories permeated most early American sociological thought. One finds Spencer's influence most notably in the work of Sumner, one of the most prominent and theoretically influential American social scientists. This school of thought "scientifically" documented and justified the enslavement of AfricanAmericans and their continued consignment to the lowercaste. Proponents of this framework perceived AfricanAmericans as incapable of comprehending liberal democratic culture because of biocultural backwardness, meaning AfricanAmericans are the cultural descendants of a recently- or mis-evolved preliterate, tribalistic, animistic people. This school believed

Africans to be linguistically limited, technologically simple, religiously paganistic, and cranially "underdeveloped" (lacking a full-sized human brain), thereby being both biologically and culturally unable to comprehend and absorb sophisticated, complex, scientifically advanced liberal democratic culture. Thus, this school justified slavery and the subsequent quasi-feudal tenant farming system imposed in the South on the basis that these impositions constituted a humane means of gradually "uplifting" people of color from "darkness" and a particularly intractable African primitiveness into the "light" of western civilization.

In essence, then, EuropeanAmerican oppressors perceived themselves as good Christian missionaries granting "these people" a favor out of the "goodness" of liberal hearts, and benign concern for the oppressed's moral, spiritual, and cultural development. EuropeanAmericans considered themselves to be protectively and supportively socializing backward, quasi-human beings for participation in the modern world, spoon-feeding civilization to Africans who possessed minds like those of children. Gossett demonstrated that when the Southern White apologists eventually set aside the Bible as a justification for slavery, they merely turned to the prestigious colleges and universities (Harvard, Yale, Princeton, Stanford, University of Chicago, and so forth) whose fledgling social science divisions or sociology and anthropology departments were bastions of "scientific" racism.[1]

The abolitionist-influenced liberal humanists who argued for accepting the humanity of AfricanAmericans challenged this position. The presence of many AfricanAmericans who had demonstrated the ability to be functioning, "normal," even materially successful American citizens reinforced the abolitionists' arguments. From this group's perspective, the more culturally backward, irrational White Southerners who had to be forced to free their enslaved Africans created the caste system through racial prejudice and discrimination which determined the status of AfricanAmericans in this society. These abolitionists portrayed the South as culturally behind and subordinate to the North, Midwest, and the West. They saw this backwardness reflected in the South's outdated, anti-democratic, socially and culturally fragmented political-economic system. So, even though the North had beaten the South into submission and forced it to subordinate its regional political-economic system to the expanding, northeastern liberal, capitalist ruling class, the South still retained its traditional, irrational attitudes, beliefs and values regarding the "Negro." That the entire Southern region suffered from "cultural lag" (due to its retention of European feudal forms of political-economic organization and its "uneducated," irrational emotions and practices toward the "Negro") served as the underlying implication in this approach.[2]

Social analysts developed the caste concept to describe and explain the peculiar position of AfricanAmericans in the United States. As mentioned in the preceeding chapter, much of American sociological theory derived from Weber its explanation the nature of the U.S. system of inequality. Yet, although Weber used the concept of caste in his discussion of ethnicity and social class, few, if any, American sociologists indicated an awareness of his position. Weber observed that society stratified status groups (as opposed to commercial acquisitive groups) according to their lifestyles as reflected by their ability to acquire material goods, *i.e.*, essentially how conspicuously they consume. However, status group stratification became caste stratification, especially if society bestowed upon some or more of the ethnic groups a "pariah" identity:

> ... the caste structure transforms the horizontal and unconnected coexistencies of ethnically segregated groups into a vertical social system of super- and subordination. ... [E]thnic coexistencies condition a mutual repulsion and disdain but allow each ethnic community to consider its own honor as the highest one: the caste structure brings about a social subordination and an acknowledgement of "more honor" in favor of the privileged caste and status groups. This is due to the fact that in the caste structure ethnic distinctions as such have become "functional" distinctions within the political societalization.[3]

Weber's conceptualization of the relationship between ethnicity and caste suggests the permanence or the persistence of a system of inequality. Although the creation of an ethnic caste system accurately describes what happened in many instances when ethnic and status groups found themselves competing for highly valued goods and services in the same geographical area, theorists perceived this system of inequality as being characteristic of a more traditional society; that is, feudal Europe. To have accepted Weber's concept of a functional, subordinate ethnic caste system would have contradicted all the liberal democratic myths most American social scientists had been socialized to accept regarding the nature of their society and the rights and freedoms of individual citizens. Thus, they chose to use caste in the anthropological sense of the term to describe the distinct condition of American "Negroes." In so doing, they could remain true to the liberal democratic ethos and discuss the experience of AfricanAmericans as a transitory aberration. Rose's observations regarding the position of AfricanAmericans reflected this choice:

> ... the present positions of the Negro is more like that of the European lower class than it is like that of the white American lower class, at least in the Northern and Western states. For this reason it is justifiable to speak of Negroes as the only American lower class (using the term in the European sense), or to use a more precise anthropological term — "caste" — to designate them. I prefer the latter approach, especially as it permits recognition of the significant status and other differences within the Negro group.[4]

In this observation, Rose provides a classic confirmation of the cultural biases inherent in American sociological theory that I mentioned above. Sociologists portrayed America as having transcended the European class system to the point where "only" the Negro occupied a lowercaste. No White lowerclass ethnic group in this sense existed, especially in the North and West. They acknowledged that AfricanAmericans, a racial group, held a permanent subordinate class position in America, but even AfricanAmericans have some internal differentiation within their communities. This interpretation affirmed that the racial caste and class systems were present only in the quasi-European feudal culture of the southern United States.

Although the caste school of race and class relations in the South used Warner's much criticized anthropological approach, many sociologists accepted this description and interpretation of southern small town culture. This interpretation and description of southern life reinforced the northern, liberal democratic, bourgeois elites' perception of themselves as culturally and morally superior to traditional European society. The caste school attacked Warner's description of northeastern villages and small towns in part as a reaction to his negative portrayal of these communities in the sense that they were similar to southern communities. That is, the system of inequality in northeastern communities reflected the same permanent character as the southern communities with the notable exception that in the South, the lowercaste was composed only of AfricanAmericans, the pariah group. Specifically, Warner described the class cultures of New England as similar to Dollard's, the Gardners' and Davis' portrayals of the White caste/class system in the South. Thus, Warner's theory was considered as biased and subjective when used to describe permanent class cultures among *white* New Englanders, but accurate and acceptable for describing the position of AfricanAmericans in southern small town societies. This reflects the northern bias toward the South as backwards, more closely akin to its European antecedent than the supposedly more liberal and progressive Northeast.[5]

This criticism of Warner's approach becomes even more difficult to comprehend when one remembers that Warner's model of class and ethnic relations essentially resembles that of the functionalist-assimilationists. In his analysis of Warner's theory, Gordon observed that one of its principal theses asserted that members of ethnic groups could participate comfortably in the ethnic subsystem as long as they did not rise above the lower middleclass, because

> ... an upper-middle or higher class position implies breaking away from the ethnic group to a position initially of marginality and eventually of incorporation into the dominant group. Thus, his prognosis for nonracial ethnic groups on the American scene is that most of them will decrease in size and importance and probably disappear.[6]

The principal difference between White ethnics and AfricanAmericans and other racial or "colored" minorities lies, therefore, in the latter's total lack of access into the higher classes by virtue of their skin color and sociocultural characteristics. This situation of being permanently blocked from access to the dominant culture also figures in Myrdal's definition and description of the American caste system. While focusing on the inappropriateness of the concept of "class" in discussing racial differences, he made the following observations:

> The ... term,"class," is impractical and confusing in this context since it is generally used to refer to a nominal status group from which and individual can rise or fall. There is class stratification *within* each of the two groups. When also used to indicate the difference *between* the Negro and White groups, the term "class" is liable to blur a significant distinction between the two types of social differences. The recently introduced term "minority group" and "minority status" are also impractical ... since they fail to make a distinction between the *temporary* social disabilities of recent White immigrants and the *permanent* disabilities Negroes and other colored people. We need a term to distinguish the large and systematic type of social differentiation from the small and spotty type and have throughout this book used the term "caste."[7]

Prior to Myrdal's massive study, most American sociologists willingly accepted the Warner school's portrayal of Black-White relations in the South as a caste system but refused to accept this situation as reflective of race relations in the more liberal, enlightened North and West. But,

Myrdal recognized that American observers of the race scene tended to lump the peculiar, unique problems of AfricanAmericans together with those of the then recent European immigrants. Instead, they claimed AfricanAmericans would enter what the Chicago school of social theoreticians defined as the "urban assimilationist cycle." This model reached prominence through the work of Robert E. Park and his students, including Black social scientists E. Franklin Frazier, Charles Johnson, St. Clair Drake, Horace Cayton, and others.[8] In Park's theory, recent ethnic and racial immigrants to the urban areas usually began their acculturation/ assimilation journey into mainstream America from their lower class, homogeneous, slum communities, and gradually through their ethnic political participation achieved political-economic and sociocultural progress. Consequently, by the third generation, they generally had become more culturally "American" than ethnic.

Myrdal challenged this assertion by noting that the entire nation maintained caste barriers to AfricanAmerican progress, not just the South — though, possibly, it was more visible in that area. He noted further that the Park school's opposition to the use of caste in describing and explaining the AfricanAmerican experience emerged as a consequence of its tendency toward theoretical "hair-splitting," emphasizing the differences between the nature of "classical" caste systems and the more "liberal" manifestations of prejudice and discrimination characteristic of American race relations.

> It should ... be clear that the actual content of the Negro's lower caste status in America, that is, the social relations across the caste line, vary considerably from region to region within the country and from class to class within the Negro group. It also shows considerable change in time.... It will only have to be remembered constantly that when the term "caste relations" is used in this inquiry to denote a social phenomenon in present day America, this term must be understood in a relative and quantitative sense. It does not assume an invariability in space and time in the culture, nor absolute identity with similar phenomena in other cultures. It should be pointed out ... that those societies to which the term "caste" is applied without controversy — notably the Antebellum slavery society of the South and the Hindu society of India — do not have the "stable equilibrium" which America sociologists from their distance are often inclined to attribute to them.[9]

Here Myrdal responded in large part to Oliver Cox's critique of the caste school. It seems somewhat ironic, within the context of the PanAfrican communalism model, that a Black sociologist would challenge the caste school on the basis that it misrepresented the nature of AfricanAmerican-EuropeanAmerican relations in the United States. Yet, Cox's criticism of the caste school provides us with additional insights into the nature of capitalist culture and its impact on the AfricanAmerican community. Furthermore, this debate introduces the central concept underlying this discourse, that of cultural conflict, the power struggle between subordinate and superordinate cultures. Cox basically disagreed with the caste school due to his commitment to a Marxist approach to the study of human society. As such, he attacked the caste school from the Marxian evolutionist position. He described caste societies as tradition-bound, static societies with a certain mode of production while the liberal-democratic, individualistic capitalist culture had another, superior, mode of production.

> As distinguished from bipartite interracial adjustment, the caste system is ancient, provincial, culturally oriented, hierarchical in structure, status conscious, nonconflictive, non-pathological occupationally limited, lacking in aspiration and progressiveness, hypergamous, endogamous, and static.[10]

One sees from this description that Cox perceived capitalist culture and its race problem to be vastly different from a pre-capitalist caste system. He defined capitalist cultures as cosmopolitan, heterogeneous, modern, conflict-oriented, pathological, competitive, and progressive with unlimited occupational mobility. Cox took the position that equating race relations in modern, liberal-democratic, capitalist America with relations in an ancient caste system is like saying that an apple "under certain circumstances" is an orange:

> In Western civilization, there is basically a limitless urge to exploit the means of production. In a caste system, this is not nearly so pronounced. Production... is based upon hereditary monopoly rather than upon competitive opportunities ... race relations or problems are variants of modern political class problems — that is to say, the problems of exploitation of labor together with the exploitation of other factors of production. In a caste system, there is no proletariat, no class struggle — indeed, no need for the proletarianization of the workers. We shall assume "judicial notice" of the fact that the race problem in the United States arose from its inception in slavery, out of the need to keep Negroes proletarianized.[11]

Cox, in the true Marxian tradition on the race question, emphasized the differences in the cultural modes of economic production. In so doing, he supported the Marxian thesis that racism, a rather recent phenomenon in human history, correlates with the evolution and development of the capitalist mode of production. As indicated in the preceding discussion of Marxist theory, the works of several historians and social analysts challenged this position. Nevertheless, while Cox's distinctions have some theoretical validity, he based them on "ideal-type" constructs. He compared two systems in terms of how they *ought* to work as opposed to how they *actually* work. Note the distinctions he makes between a caste system and a capitalist system in the following passage:

> Production in a caste economy ... is carried out by hereditarily specialized producers associations which have not only the right to the peaceful enjoyment of their specialty but also the sacred duty to execute it faithfully and contentedly. Castes do not have the alternative opportunity of working in those industries which yield the largest returns. A significant point of difference here is that there is no "boss" employing castes at stipulated wages to produce commodities which belong to an entrepreneur and which he expects to sell at a profit. The material products of a caste belong to the caste; and it ordinarily disposes of them according to certain established rules of the community.[12]

Having established the theoretical "ideal-type" political-economic characteristics of a caste system, Cox then attempts to demonstrate, again theoretically, how the position of AfricanAmericans in the U.S. cannot be compared or equated with that of caste:

> On the other hand, Negroes in the United States have the right to sell their labor in the best market. The competition of different varieties and especially open exploitation tend to keep Negroes out of many employments: in so far as the occupation is concerned ... both Negroes and whites are on equal footing. Thus, not only are the races not identified with any particular occupation but there is also no accepted plan for the sharing of occupations.[13]

The fact that in capitalist culture, "Negroes" are as "free" to be exploited as other workers is one critical difference between Cox's ideal construction of caste culture and capitalist culture. However, he did concede that AfricanAmericans "may be" prevented from participation in "certain" occupations due to "competition" and "open exploitation."

Cox's work is a classic revelation of the "Achilles heel" of Marxian theory on race and class. As Myrdal observed, class relations *are* fundamentally different from those of race. True, they do have some overlapping behavioral manifestations, yet they remain separate and distinct. The fact that Cox (an AfricanAmerican) attempted to subsume the issue of race in the United States under the so-called "broader" issue of class strikes me as another example of a "scientist" circumscribed by ideology, an ideology that negates his cultural being in the same Western chauvinistic manner as that of liberal-democratic universalism.

Initially, Cox's conceptual distinctions between modern capitalism and the ancient Hindu caste system were quite impressive because of the important critical differences in their respective cultural organization. Yet, Cox takes a position essentially the same as that of a bourgeois intellectual. Despite his Marxian perspective, his argument parallels those I have previously identified as representing the ruling class ideas as presented by functionalists. He failed to "ground" his argument in the "real" world of Jim Crow segregation: racial lynchings by police or mobs, restrictive covenants in the North and neighborhood segregation in the South, with an equal opportunity for occupational discrimination, and political and economic disenfranchisement for all persons of color — all of which existed during the period in which he wrote.[14]

To ignore the unique, gross inequities and injustices being perpetrated upon members of his racial/cultural group and to "lump" this phenomenon under the umbrella of proletarian class struggle reflects another type of intellectual blindness that often afflicts educated members of oppressed racial groups. Fanon labelled this type of pathological personality a "colonized mentality." Individuals suffering from this peculiar psychological disease often adopt a radical and/or critical theoretical orientation while failing to acknowledge or even perceive the underlying implications that the theory poses for the survival and perpetuation of their group's culture.[15]

Cox's inability to see the convergence between Marxian theory and liberal democracy on the issue of AfricanAmerican culture reflects the persuasive power of liberal progressivism. We often find ourselves supporting the basic premises of liberalism even in the midst of our critical attacks upon it. To deny the existence of a racial caste on the basis of illegality or inconsistency with the capitalist mode of production is analogous to the functionalists arguing that America is a fluid, open, class system. In either case, the proponents assume the ideal to be real.[16]

Myrdal appeared to respond directly to Cox when he noted that many observers of America's race relations confuse caste relations with the caste line:

> The changes and variations which occur in the American caste system relate only to caste relations, not to the dividing line between the castes. The latter stays rigid and unblurred. It will remain fixed until it

becomes possible for a person to pass legitimately from the lower caste to the higher without misrepresentation of his origin. The American definition of "Negro" as any person who has the slightest amount of Negro ancestry has its significance in making the caste line absolutely rigid. Had the caste line been drawn differently — for example, on the criterion of the predominance of white or Negro ancestry or of cultural assimilation — it would not have been possible to hold the caste line so rigid. [17]

For Cox, the existence of the racial caste line occurred as a temporary phenomenon. He noted, in an article published prior to the one cited above, that when society isolates two or more racial or nationality groups as a consequence of a situation of sustained conflict or basic repugnance, these groups should not be construed as castes even though their relationships equalled one of superordination and subordination or "conqueror and conquered." He termed these situations "latent power relations," situations which occur when a society (culture) fails to fully integrate the various groups within its population. Cox observed further that since the South was not a fully integrated society, caste theory was not applicable. The unstable relationship between the races remained subject to change:

... Negroes and whites in the deep South do not constitute an assimilated society. These are rather two societies. Thus we may conceive of Negroes as constituting a quasi or tentative society developed to meet certain needs resulting from their retarded assimilation. Unlike the permanence of caste, it is a temporary society intended to continue only so long as whites are able to maintain barriers against their assimilation.[18]

The question here, of course, becomes when does Cox expect this "temporary," "latent power group situation" to change? He admitted that the legal barriers to the assimilation of AfricanAmericans had been eradicated, but their "tentative" society still appeared to be subordinate. Cox apparently willingly ignored what Gerald Berreman perceived as the essential similarity of the two systems — that caste rules function to maintain indefinitely the caste system with its institutionalized inequality:

In the United States, color is the conspicuous mark of caste, while in India there are complex religious features which do not appear in America, but in both cases dwelling area, occupation, place of worship, and cultural behavior, and so on are important symbols associated with caste status. The crucial fact is that caste status is determined and therefore systems perpetuated, by birth: membership in them is ascribed and unalterable. Individuals in the low castes are considered inherently inferior and relegated to a disadvantaged position, regardless of their behavior. From the point of view of the social psychology of intergroup relations, this is probably the most important common and distinct feature of the caste systems.[19]

On these issues, Cox can be categorized as an optimistic Marxist assimilationist. He had little regard for AfricanAmerican culture and appeared to look forward to the day when the Black "quasi" society would cease to exist, thereby demonstrating its complete (as opposed to "retarded") assimilation into American mainstream culture and—if I read him correctly—active involvement in the anticipated Marxian class struggle. As previously noted, Cox's description of AfricanAmerican culture as tentative, retarded, and temporary, as well as his proposed solution to this "latent power group conflict" are essentially the same as the pro-caste, liberal humanitarians. Both Cox's and Myrdal's forecast or prognosis for the AfricanAmerican community involved gradual absorption into liberal, democratic America. Their assessments represent a good example of the accuracy of Cruse's assertion regarding the similarity of goals for both liberal Marxist and liberal non-Marxist (the theoretical "gurus" who interpret and defend the capitalist status quo), to wit: the cultural negation of the AfricanAmerican community.

The fact that these two different schools of thought arrived at the same conclusion with respect to the ultimate fate of the AfricanAmerican community deserves special treatment. It demonstrates an unusual amount of "faith" in liberal democratic culture and the "American Creed." It also demonstrates some rather naïve notions regarding the nature of both AfricanAmerican and EuropeanAmerican culture. A major contribution made by the caste school was its introduction of the element of cultural conflict. Emphasizing the fact that Whites and Blacks existed in separate caste cultures, with one cultural group superordinate and the other subordinate, actually provided an acknowledgement that both groups maintain and perpetuate *cultural* differences over time.

The caste school confirmed Herbert Blumer's thesis stressing race relations as a sense of group position.[20] From this perspective, theorists cannot confine racial prejudice and discrimination to the acts or attitudes of individuals. Rather, racism, the feeling or sense of cultural and biological superiority, must be acknowledged as much a part of American culture as "mom and apple pie." As such, American institutional life inherently requires the catechism of racism. It is taught to and internalized by children as they acquire the ability to read, write, and speak. Once children leave their families and enter the major socializing agent in American society, the educational system, this sense of superiority over "colored" groups is reinforced. In this setting, AfricanAmerican and other racial minorities become quite conspicuous by virtue of their absence, both in the physical setting (segregated classrooms) and the content (a white-supremacist curriculum). When present in either or both, the society presents AfricanAmericans and other people of color as inferior.

The caste school's perspective also confirmed and reinforced Warner's conception of the nature of capitalist America's cultural class structure. This approach, as noted above, documents the presence of stable social classes among both groups distinguished by class-specific cultures, each a variant of the general culture. This position on the relationship between class and culture also reflects (and reaffirms) the work of Lucio Mendieta y Nuñez, a sociologist from Mexico. According to Nuñez, social classes differentiate by their peculiar lifestyles based on their position in the economic structure:

> In the same way we find that there is a culture of the higher class, another of the middle-class, and still another of the proletarian class within every civilized society, as aspects or phases of its general culture; and that with the essential characteristics of these cultures well defined, permanent units or circles can be formed in spite of the incessant changes operating in the persons living within them. But the social class is not constituted either by the individuals regarded as such or by the cultural contents of each circle, but by uniting both elements into a living, always actual synthesis.[21]

Nuñez's emphasis on class cultures as aspects of a society's more general culture closely resembles that of the PanAfrican communalism model informing the present discourse. However, he omitted a discussion of race and ethnic oppression or assimilation in his theory. Thus, his descriptions of the politics, economics, and values of the various classes comprising modern, civilized (read capitalist) society holds true only for ethnically homogeneous societies. Applying his model to the United States, one must emphasize that the generalized class-cultural portraits he presents reflect aspects of the White Anglo-Saxon Protestant cultural system which functions as THE American culture. This qualification becomes essential since, as both Cruse and Gordon have demonstrated, America is stratified by class, race, and ethnicity.

Nuñez's model (like Weber's and Mills') emphasizes both the political-economic dimension of class as well as that of culture or lifestyle. In his description of the upper or higher class, he notes that pride of blood or wealth exists as a dominant characteristic although modern bourgeois society bases this pride more on wealth and power independent of any consideration of blood. He delineates several distinctive features or cultural traits characteristic of the capitalist upperclass. These are: (1) possession of wealth and capital power; (2) a refined form of material and moral living permitting the satisfaction of human needs through its access to the best things; (3) a feeling of safety and pride of class; (4) social conduct constrained by rigorously observed conventions; (5) a constant preoccupation with keeping up appearances; and (6) a reactionary and conservative spirit.[22]

Nuñez perceived these cultural attributes of the upperclass to be constants, meaning, they exist as Durkheimian "social facts," external to the individual, yet constraining h/er. In essence, before society considers an individual to be wholly or completely "higher" or "upperclass," s/he must possess and internalize most or all of these cultural and material prerequisites. Nuñez differs from Warner because he includes the elements of power, especially economic power, as an inherent element in upperclass culture. Warner and his disciples concentrated more on the behavioral and blood dimensions while underemphasizing or omitting a discussion of the importance of wealth and power. However, both Nuñez and Warner perceived these class cultures as being open and more fluid than caste stratification. One can also consider Nuñez a Darwinistic evolutionist in his perception of modern "civilized" society's class organization as being an "advance" over backward, rigid, traditional caste-stratified societies or cultures.

Nuñez's cultural portrait of the middleclass is classic in that it captures the unity or organic wholeness of capitalist culture, which is the cement which binds the classes together into a stable, harmonious system, a condition contrary to Marx's predictions. Nuñez began by noting that the middleclass copies the ways of living of the higher class, which in this purely material aspect, seems to be its constant ideal: dress, furniture, living quarters, recreation, homeowner, and so forth. Secondly, the middle-class bestows great importance on culture, the sciences, technology, the professions, and so on, as means for the attainment of economic well-being and moral satisfaction. Nuñez postulates further that the middleclass also possesses a high ethical and religious sense, with ambitions limited to obtaining this well-being and moral satisfaction mainly by means of work. The middleclass does not make a point of accumulating riches.[23]

Politically, Nuñez observes that the middleclass exists in an ideological contradiction. It values the rights associated with the ownership of private property, yet it recognizes the vast difference between its limited wealth and that of the upperclass:

> It loves and respects private ownership on account of having acquired it by way of patient efforts and privations or because it hopes to acquire it, and naturally feels fearful and indignant at the very idea of being dispossessed of what it justly holds to be the product of its work. The justification of its right to the small property it owns leads it to justify every right to ownership without taking into account the fact that the enormous properties of the higher class do not have the same foundation.[24]

As a consequence of its allegiance to the principles and rights of private property, Nuñez perceives the middleclass' role as that of moderator, helping to maintain equilibrium in the class system. The higher class sees this "buffer" role the middleclass plays as essential for the stability of the social system; for, without the latter, the former would be soon destroyed by the proletariat. On the other hand, the proletariat holds the middleclass responsible for delaying the triumph of the revolution due to its conformist, cowardly counterrevolutionary tendencies. However, Nuñez also noted that the high cultural, ethical, and religious sense of the middleclass led many of its members to a critical analysis of human societies. Thus, the middleclasses produced, in all historical periods, great revolutionaries, great reformers, and apostles of social justice.

Nuñez concludes the discussion of the cultural traits of the middleclass by commenting on its commitment to maintaining appearances, even at the cost of great sacrifices — the "keeping up with the Joneses" syndrome. It derives its economic foundation from rent on small property, or revenue from limited capital, from personal work, or from both. Some sectors of the middleclass possess a certain amount of luxury and comfort but these do not approximate that of their more ostentatious reference group and social superiors. Consequently, service workers or "caretakers" — the bureaucrats, technicians, professionals, administrators (public and private), and so forth — compose the middleclass. In other words, Nuñez's portrait fits essentially what recent neo-Marxian theoreticians have labelled the "new working class."

This portrait of the middleclass in modern "civilized" societies, or capitalist cultures, confirms in form and content the proposition that the middleclass represents the cultural bedrock of capitalist societies. Support for the right of private ownership, imitation of and aspiration to become members of the "higher classes," ritualistic observance of the cultural and ethical values of capitalist culture, management and manipulation of the lowerclass to serve the interest of the upperclass as well as to maintain its middle-level niche comprise the beliefs, values, and behavior that serve to perpetuate the liberal democratic myth.

I will return to this portrayal of the role, function, and cultural values of the middleclass in a subsequent discussion which compares and contrasts the AfricanAmerican and EuropeanAmerican middleclasses. In clarifying the cultural attributes of the middleclass as well as delineating its political-economic status within the broader cultural system, Nuñez has provided an excellent model for analyzing the cultural complexities inherent in the AfricanAmerican-EuropeanAmerican cultural struggle. However, before elaborating on this issue, let me briefly summarize Nuñez's cultural portrait of the lowerclass in capitalist societies. This summary will provide additional insight into the nature of capitalist culture and the dynamics of racial-cultural struggle in the United States.

Nuñez described the lowerclass as a group of inadequately educated (often illiterate), economically struggling, manual laborers with crude manners of speech and social conduct. He calls them present-oriented and very religious; they attend church regularly in order to meet certain emotional needs. Politically, they tend to be conservative or aggressively patriotic. They are disproportionately represented in the army — even in countries where military service is not compulsory. Although they have the power in terms of numbers to launch a successful revolution at any time, they tend to be the staunchest supporters of class-divided, legally structured social inequalities and elite-dominated capitalist "democracy": "In spite of its economic situation it accepts the existing state of things, reacting and rebelling only when guided and given a program and a banner by individuals from the other social classes especially from the middleclass."[25] Nuñez observed that this paradox can be explained only on grounds of religion and culture.

This analysis of the lowerclasses in capitalist cultures confirms the theses of several social analysts (Harold Cruse, James and Grace Boggs, and C. Wright Mills, among others[26]) regarding the folly of American

Marxists' attempts to forge an alliance between AfricanAmericans (and other peoples of color) and the White workingclass. As Nuñez correctly notes, workingclass culture in capitalist society constitutes THE most reactionary, conservative element for the maintenance of the status quo. Its members consist of the front-line, "cannon-fodder," supporters of the capitalist system. They place their lives on the line for its protection and perpetuation, be it in Japan, Korea, Vietnam, Western Europe, Johannesburg, Nicaragua, Boston, Little Rock, Oakland, Memphis, and so forth. The AfricanAmerican cultural struggles directed towards assimilation or separation in the U.S. inevitably challenge the cultural-economic interests, loyalties, and racial privileges of this group.

Nuñez's observations also provide additional support for the thesis offered above regarding the relationship between capitalism and the Protestant Ethic. The fact that the lowerclasses in America maintain their deeply devoted loyalty to capitalist culture despite their obvious and unnecessary material and social deprivations can only be attributed to religion and culture. This important point counters the functionalists' profit-motivated theory of stratification. If one accepts the functionalist thesis, one would conclude that the elite of the system—those deriving the greatest amount of wealth, power, privilege, and prestige—would be the first to join the army, man the tanks and planes, first on the "old battle line." Yet, this is not the case. The elite may be the ones to decide that *someone* will man the war machinery, but *they* will not be the ones.

If one accepts the postulate that the greatest service one can render to the perpetuation of a particular group or collective way of life is to offer h/er life, it is ironic to find that altruistic loyalty most often amongst those who benefit the least from the status quo. Clearly, then, culture, given its religiously-backed moral ethos, proves to be greater than the sum of its individual parts. One could not persuade the rational economic man implicit in functionalist stratification theory that their economic interests involved risking their life in war for a salary lower than that of a corporation president, who would probably earn excess profits as a consequence of the war. The loyalty of the lowerclasses of capitalist culture reflects the power of commitment to the prevailing moral/spiritual ethos in maintaining cultural integrity and autonomy. Thus, the intervening effect of culture, a collective commitment to the maintenance and perpetuation of capitalist cultural social life with its accompanying racial and class privileges, negates what appears to be the perfect setting for the Marxist class struggle.

Nuñez's analysis, however, does not eliminate the possibility of Marxian-style class struggle. Rather, he notes that the leadership and program for such a movement must come from the middleclass. He considers the lowerclass usually incapable of organizing ideological movements. Several social theoreticians have expounded this concept of the middleclass as the "new working class" with the potential for creating and implementing strategies for radical socialist-oriented social transformation.[27] The difficulty with this position essentially reflects that of traditional Marxian theory. It ignores or refuses to accept the importance of the racial-cultural question. Its Western vision of scientific socialism essentially negates other forms of socialism: that is, forms of socialism such as NativeAmerican communalism or African Socialism (as developed by former President Julius Nyerere of Tanzania and refined/extended by Chinweizu in his provocative monograph, *The West and the Rest of Us*). These concepts suggest that socialistic, or more specifically, communalistic forms are culturally consistent with African peoples and would be more easily grasped and possibly acted upon by the AfricanAmerican masses than European Marxism-Leninism.

Nuñez's analysis of the class system and the subcultures contained therein prove consistent with that of Warner and the caste school. Both models' delineation of the various classes and the relationships between and within the class groupings contradict and refute the functionalist stratification thesis. As their models vividly demonstrate, the American capitalist cultural class structure is neither open nor fluid. On the contrary, it is stable and inherently perpetuates social inequality. This analysis of the class system also contradicts the liberal democratic ethos which serves as the cornerstone for American culture.

Nuñez's assertion regarding the cultural unity of the system also remains consistent with the racial-cultural struggle model guiding this discussion. His emphasis on religion and culture as the cement which holds what appears to be disparate and contradictory elements together coincides with the major thesis informing this discourse: capitalism as a cultural system includes a moral and spiritual dimension, it is not merely a political-economic system. Its vision or worldview uniquely includes individualism, competition, and materialism as its core elements. As such, it stands in direct opposition to other more communalistic, cooperative societies and cultures.

As a consequence of accumulation of immense wealth and power, the leading capitalist economic countries (with Japan as the notable exception) dominate and exploit peoples of color. This political-economic dominance is generally justified by and attributed to these countries' presumed cultural superiority, which often they cast as biological superiority. In this, they are joined by the elitist Japanese political-economic leaders. Once perceived as a cultural system which bestows special racial privileges and benefits on its constituents, the so-called race-class struggles within the capitalist state take on new meaning. For while a continuous class struggle may be occurring among the superordinate groups, a larger need to remain in ascendance at the expense of peoples of color controls and constrains that struggle. Thus, racism provides a crucial element for maintaining unity within the dominant culture. Nuñez, Warner, and the caste school neglected to emphasize this critical dimension of capitalist culture.

Nuñez's description of the role of the middleclass in capitalist culture significantly contributes to the concept of cultural struggle. Several researchers and social critics have emphasized the importance of achieving middleclass status, especially for people of color in North America. The assimilationist/integrationist model for race relations in American sociology generally uses the middleclass as the norm for determining the "progress" of racial and ethnic groups. If these researchers demonstrate that the majority of a racial or ethnic group acquired the attributes of the middleclass, they generally concede that the group has become "American," sharing the values, beliefs, and behavior Nuñez described.

When applying Nuñez's model to the AfricanAmerican community, the analysis reveals that the majority of AfricanAmericans belong to the lower and/or underclass (to borrow Billingsley's concept). They remain outside of mainstream American life. Thus, many liberal policymakers adopted a national objective to increase the number of Blacks in the middleclass. If the policymakers succeed — and they haven't thus far — the AfricanAmerican community will cease to exist in any culturally distinguishable way. From the perspective of cultural struggle, the realization of this middleclass objective would be construed as a defeat for AfricanAmericans. However, due to the tenacity of the racist element inherent in capitalist culture, the possibility of achieving this objective does not constitute an imminent danger.

The contemporary middleclass orientation toward cultural struggle presents the more pressing problem confronting the AfricanAmerican community. As Warner and the caste school demonstrated, the Black middleclass traditionally identifies with the dominant culture's middleclass. Policymakers and the caste school present this group in the AfricanAmerican community as the model to be emulated by its lowerclass brethren. In other words, for many social theorists and politicians, the Black middleclass represents the "best" of the race. This desire and description emanates in large measure from the Black middleclass's conventional public behavior, its material possessions, lifestyle, participation in mainstream politics, and often heroic struggles against apartheid-type discrimination of the "old" South. Members of the AfricanAmerican middleclass struggle very aggressively in their efforts to become accepted, to get in the door to prove their humanity by competing as equals with their White counterparts.

From the perspective of cultural struggle, the pursuit of these objectives places members of this group in the enemy's camp politically in comparison to their non-assimilated racial brethren. For, as Nuñez clearly and decisively demonstrated, the middleclass stands as the bedrock of capitalist culture. They become the "caretakers" of the system, the guards at the gates to the castle, the interpreters, definers, and justifiers of capitalist cultural hegemony. In order to be accepted into this group, AfricanAmericans must become culturally White (BASPs: Black Anglo-Saxon Protestants). In so doing, they become the cultural enemy of their racial-cultural group. This theme is pursued in greater depth in a subsequent chapter. However, as noted in the "Introduction," I consider the cultural assault perpetuated on AfricanAmericans one of the gravest problems confronting our community. If committed to fulfilling its historical mission as outlined by DuBois, the Black middleclass plays an important role in this continuing struggle:

> So far they are justified; but they make their mistake in failing to recognize that, however laudable an ambition to rise may be, the first duty of an upper class is to serve the lowest classes. The aristocracies of all peoples have been slow in learning this and perhaps the Negro is no slower than the rest, but his peculiar situation demands that in his case this lesson be learned sooner.[28]

DuBois made this statement in 1899. Since then, it appears that the African American middleclass has been rather slow to assume its proper role.

Before concluding this critical review of caste, class, and race relations in capitalist culture, I will discuss briefly a very controversial work which supports the thesis advanced here regarding the nature of cultural struggles. I refer to both an article and the first volume of

Immanuel Wallerstein's work which focuses on the rise (and hopefully demise) of the capitalist world economy. Wallerstein's thesis regarding the evolution and ascendance of the capitalist world economy and its exploitation/domination of semi-peripheral and peripheral areas or nation-states affirms the arguments presented here regarding Western European cultural and economic imperialism.

Wallerstein documented the evolution of capitalist political-economy in Western Europe through its various stages culminating in the emergence of the current core nations, that is, the United States, Japan, West Germany, France, Britain and other nations comprising the European Common Market. These nations constitute the so-called developed countries because of their advanced technological development, modern industrial production facilities, accumulation of finance capital, and generally high standards of living, among other factors. Excluding the socialist nations, the remaining nation-states were categorized according to their economic value to the core. Thus, those nations possessing natural resources essential to maintaining and/or expanding the economies of core capitalist states Wallerstein considered to be prime areas for investment. As a consequence of the increased level of investment as well as greater capital or cash flows derived from the sale of their valuable natural resources, the semi-peripheral countries develop (or industrialize) at a much faster rate than those countries categorized as peripheral. The nations on the periphery possess few, if any, natural resources vital to current capitalist productive needs. Thus, Wallerstein considered them poor investment risks and marginal to the core's economic interests.

Needless to say, rampant poverty, political instability, and a welfare-type dependency on the largesse of the core nations characterize their political-economic existence. The economic exploitation and dependency is accompanied by an intense emphasis on cultural change. The core nations attempt to impose their capitalist cultural definition of "modernization" and development on both the semi-peripheral and peripheral nations. That is, the core nations pressured the dependent nations to accept and internalize capitalist values and orientations: rationality, efficiency, materialism, competition, individualism, Christianity, and so forth. The core nations imposed elements of capitalist culture on the peoples and cultures of the "Third World"; sometimes ruthlessly.

From a PanAfrican communalist perspective, the essential point in Wallerstein's analysis involves the semi-peripheral and peripheral countries composed of peoples of color—Africans, Arabs, Latin Americans, Asians, the Caribbean Islanders, and others. The core nations exploit and plunder the land and use the people as laborers/consumers in order to fuel the development of the core capitalist states.[29] In essence, the capitalist modern world system offers a macrocosm of the racial-cultural struggles occurring within the United States. The most oppressed and exploited racial groups in this nation are descendants of the most oppressed peoples internationally. The significance of this parallel between the past and present experiences and social conditions of AfricanAmericans and their African racial-cultural brethren becomes clearer during the forthcoming discussion of the PanAfrican continuum.

In concluding this discussion, I wish to note Wallerstein's valuable contribution to the development of the PanAfrican communalism perspective. His work documents and affirms the fact that capitalist racial-cultural relations and struggles *within* core nations are reproduced not only in predominantly White "developed" nations but also in "underdeveloped" predominantly "colored" nations. Wallerstein further provided scientific documentation for the observation of the brilliant PanAfrican Nationalist, Malcolm X, regarding African Americans and other peoples of color: We are all in the same boat, victims of White people's greed and racism.

CHAPTER VII

INTERNAL COLONIALISM AND BLACK CULTURE — THE PANAFRICAN CONTINUUM

As I noted at the outset, the major purpose of this discourse is to clarify the position of the AfricanAmerican middleclass in American capitalist culture. To do this, I used the PanAfrican communalism perspective for critiquing several sociological schools of thought on the problematic confluence of race, class, and culture. I now begin a discussion of the nature of the relationship between the capitalist cultural/class system and the AfricanAmerican community. In order to establish the connection between the preceding discussion and the Black middleclass, I will use the concept of domestic or internal colonialism.

Although Black social analysts (especially Harold Cruse in *Rebellion and Revolution,* Kenneth Clark in *Dark Ghetto;* and Charles V. Hamilton and Stokley Carmichael/Kwamé Turé in *Black Power*) used the concept of domestic or internal colonialism to describe the position and social conditions of AfricanAmericans, the concept did not receive serious academic attention until Robert Blauner published a critique of the McCone Commission's report on the causes of the Watts riot (or insurrection). In an article appearing in one of the respected professional social scientific journals, Blauner argued that AfricanAmerican activists' perception of their colonized status in the United States caused the Watts insurrection.[1] To the empirical data obtained by the Commission, he applied the theoretical constructs of Fanon and Memmi which he appropriately modified to reflect the unique position of AfricanAmericans. His thesis contradicted the Commission's conclusion that the insurrection/ riot occurred spontaneously and was exacerbated by the presence of outside agitators or "would-be" Black revolutionaries. Blauner's interpretation of the data emphasized that the AfricanAmerican community used the riot as another strategy or tactic to express its discontent with its colonial status. In essence, he perceived the "riot" as a part of the liberation movement which had begun with the freedom rides, SNCC-initiated sit-ins, freedom marches, wade-ins, voter registration drives, the Martin Luther King, Jr./SCLC marches, and so on: all efforts directed toward achieving full citizenship recognition and rights in the United States.

Needless to say, the liberal academic establishment received Blauner's analysis with a great deal of skepticism, criticism, and torment. While most recognized AfricanAmericans as an exploited, victimized group of second-class citizens, few would accept the premise that the Black situation in America resembled that of a colonized people of color. After all, the reasoning went, AfricanAmericans were United States citizens. They had made great strides in their efforts to become fully integrated into the mainstream of American institutional life. And, eventually, like other immigrant groups, they too would be fully accepted.

The domestic colonial thesis shattered the liberal image of the United States. Blauner's distinctions between the ethnic immigrant experience and that of AfricanAmericans and other racial minorities "ripped the covers off" of America's "land of the free, home of the brave" liberal democratic image. He noted that EuropeanAmerican ethnics had come voluntarily, often to escape economic and political difficulties in their "mother" country. They came seeking the new freedoms, the new economic prosperity which the United States had come to symbolize. Although many of them experienced initial difficulties, they persevered and ultimately transcended the overt prejudice and discrimination imposed upon them by both the preceding immigrant groups and the culturally dominant WASPs. Gordon observed that White ethnics could choose to remain merely acculturated; that is, speak the language, obey the laws, and so on. Or, they could choose to assimilate structurally with the dominant group's culture; that is, intermarry, join the private social clubs and cliques, and so forth.[2] They could change their names, have their noses altered to more closely approximate the WASP "ideal type," drop their immigrant accents, move out of the original ethnic enclave and into the amorphous WASP middleclass. AfricanAmerican and other *peon*ized racial groups — notably NativeAmericans, AsianAmericans, MexicanAmericans and Puerto RicanAmericans — did not have that option unless they had features very similar to EuropeanAmericans and could thus pursue the precarious role of "passing."

Blauner described AfricanAmerican urban ghetto communities as externally controlled, political-economic dependencies maintained and perpetuated through institutionalized racist practices and policies. His description essentially merged the somewhat separate observations of Cruse, Clark, and Hamilton and Carmichael. His analysis confirmed Hamilton and Carmichael's thesis regarding institutionalized racism as not merely a pathological component of a given White individual's personality, but a systematic constellation of practices and policies which remain endemic to American society.[3] Defining racism in this manner, Blauner eradicated one of the popular liberal responses to African-Americans' charges of racism: the old "I'm not responsible for the deeds and actions of my predecessors" line. He (as well as Hamilton and Carmichael) asserted that as long as any EuropeanAmerican in U.S. society accepted the racial status quo, s/he derived benefits and privileges accrued at the expense of AfricanAmerican subjugation and exploitation. In essence, an individual White person need not be overtly racist to benefit from and support racist activities and practices.

Blauner's definition of racism relieved Southern EuropeanAmericans of their local variant of the "White man's burden." He exposed the hypocrisy inherent in the northern liberal tradition. While northern Whites arrogantly condemned their southern brethren for their outmoded, conservative, irrational, backward views on race, they simultaneously maintained and created Black ghettoes through restrictive covenants, gerrymandering, block-busting, employment discrimination, and other forms of legal subterfuge which had the effect of keeping AfricanAmericans at the bottom of the economic order.

One example which readily comes to mind involved the use of the merit system for Civil Service employment. As AfricanAmericans migrated to northern urban areas in large numbers, the "old" political patronage system which had served EuropeanAmerican ethnics so effectively was replaced by the more democratic and "fair" merit system.

Knowing the effects of Jim Crow segregation on Black education in the South, one could easily predict how the vast majority of AfricanAmericans would score on a civil service examination. Therefore, although the merit system appeared to be more democratic and less discriminatory, it proved democratic only for EuropeanAmericans, since poorly educated AfricanAmericans were in no position to be competitive. This system represents a classical example of institutionalized racism of the Northern liberal variety.

The domestic colonial model proved to be a major innovation in race relations theory. Robert Staples noted that this model provides Black social scientists (and Whites, if they can accept its assumptions) with a framework for merging what many often present as contradictory ideological or theoretical approaches: PanAfricanism and Marxism.[4] He argues that the ideology of PanAfricanism serves the vital political function which connects the AfricanAmerican cultural nationalist struggles with similar struggles of African peoples on the continent and elsewhere in the Diaspora, usually thought of as being the Caribbean and Latin America (but one should not ignore the struggles of African peoples in Britain as well), while Marxism, on the other hand, documents the similarities between the class exploitation of African people in the United States (and England) with that experienced by the other AfricanAmericans in the Western Diaspora.

Blauner's merger of these two ideological frameworks within the domestic colonial model represented a major accomplishment and theoretical advance. It challenged the scholars and political activists committed to one or the other positions to refine their arguments and include relevant elements from the opposition's perspective and analysis. James Turner and W. Eric Perkins noted that advocates of these positions tended to engage in unnecessary polemics which retard the development of a social scientific theoretical model which explains the AfricanAmerican experience.[5] What follows represents an attempt to develop such a model. However, to accomplish this objective requires a critical appraisal of Blauner's original formulation. I focus specifically on the ahistorical nature of the model and its limited emphasis on AfricanAmerican culture.

Although Staples, in his excellent article, summarized some of the criticisms I raise, I will approach the model from a slightly different angle. One of the major areas of difficulty in Blauner's formulation stems from his distinction between classical colonialism and the domestic variant. While I have no problems with the obvious structural differences, I find the differentiation historically discontinuous. In emphasizing that an internal colony structurally inverts the classical colonial situation, he obscures the relationship between the classical and the domestic. Let me elaborate. In the classical colonial situation, a large native population is dominated, subjugated, and exploited by an external, usually White, Western European power, whose emigrants in most cases remain a numerical minority in the colony. On the other hand, the domestic colonial situation is characterized by a "colored" minority residing in a country dominated and controlled by a White majority. Thus, in classical colonialism, the colonizer occupies and annexes the people's land, while in domestic colonialism (especially in the United States' variant), the colonizer brings the people of one land involuntarily to the colonizer's recently usurped land, land acquired from the indigenous group, which simultaneously suffers the victimization of classical colonialism, and in the case of the United States, eventual genocide.

I disagree with Blauner because he mentions both of these processes as aspects of Western European colonial expansion but fails to emphasize them sufficiently. His neglect can be accounted for by the tendency of EuropeanAmerican historians and social scientists to separate the slavery era from the era of European colonial expansion, which is a significant intellectual error. It should be remembered that when Columbus "discovered" America, he claimed the land for the King and Queen of Spain. A parallel claim held when the Portuguese explorers "discovered" West and East Africa. As the Nigerian social critic Chinweizu noted, the Papal *Bull* divided the New World into Spanish territories, on one hand, and Portuguese on the other.[6]

England's emergence as the heir-apparent to Spanish domination of Europe and the high seas initiated a new era of European expansion and colonialism. From this perspective, the northern lands in the Americas were colonies; the indigenous people, NativeAmericans, were colonized. The European invaders overpowered and subjugated the indigenous people, a practice consistent with the various forms that racial and cultural contacts assumed during this period. E. Franklin Frazier observed that the initial contacts assumed a variety of forms; sometimes mutual respect, sometimes initial warfare, sometimes one leading to the other, sometimes a mixture of both.[7] The results always followed the same pattern: in the case of Africa, Asia, and South America, the European and in the case of North America, the EuropeanAmerican emerged as the colonial rulers of subjugated indigenous peoples and used their labor in order to pursue

European economic interests.

Frazier and Chinweizu both noted that the colonizers commonly moved their subjects around; that is, if they needed a supply of cheap labor in one of their colonies (the United States, for example), they could and did transport the colonized from one geographical location to another. When one perceives the European slave trade of Africans in this manner, one sees the relationship between classical colonialism and domestic colonialism more explicitly as no more than aspects of the same continuous historical process; thus, domestic colonialism becomes a subtype within the classical colonial process.

Variations on the this subtype exist. For example, the racial situation in Azania (South Africa) constitutes another type of domestic colonialism. Here, the ruling White regime represents a minority of the population forcing the Black majority into the status of an internally colonized power minority group (or groups) on the Blacks' original land. This pattern also prevailed in Zimbabwe, the former racist state of Rhodesia. In this sense, one can see the similarity between the Southern African colonial experience and that of the United States. The major difference with Azania and Rhodesia is that the Whites did not pursue a policy of total annihilation of the indigenous population. Whereas Europeans in North America, in particular, essentially decimated the Native Americans in the North American and Caribbean colonies.

At any rate, this revision of the internal colonialism model lends credence to the PanAfricanist communalism perspective for explaining or accounting for the experiences of African peoples on both the continent and in the diaspora. It provides the social scientist with a theoretical model which delineates both the unity, as well as the diversity, of these experiences — to paraphrase Blackwell's title of his text on the AfricanAmerican community— *Unity-in-Diversity*; a very African concept.

This perspective also compliments and parallels Wallerstein's thesis regarding the relationship between "peripheral" (Third World nations and, especially for this discourse, Africa) and "core" areas (Western nations) in the expanding capitalist world economy and culture.[8] The peripheral areas are perceived and function as sources of raw materials, which these areas provide at minimal cost because of the presence of large, reservoirs of cheap labor. The "core" nations export the raw materials to the metropole, convert them into finished products, and sell them at handsome profits. Additionally, it became apparent that the colonized and enslaved natives could be influenced by Western European cultural values, especially those related to materialism. Thus, the peripheral areas also became markets for capitalist cultural products. With the exception of the those in the oil cartel, increasing imports of these products created the classical economic bind encumbering all peripheral nations with huge trade and balance-of-payments deficits resulting from the high cost of imports which far exceed the income received from the low (via "hidden" controls) prices of exports.

Again, one sees how the internal colonial model as elaborated here combines the PanAfricanist and Marxian theoretical interpretations of the AfricanAmerican experience. The internal colony thesis demonstrates that Western nations forcibly uprooted African peoples from their homelands, much like raw material resources, and sold them in the so-called "New World" for profit to enhance and enrich the capitalist elite in an expanding capitalist world economy and culture. The Western nations justified and rationalized their actions on the basis of racism and cultural chauvinism—what Wilson referred to as "cultural racism." [9]

Sydney Mintz noted this racist dimension inherent in the capitalist world economy and culture in his review of Wallerstein's first volume.[10] He challenged certain aspects of Wallerstein's Marxist position on the relationship between the proletarian status of slaves and that of the Western European peasants. While agreeing that both groups were indeed proletarian in their role and function in the expanding capitalist world economy or culture, Mintz signalled an important difference in their status: the peasants were "legally" and culturally-ideologically "free," and the slaves were legally unfree in all respects.

A significant distinction existed between slavery "pure and simple" and "veiled" slavery. The capitalists forced the "pure and simple" slaves to provide their labor for no wages, but allowed the peasants to sell their labor voluntarily, or forced them into selling it because of a lack of alternatives. However, the racism inherent in capitalist ideology was instrumental in convincing the "veiled" European wage-slaves of their superiority over the non-free African and NativeAmerican slaves because of both skin color and Western cultural heritage. Therefore, through psychological indoctrination, the expanding capitalist culture with its liberal-universalistic, progressive-democratic ideological superstructure not only altered class relations in the "core" Western European nations, but also generated an international caste system, relegating indigenous populations to the periphery and to inferior, pariah castes and securing for the lowerclass Western Europeans a sense of superiority over the lowercaste peoples of color.

Using the PanAfrican communalism perspective on internal colonialism, I recognize AfricanAmericans as a political-economic, racial and cultural caste within the American capitalist culture analogus in domestic status to that of African and other Third World nations and peoples in the World capitalist system. In other words, AfricanAmericans belong to that world group of racial, political-economic castes on the periphery (again, "unity-in-diversity"). Seeing AfricanAmericans as a domestically colonized racial caste leads us to another PanAfrican communalism reappraisal of Blauner's model: his analysis of AfricanAmerican culture.

In the original article, Blauner delineated another major difference between classical colonialism in Africa and the domestic colonialism of AfricanAmericans. In the classical situation in Africa, the indigenous group maintained its cultural integrity, meaning that colonization did not disrupt traditional institutions and values as thoroughly as internal colonization in America destroyed those of imported Africans. The indigenous people in the African colonial situation retained a "stronger" sense of cultural unity and cohesiveness. It is worth noting, in passing, that AfricanAmerican culture, though not as cohesive as that of its African predecessor, experienced a "renaissance" in the 1960s; a revitalization which contributed to a more systematized and consciously articulated culture.

In a subsequent article, Blauner elaborated upon his concept of AfricanAmerican culture and identified the major social processes and factors which shaped Black American culture.[11] While I take exception to his characterization of AfricanAmerican culture as "emerging," I still consider his analysis one of the best and most systematic sociological treatments of AfricanAmerican culture.[12] Recently, several interpretations of African American life and culture affirmed my original displeasure with Blauner's view. AfricanAmerican culture came with us and has existed from the time of our landing on these shores. It neither was nor is an "emerging" phenomenon, except insofar as its bearers have more legal and social freedom to express and evolve it. These more recent works present both theoretical and substantive support of the PanAfrican communalism theoretical model.

AFRICANAMERICAN CULTURE AND CULTURAL STRUGGLE

When Blauner published his provocative essay, much controversy surrounded the issue of AfricanAmerican culture in academia as well as in the larger society. The Civil Rights Movement phase of the African American decolonization struggles had transformed into the Black Power Movement, a movement subdivided by an intracaste-cultural struggle: the revolutionary nationalists (*e.g.*, the Black Panthers, Revolutionary Action Movement) versus the cultural back-to-the-African-roots nationalists (*e.g.*, Karenga's United Slaves or "US" and Baraka's "Kawaida" organizations). The revolutionary nationalists tended to adopt a Marxian approach while the cultural nationalists moved toward a PanAfrican orientation.

Their ideological differences sometimes led to violent confrontations. While one could justifiably deplore the internal violence, its presence reflected the intensity of the intracaste-cultural struggle as AfricanAmerican activists and scholars grappled with complex issues, definitions, aims, and objectives. However, that internal community-based struggle—fortunately and unfortunately, in different senses—waned. Yet, the concept of AfricanAmerican culture continued to be a very political issue in both academia and the public policy-making bureaucracies of America. The Black Studies movement in America's colleges and universities contributed immensely toward keeping the cultural issue alive and challenged Black activist intellectuals to seek resolutions to this intracaste cultural polemic. The PanAfrican communalism perspective is what emerged from this continuing debate.

Sydney Mintz and Richard Price's *An Anthropological Approach to the Afro-American Past*, a timely monograph on AfricanAmerican culture; Eugene Genovese's epic revisionist treatment of AfricanAmerican slavery in *Roll, Jordan, Roll*; Vincent Harding's 1981 publication *There Is A River*; and Lawrence Levine's *Black Culture and Black Consciousness* are creative and innovative works which help to clarify the PanAfrican communalism approach. I will discuss the Mintz and Price monograph first because it raises the questions and sketches the approach one must use if s/he seeks to understand and explain AfricanAmerican culture in the United States and other parts of the "New World." Following the discussion of Mintz and Price is a summary which emphasizes the racial-cultural conflict inherent in the master-slave relationship highlighted by Genovese's novel interpretation of slavery.

In essence, these works document and support the PanAfrican communalism thesis regarding the nature of the relationship between AfricanAmericans and EuropeanAmericans. They also support the previously raised contention that both the classical and internal domestic colonial models tend to present this struggle as occurring in only one direction, the cultural imposition of the colonizer on the colonized and its consequences for the colonized. The PanAfrican communalism approach emphasizes that this was and continues to be a dialectical struggle. Mintz and Price, Genovese, Levine, and Harding present evidence which supports the thesis that enslaved and emancipated AfricanAmerican peoples not only maintained elements of their essentially African culture but also sought to impose their cultural definitions of the situation in contacts with EuropeanAmericans. When viewed in this perspective, we see colonialism and its domestic variant as the catalyst for both intercultural struggle between Africans and Europeans and intracaste-cultural struggle among Africans in America as they modified and adapted their cultural apparatus to adjust to or confront the challenge posed by slavery and colonialism.

Mintz and Price's stimulating and incisive monograph, *An Anthropological Approach to the Afro-American Past:A Caribbean Perspective*, extends Blauner's analysis of Black culture and suggests a new, more flexible framework for analyzing the origins and subsequent vitality of AfricanAmerican cultures in the "New World." Blauner acknowledged Melville Herskovits' original thesis and contribution but chose not to pursue the dimension or implication of African cultural continuities. He primarily wished to document the existence and content of African American culture. And, to his credit, he indicated quite clearly why AfricanAmericans reluctantly identify with their African past:

> From the beginning, Africa's role was consistently obscured by the depraved racist imageries of the continent as a cesspool of savagery and barbarism. The Western nations have until recently assumed that Africa had no history and that Afro-Americans were people without a past. The stigmatization of Africa was evidently more pronounced among Protestant nations. Though racist in their own way, such countries as Brazil and Cuba have officially recognized African contributions to their national cultures.[13]

Domestic colonialism systematically cut AfricanAmerican cultural connections to their African past by exposing them to very little about Africa except in a negative, racist, and distorted manner.[14] While agreeing to a certain extent with the Herskovits thesis regarding the presence of African retentions, Blauner noted that most scholars generally referred to African values and cultural traits as "Negro" values and behaviors, still omitting any reference to Africa.

Mintz and Price, however, used Africa as the starting point. Their work begins with a discussion of a highly controversial assumption, one contradicting the prevailing distinctions between the EuropeanAmerican ethnic group experience in the "New World" and that of AfricanAmericans. Several race relations theoreticians observed that in relation to AfricanAmericans and other racial-cultural groups, EuropeanAmerican ethnics are unique because they retained their ethnicity, their former national cultural traditions, and their values. Even Blauner accepted this distinction between racial and immigrant groups. Lucille Duberman's[15] and James Geschwender's[16] more recent works support this assessment which also appeared in the works of Nathan Glazer and Daniel Patrick Moynihan (*Beyond the Melting Pot*), Milton Gordon (*Assimilation in American Life: The Role of Race, Religion, and National Origins*) and Gunnar Myrdal (*An American Dilemma*).

These same analysts portrayed racial/cultural groups, on the other hand, as having no cultural traditions. They considered them recognizable groups by virtue of physical features and the dominant group's definition of them as racially different. These scholars claimed that racial groups lack the internal cohesion, sense of "we-ness" and pride in their national origins associated with ethnocentric Whites.[17] These theorists usually justified these assumptions by claiming that slavery separated AfricanAmericans from their cultural heritage. Mintz and Price acknowledged that their revision of this model is in many ways speculative, with many generalizations based on inadequate or insufficient data. Nonetheless, they sought to refute many of the prevailing myths regarding the AfricanAmerican past as well as to clarify and expand the interpretations of those studies which adopted a similar perspective.

Before presenting a more detailed summary of Mintz and Price's theory, I should note that their argument derived primarily from their reinterpretation of studies conducted among African societies and cultures in the West Indies and Latin America. They attempt to demonstrate that these quite diverse societies and cultures share certain cultural elements attributable to their common African origins. To the untrained and/or less sensitive observer, these societies appear to be totally unlike one another, each a unique and distinct cultural group. However, Mintz and Price argue that to the trained and sensitive observer who possesses extensive research experience among both West African and Diasporan ethnic groups, the similarities, parallels, and continuities are remarkable. While the crucibles of the Middle Passage, different physical environments, and different European colonizers and slave masters seriously disrupted AfricanAmericans' original cultural heritage, Mintz and Price presented evidence strongly supporting the existence of both visible and extensive African cultural continuities.

These authors do not deny the importance of the diversity and heterogeneity found among and within the cultural groups. They argue instead that if researchers approach such comparative studies with the appropriate training and preparation, they will find numerous, shared cultural traits traceable to the West and Southern African origins— "unity-in-diversity." As noted earlier, the scarcity of theoretical and substantive work in this area can be attributed to the racist and cultural chauvinistic biases inherent in EuropeanAmerican social theory and practice.

Mintz and Price begin their revisionist interpretation by challenging the prevailing myth regarding the supposed cohesiveness of transplanted European cultures:

> Though it may appear at the outset that the continuity and strength of transferred cultural materials weighed much more heavily in favor of the Europeans than of the Africans, we would contend that a more sophisticated treatment of the content of transferred materials would fail to support so simplistic a conclusion. In fact, the character of transfers and their subsequent transformations may argue at times for greater continuity in the case of Afro-America than in that of Euro-America, considering the circumstances under which the transfers occurred, and the settings within which they took root.[18]

Their analysis contends that transplanted Africans retained more of their culture than Europeans despite the greater homogeneity of Europeans who generally came from the same geographical areas, who had a common religious heritage, who had a monopoly over military and police power, and who had the freedom and power to establish and develop their own legal, educational, political, and economic systems. On the other hand, Europeans drew Africans from a variety of ethnic and linguistic groups, from different regions and transplanted them to many different places in the Americas. These authors sought to answer how African peoples maintained their cultural practices under less than optimal conditions. One critical factor contributing to the phenomenon of African retentions involved the European colonizers and slave masters imposing enforced segregation of the races and creating a racial/cultural caste system. Mintz and Price further suggested that this enforced separation resulted in the creation of social systems "marked by different ladders of status, different codes of behavior, and different symbolic representations for each sector."[19] Therefore, the enforced segregation provided African slaves with the social space required to perpetuate many of their cultural beliefs and practices.

Reviewing the theoretical models which supported the cultural continuities thesis for analyzing and interpreting the experiences of "New World" AfricanAmericans, Mintz and Price observed that two basic arguments exist:

> (1) to posit the existence of a generalized West African cultural "heritage," which Africans of diverse background brought to a given colony; or (2) to argue that the bulk of Africans in that colony came from some particular "tribe" or cultural group.[20]

They considered both of these positions inadequate and outdated. Many contemporary anthropologists have presented convincing evidence which supports the thesis that no generalized West African cultural heritage of the formal sort Herskovits attempted to document exists currently nor existed during the slave era. Furthermore, they offered evidence which supports the thesis that the patterns of enslaving Africans allowed the Africans to exist as homogeneous groups in certain colonies or on plantations which only imported Yoruba or Ashanti peoples. Consequently, although they constituted radical departures from the prevailing racist and cultural chauvinistic approaches, Mintz and Price seriously challenged and increasingly discredited preceding explanations regarding the origins of the highly cohesive AfricanAmerican cultures.

Mintz and Price's reformulation of the African continuities theory asserts that while it is inaccurate to state that enslaved Africans brought intact cultures with them, they did bring a reservoir of similar cultural resources which they used in shaping new African-centered cultures. The authors borrowed a term, "cognitive orientations," from another researcher to characterize this cultural reservoir. They defined "cognitive orientations" as basic assumptions about social relations — for instance, what values motivate individuals and how one deals with others in social situations and matters of interpersonal style — and basic assumptions and expectations about the way the world functions phenomenologically, for instance, beliefs about causality and how particular causes are revealed. "We would argue that certain common orientations to reality may tend to focus the attention of individuals from West African cultures upon similar kinds of events which may seem quite diverse in formal terms."[21]

Mintz and Price, therefore, shifted the debate on AfricanAmerican cultural continuities from a focus on concrete, formal cultural forms such as language, family system, and religious practices to an emphasis on values. They asserted that West African cultural unity occurs at different levels and that in order to comprehend the "Africanness" of New World AfricanAmerican cultures, researchers and analysts must look beyond the obvious and the concrete. They noted further that while their reappraisal of preceding works was quite critical, they understood that anthropologists lacked the conceptual tools to undertake this kind of research until quite recently. Indeed, anthropologists continue to be limited in the present by this inadequacy, although I am confident that Mintz and Price's innovative approach will contribute immensely toward generating new concepts and methodologies appropriate for the task.

Mintz and Price suggested performing comparative studies of the peoples' attitudes and expectations about "sociocultural change—their orientations towards 'additivity' in relation to foreign elements, or expectations about the degree of internal dynamism in their own culture" as one means of "getting at" the complicated underlying dimensions of West African culture. More generally, for almost any aspect of culture, one could probably identify abstract principles which are widespread in the region. For example, though "witchcraft" may figure importantly in the social life of one ethnic group and be absent in that of its neighbor, both communities may still subscribe to the widely-held West African principle that social conflict can produce illness or misfortune by means of mechanisms we would class as "supernatural," and of which witchcraft is only one variant.[22] While they recognized that these underlying principles would be difficult to ascertain empirically, Mintz and Price asserted that present and future research must move in this direction:

> ... it seems reasonable to assume that, if the perceived similarities are real, there must exist underlying principles (which will often be unconscious) that are amenable to identification, description and confirmation. From the perspective of Afro-American cultural continuities, the more formal elements stressed by Herskovits may well have exerted less influence on the nascent institutions of newly enslaved and transported Africans than did their common basic assumption about social relations or the workings of the universe.[23]

Although Mintz and Price oriented their observations towards AfricanAmerican cultures in the Caribbean, obviously their approach holds great relevance for the study of AfricanAmerican culture in the United States. The assertions of liberal social scientists regarding the absence of an AfricanAmerican cultural heritage, relegating AfricanAmericans to a non-ethnic group status, becomes "inoperative." Mintz and Price's assertions, on the other hand, about the origins and development of AfricanAmerican cultures from slavery to the present reinforce the thesis of PanAfricanist Black scholars regarding the cultural unity of Africans on the continent and those in the Diaspora. These Black scholars argue that African slaves ably created new cultural forms within the constraints of their oppressed status, cultural forms which not only ordered and shaped their lives within the slave community, but also provided them with the "weapons" needed to wage cultural conflict with their slave masters. For, as Mintz and Price noted and Genovese convincingly argues, enslaved Africans forced their masters to recognize the African humanity despite having a legal definition as chattel property and work animals:

> Animals cannot learn to speak a new language, to employ tools and machinery in the manufacture of sugar, to direct crews of their fellows in completing a task, to nurse the sick, cook elaborate dinners, compose dances and verse — or, for that matter, to become adept in ridiculing with impunity the inanities of those who abuse them. Nor do animals organize resistance, poison their oppressors, lead revolutions, or commit suicide to escape their agonies.[24]

This characterization of AfricanAmericans' cultural heritage challenges the myth perpetuated in the more overt racist literature which asserts that enslaved Africans docilely, happily, and contentedly accepted their status and became pathological caricatures of their omnipotent White slave masters. Rather, it argues that a true portrait of slavery requires one to be aware of the Africans' cultural heritage; to know how European slave systems functioned. Mintz and Price's approach suggests that one underlying consistency in the West African region involved a set of attitudes and expectations regarding how slaves were supposed to be treated. Enslaved Africans fashioned an African-centered culture which confronted and challenged the dominant, powerful masterclass.

As Mintz and Price's perceptive discussion of the reciprocal dependency relationship and Genovese's concept of paternalism argue that the White slavemasters' monopoly on power was constrained by the desire to acquire profits. This need for a productive, efficient labor force created the "crack" in the oppressive system which the slaves were able to manipulate to their advantage. Mintz and Price most eloquently stated their observations on this relationship in the following passage.

> That the master class served both as teachers — and as intimidators — of the slaves, as regulators of their conduct, has always been matter-of-factly accepted and was doubtless usually true. But the role of the powerless in affecting and even controlling important parts of the lives of the masters was also typical of slave colonies, and has not received enough attention.[25]

Genovese arrived at a similar conclusion through a different analytical route. His Marxist orientation led him to deny that slavery with its racist subordination, subjugation, and oppression constituted a caste system. He persisted in the usual Marxist manner of analyzing and interpreting the master-slave relationship as a unique category of class relationships: "American slavery subordinated one race to another and thereby rendered its fundamental class relationships more complex and ambiguous; but they remained class relationships."[26]

In order to demonstrate this peculiar racial superordinate-subordinate relationship as a unique example of class conflict, he introduced the concept of "paternalism." He observed that the "old" South was a unique kind of paternalist society as a consequence of the Black versus White class struggle. He further emphasized that in discussing slavery as the manifestation of a peculiar paternalistic class struggle, he was not reducing the importance of racism or denying the intolerable contradictions inherent in "paternalism" itself:

> Southern paternalism, like every other paternalism, had little to do with ole massa's ostensible benevolence, kindness, and good cheer. It grew out of the necessity to discipline and morally justify a system of exploitation. It did encourage kindness and affection, but it simultaneously encouraged cruelty and hatred.[27]

However, as Genovese elaborated on his concept of paternalism, it became increasingly apparent that he was describing cultural struggle as opposed to Marxian class struggle. He claimed that in order for this paternalistic social formation to work, both masters and slaves had to accept it; but each group had radically different interpretations of slavery as an institution. For the masters, "paternalism" represented their desire to overcome the fundamental contradiction in slavery: "the impossibility of the slaves' ever becoming the things they were supposed to be."

> Paternalism defined the involuntary labor of the slaves as a legitimate return to their masters for protection and direction. But, the masters' need to see their slaves as acquiescent human beings constituted a moral victory for the slaves themselves. Paternalism's insistence upon mutual obligations — duties, responsibilities, and ultimately even rights — implicitly recognized the slaves' humanity.[28]

Genovese believed that the mutual acceptance and mutual obligations inherent in the concept of paternalism as well as the radically different interpretations of these processes suggest the presence of cultural conflict. To him, the masters reflected their value and normative belief systems in their definition of the paternal relationship while the slaves relied on their cultural system to create their definition of the masters' role. Genovese's commitment to perceiving AfricanAmerican culture as a peculiarly U.S. phenomenon prevented him from engaging the question of African cultural continuities. He acknowledged that the argument held some degree of validity but did not consider it especially relevant to his portrayal of "the world the slaves made."

From a PanAfrican communalism perspective, Genovese committed a grievous error in an otherwise excellent analysis. If Genovese had pursued the cultural continuities thesis, he would have been compelled to investigate the slave practices in West African societies. No serious scholar would suggest that the African slaves transported to the colonies in the Americas and the Caribbean came "tabula rasa" (minds that contained no cultural content). As Mintz and Price and others noted, slaves came from intact, cohesive, complex African societies which in many cases practiced a form of slavery. They came with a set of cultural norms, values, and expectations associated with slave status. Connecting his research with those studies of slavery in West African societies possibly would have led Genovese to discover that AfricanAmerican cultural interpretations of the duties, obligations, and responsibilities of slavemasters originated in Africa. Given the various geographical contexts and ethnic heterogeneity of the colonizers, slaves may have changed these definitions as they adjusted and adapted to particular circumstances. Yet, the evidence suggests that much "unity" existed in the "diversity" of the "new world" Africans' adaptations to chattel slavery.

Genovese also suggested that the paternalistic "class" relationship accounted for the relative stability of Old South slavery. He observed that paternalism undermined solidarity among the oppressed by linking them as individuals to their oppressors:

> The slaves of the Old South displayed impressive solidarity and
> collective resistance to their masters, but in a web of paternalistic
> relationships their action tended to become defensive and to aim at
> protecting the individuals against aggression and abuse; it could not
> readily pass into an effective weapon for liberation.[29]

While one cannot deny the partial accuracy of Genovese's assertion,
I would contend that greater knowledge of West African cultural traditions reveal an alternative explanation. Enslaved individuals in West
African societies could achieve their freedom, marry into the master's
ethnic group, and become a member of the master's family and clan.[30]
Loyalty to a master, then, could result in a desired objective, freedom and
acceptance. In addition, I would contend that understanding Africans'
concepts of time, morality, and religion is essential before one analyzes
enslaved Africans' behavior in relation to their masters. One must
remember that enslaved Africans in the U.S. were separated from members of their group. Thus, those on plantations could be from ethnic groups
which were traditional enemies. Creating a sense of solidarity would have
been much more difficult in this situation. Resorting to individual solutions would be expected and would have been logical outcomes in those
circumstances. A more important question from a PanAfrican communalist perspective would be "How did the enslaved Africans create the unity
and solidarity exemplified in their collective resistance efforts?"

The stability of the Old South slave system which Genovese attributed to the cooperation of the enslaved Africans with the system of
"paternalism" could also be explained by examining West African moral
and ethical beliefs and practices. For example, if West Africans believe
that God intervenes in the day-to-day activities of humans, one could
argue that their submissive behavior and emphasis on religious rituals for
nurturance, sustenance, and ultimately freedom were forms of resistance
in that they believed that correcting their relationship with the "Higher
Power" would be rewarded. As such, they would appear to be patient,
long suffering, but expectant and hopeful, confident that a "Power"
greater than the master's would intervene on their behalf. I am certain that
as they witnessed small increments of change, they attributed them to
their gods' powers and presences, answering their prayers and calls for
assistance to force their earthly "masters" to treat them in a more humane
manner, or suffer the consequences.

Genovese acknowledged this possibility in his discussion of the
religion amongst enslaved AfricanAmericans but failed to connect that

religious behavior and beliefs to their African cultural heritage. Had he done so, he would have contradicted his Marxist class struggle model even more. Although Genovese presented an excellent analysis of the cultural struggle as it occurred during the slavery period, his Marxist orientation precluded his acknowledging that slavery brought two very different peoples and cultures together in a conflict situation. He tried to reduce a cultural system which includes class organization and structure to mere class. Except for this serious flaw, Genovese made a valuable contribution to account for race and ethnic relations in the U.S. and to the PanAfrican communalism model of cultural struggle.

The cultural struggle perspective represents a radical departure from past conceptualizations of master-slave relations and Black versus White relations. Most of the social science literature ignores and/or omits the oppression of AfricanAmerican culture, preventing most European-American scholars from appreciating its impact and influence on the dominant culture. EuropeanAmerican scholars developed their biased, distorted interpretations due their inability to perform what Weber referred to as *Verstehen*, putting oneself in the role of the other and seeing how s/he might define the situation. If they had used this methodological technique, they would have been able see, as Mintz and Price did, "that the points of contact between persons of differing status, or different group membership, did not automatically determine the direction of the flow of cultural materials according to the statuses of the participants but according to other variables instead."

The status of the master's child vis-a-vis his slave-governess would surely affect his learning of a style of command in dealing with slaves. But his speech, his food preferences, his imagery, his earliest ideas about men and women and a good deal more of what became his characteristic qualities as an individual would be learned from someone far below his status but otherwise very much in control of him.... Although we choose not to pursue this part of the argument further here, any reflection upon the music, cuisine, folklore, dance, or speech of the American South ought to make clear that it is anything but a perfect case of Europeans successfully "Americanizing" their slaves, merely because they held a monopoly of power over them.[31]

Mintz and Price's concept of cultural style needs greater clarification as an analytical construct for studying and interpreting AfricanAmerican culture. I have been intrigued by the repeated observations of White racist colonizers regarding the passivity and docility of Africans, whether on the continent, in the Caribbean, or in the Southern United States. The cultural continuities theory suggests that we should look for the origins of this behavioral style among West African ethnic groups.

I encourage AfricanAmerican historians and anthropologists to explore West African peoples' attitudes and expectations toward authority figures. I would argue, based on personal observations and conversations with West African friends and colleagues, that West Africans treat authority figures with deference, respect, and loyalty. However, the authority figure's proper, culturally prescribed enactment of h/er role determines this deferential behavior. If the authority figure violates these cultural constraints, s/he loses the right to this deference. If this pattern indeed reflects an underlying cultural continuity, it would, in part, account for slaves' attitudes and behavior towards their masters, their loyalty and devotion to some and absolute hatred of others.

I have attempted to demonstrate that social theoreticians cannot consider AfricanAmericans as merely a racial group whose cohesion resulted primarily from their oppression and exploitation. On the contrary, AfricanAmericans possess a unique ethnic culture (or cultures, to be accurate) and a rich cultural heritage. One can view AfricanAmerican culture as "emerging" only in the sense that it is a unique variant of African cultures in the "new world." That the dominant culture has not acknowledged and, therefore, not transmitted it through the established institutional apparatus only reflects and confirms the AfricanAmericans' colonized status. In addition, the EuropeanAmerican colonizers have maligned, denied, and distorted AfricanAmerican culture because they perceive its African-derived style as foreign to most observers, Black and White. This denial of the African roots of AfricanAmerican culture became a political decision on the part of liberal Whites and Blacks to counter the racist assertions of EuropeanAmerican political conservatives. However, few Whites and practically no Blacks had actually conducted studies in Africa. Instead, they developed a theoretical position based on minimal empirical evidence. In addition, AfricanAmerican scholars trained in EuropeanAmerican academic institutions became victims of the itellectual "brainwashing" which characterizes that of their White counterparts.

This AfricanAmerican cultural style, though greatly influenced by the constraints of slavery and domestic colonial practices and policies, proved to be a worthy opponent to EuropeanAmerican capitalist culture. It succeeded in creating an institutional life which provided AfricanAmericans with the sustenance necessary to survive in European America with dignity. And, as Mintz and Price emphasized, African-Americans not only survived, but retained as much, if not more, of their African heritage as EuropeanAmericans retained of their European culture. While this is a difficult thesis to validate empirically, it could be substantiated by researchers with appropriate training and sensitivity.

AfricanAmericans in the U.S. and other parts of the Americas exist outside of the dominant, mainstream cultures of their colonial oppressors. This cultural isolation permitted the development of "new" indigenous, unique cultural systems composed of various West African cultural traits which they modified in the process of adjusting and adapting to the respective physical and socioeconomic realities. An expanding body of literature documents the West African origins of AfricanAmerican speech patterns, dialects, humor, religious behavior and orientation toward the sacred, music, attitudes toward the preparation of food, and so forth.[32] Based on conversations with and personal observations of several AfricanCaribbeans residing in North American urban Black communities, I contend that comparative AfricanAmerican ethnic studies would reveal numerous similarities among these various communities throughout the Diaspora. At the same time, each possesses its own unique expression of these continuities.

European immigrants, on the other hand, surrendered much, if not most, of their European cultural heritage in their efforts to become WASP Americans. This pattern is exhibited especially in the middle-and upper-middleclasses, although Will Herberg's work suggested that the third generation may attempt to re-connect with its "old world" ethnic heritage.[33] However, as Arthur Vidich and Joseph Bensman noted, many members of this class descended from rural ethnic parents whose cultures the new upper-middleclass rejects [See Chapter 8, page 160*ff*, for my full discussion]. I argue that the process of assimilation as presented by Gordon[34] required European-American ethnics, especially the upwardly mobile, to reject, submerge, and/or discard their ethnic heritage; that is, to become "detribalized" (or "retribalized" as WASP Americans). Consequently, to the extent that EuropeanAmerican ethnics pursued the American dream successfully, they lost their cultural heritage.

AfricanAmericans remain, in part, culturally African while appearing to be Americanized because of what Mintz and Price referred to as the West African value of additivity:

... the context of slavery and the initial cultural heterogeneity of the enslaved produced among them a general openness to ideas and usages from other cultural traditions, a special tolerance (within the West African context) of cultural differences. We would suggest that this acceptance of cultural differences combined with the stress on personal style to produce in early Afro-American cultures a fundamental dynamism, an expectation of cultural change as an integral feature of these systems. Within the strict limits set by the conditions of slavery, Afro-Americans learned to put a premium on innovation and individual creativity; there was always a place for fads and fashions; "something new" (within certain aesthetic limits, of course) became something to be celebrated, copied, and elaborated; and a stylistic innovation brought on by newly-imported Africans could be quickly assimilated. From the first, the commitment to a new culture by Afro-Americans in a given place included an expectation of continued dynamism, change, elaboration, and creativity.[35]

AfricanAmerican culture from this perspective personifies AfricanAmerican improvisational music (a.k.a "jazz"): different musicians expressing themselves individually on their respective instruments while creating a coherent, integrated, and unified composition. Such unity within diversity could be achieved only by individuals with a shared cultural understanding, common experiences, and what Nobles referred to as their "African cultural ethos" (or Africanity).[36] Nobles saw this cultural ethos as the basis for the shared core cultural values among the heterogeneous ethnic groups in West Africa. The regional communality (Nobles' term for shared core cultural values) emanating from this African ethos provided guiding principles which determined and defined two operational orders:

> The first order concerns the notion that African people were part of the natural rhythm of nature. In effect, the people were *one with nature*. The second order is the notion of the survival of one's people. That is, *the survival of the tribe*. This author contends that African peoples share in these basic beliefs: the survival of the tribe and the tribe being in an integral and indispensable unity with nature. It is further suggested that this ethos is coupled with several philosophical principles, *i.e.*, unity, cooperative effort, mutual responsibility, *etc.* which influence most, if not every, aspect of black social reality.[37]

Nobles observed further that both the ethos and the philosophical principles became reflected in and reinforced by a deep sense of family or kinship. Thus, the AfricanAmerican improvisational music groups create "unity-in-diversity" because they belong to a cultural heritage which requires them to express themselves as individuals while affirming, enhancing, and reinforcing their African ethos or sense of kinship and family. Each hears and understands the other while simultaneously responding to one another and offering one's own voice. Looking at this example, one sees why anthropologists encounter so many difficulties defining and describing AfricanAmerican culture — or any culture — in terms of process as opposed to a static description of social structures.

In a similar vein, Mintz and Price discuss the importance of shared principles and values (ethos) concerning kinship among the enslaved Africans in the Diaspora:

> Tentatively and provisionally, we would suggest that there may have been certain widespread fundamental ideas and assumptions about kinship in West Africa. Among these, we might single out the sheer importance of kinship in structuring interpersonal relations and defining an individual's place in his society; the emphasis on unilineal descent, and the importance to each individual of the resulting lines of kinsmen living and dead, stretching backward and forward through time; or, on a more abstract level, the use of land as a means of defining both time and descent, with ancestors venerated locally and with history and genealogy both being particularized in specific places of ground. The aggregate of newly-arrived slaves, though they had been torn from their own local kinship networks, would have continued to view kinship as the normal idiom of social relations. Faced with an absence of real kinsmen they nevertheless modeled their new kin terms acquired from their masters to label their relationships with contemporaries and those older than themselves — "bro," "uncle," "auntie," "gran," *etc.*[38]

Nobles, Billingsley, Ladner, Hill, Levine, and Staples demonstrated the continued presence of these fundamental West African principles and values among AfricanAmerican families, North and South, East and West, urban and rural. The PanAfrican communalism perspective asserts that one would find these underlying principles and values among numerous, if not all, African peoples in other parts of the "new world." These new interpretations of AfricanAmerican culture confirm the nationalists' contention that AfricanAmerican people in the U.S., as well as other racial groups, possess a rich cultural heritage and a unique, dynamic, vibrant, contemporary culture.

The prevailing notion that EuropeanAmerican ethnics retain much of their cultural tradition while peoples of color have either "lost" their traditions or never had any worth maintaining should be abandoned.

Clearly, it is inaccurate and perpetuates racist stereotypes and their accompanying behaviors. A new concept which distinguishes the cultural experiences, conditions, and relationships of EuropeanAmerican ethnics from that of oppressed *racial-ethnics* must be created to correct this situation, one which does not contain these racist, cultural chauvinistic assumptions. Seeking to meet this challenge, I propose the PanAfrican communalism-derived concept of *ethcaste*.

CHAPTER VIII

ETHCASTE
AND
SOCIOCULTURAL
DIVERSITY
AMONG THE
BLACK MIDDLECLASS

I arrived at the concept of *ethcaste* after a critical review of Gordon's concept of *ethclass* and an analysis of the virtually discarded caste school approach to the study of American racial and ethnic relations. I found both approaches accurate for certain groups and for a certain historical period. However, they included numerous shortcomings as I have demonstrated in the preceding pages. EuropeanAmerican ethnics enjoy relatively open access to the socioeconomic security, prestige, and wealth of mainstream America, while AfricanAmerican and other non-European racial groups do not. This difference remains on the whole constant even though significant changes occurred during the 1960s. To the extent that White ethnics can choose to"melt" or remain within their ethnic cultural milieux, the concept of ethclass accurately accounts for their status in the United States. Since AfricanAmericans do not and never have had that option due to their antebellum bondage and continued domestic colonized status, the concept must be modified or refined to account for the Black American experience. I find the traditional caste school approach valid for explaining Black-White relations during the Jim Crow segregation era. However, as a consequence of the legal victories of the 60's, that school lost much of its pertinence. Also, the original caste school theorists tended to be ahistorical: they neglected the African past and viewed AfricanAmerican culture either as pathological or nonexistent. Their analyses correctly identified AfricanAmericans as oppressed "outsiders," a "pariah" group, but failed to recognize the vitality of AfricanAmericans' culture and its impact on the dominant culture. They also neglected the notion of cultural struggle. The original caste model implied that destroying the legal barriers would allow AfricanAmericans to finally "melt" into the mainstream of American life.

The concept of *ethcaste* provides a PanAfrican communalist framework for merging both the ethnic dimension of PanAfrican cultural continuities with the Marxist derived class analysis which sees the Black community as a domestically neocolonized political-economic racial caste. The concept of *ethcaste* incorporates the important dimensions of *ethclass* as defined by Gordon[1] and elaborated by Geschwender:

> It being the role of the analyst to determine those things that unite some members of an ethnic group while setting them apart from others with the same national origins. Similarly, it helps the analyst to determine those things that unite some members of a social class while setting them apart from the other members of the same class. It helps to focus attention on the fact that American society comprises functioning units made up of interacting networks of people who are simultaneously in the same class and ethnic group.[2]

Geschwender criticized Gordon's formulation because of its Weberian sociocultural orientation as opposed to the traditional Marxist class analysis. While I found Geschwender's critique valid, I became critical of his tendency to ignore the importance of culture and ethnicity in America's political economy. Although he cited abundant evidence indicating that AfricanAmericans constituted a racial caste, a "super" exploited group, he continued to emphasize the necessity for a Marxian class alliance with the EuropeanAmerican working class as a solution. Geschwender apparently ignored or was ignorant of Cruse's scathing critique of this strategy.

I offer *ethcaste* as a way of describing and explaining the consequences of systematic domination, exploitation, exclusion and oppression of a group on the basis of an ascribed racial trait. In this perspective, the critical factor, racism, explains or accounts for the oppressed group's position. I emphasized in the preceding discussion of caste cultural differences that racially homogeneous societies suffer *ethcaste* subordination. However, for the purposes of the present discussion, the racial factor preempts the cultural factor. This racial preemption holds especially true for the United States and other so-called technologically advanced capitalist-based democratic cultures. Groups suffering under *ethcaste* subordination also experience cultural exclusion, repression, and assault. The analysts and interpreters of the superordinate group, however, see culture as less important than race. They perceive certain groups experiencing *ethcaste* domination as having a highly developed, complex, and integrated culture, but victimized because of racial differences; in other words, in this view, it is not their cultural, but rather their racial differences which "instigate" prejudice and discrimination— NativeAmerican groups come readily to mind. These analysts and interpreters, from their self-appointed position of cultural superiority, perceive other groups as being racially different but cultureless, a type of double jeopardy in ethcaste status. AfricanAmericans are prime victims of this latter type of racist thinking and practice.

The *ethcaste* phenomenon occurred as a direct result of colonial expansion and the contemporary neocolonial relations between the United States and its Western European brethren as the bearers of the "white man's burden" vis-a-vis peoples and nations of color. Just as the domestically colonized status of peoples of color in America represents a subprocess within the "classical" European colonizing experience, the subsequent *ethcaste* status of peoples of color in the United States represents a subprocess within the larger racial caste system created by Western European colonial expansion and imperialism. The movement of large numbers of both Europeans, generally free and voluntary, and peoples of color, generally enslaved and forced, characterizes this expansion.

While many observers, especially Marxists, focus on the victimization and exploitation of proletarian Europeans during this period of capitalist colonial expansion, I am certain that none would disagree with the fundamental assumption inherent in the *ethcaste* concept: an assertion that the European proletariat enjoys special privileges as a consequence of its membership in the superordinate racial caste. No matter how much destitution, subjugation, and exploitation the members of the European proletariat experience, they are considered superior biologically, racially, and culturally to the peoples of color they encountered, subdued or eradicated. Peoples of color occupied the "bottom floor," the base upon which the capitalists erected their world system. Western European colonial expansion and imperialism, therefore, initiated both the racial caste division between Whites and peoples of color and the subsequent (and continuing) cultural struggles ensuing from those encounters. This initiation occurred for the *ethcaste* groups in the United States and other parts of the Americas as well as for the peoples of color and other caste-exploited groups and nations of the "Third World."

From this perspective, ethcaste groups in the United States, especially AfricanAmericans, are "new world" representatives of these peoples of color. AfricanAmericans' cultural heritage, and the basis for their contemporary cultural life, derive from West Africa. Our distinct identity as AfricanAmericans derives from the entire continent of Africa. The peculiar *ethcaste* status of AfricanAmericans evolved from the initial encounter and subsequent race relations which ensued from that contact. These historical relationships have remained fundamentally unchanged despite the *Emancipation Proclamation* and the victories of the 1960s Civil Rights Movement. AfricanAmericans and other ethnic groups of color occupy a lower caste (if not *out*caste) position in relation to White Americans regardless of the latter's ethnic background.

Gordon's concept of *ethclass* adequately accounts for the experiences of European ethnics who chose not to assimilate despite their status and material success in the United States. His *ethclass* concept, however, inadequately explains the experiences of AfricanAmericans, even those who experience upward mobility. While White ethnics improve their status in the dominant capitalist class structure as members of the superordinate caste, AfricanAmericans improve their status only *within* the subordinate caste. Once White ethnics achieve middleclass status, society perceives them as assimilated and accepts them as full, unequivocal members of the status group which serves as the normative foundation for American capitalist culture. That EuropeanAmerican ethnic groups had to transcend certain ethnic prejudices and/or initial economic destitution conforms to the American ethos of working hard, sacrificing (supposedly), maintaining moral purity, and taking advantage of available opportunities in an open, competitive, free enterprise system. In essence, their experiences reflect the success of this "great experiment" in democracy. Even those who choose to remain in middle- and upper-middleclass ethnic enclaves share this smug sense of satisfaction with their success, and, thus, tend to be aggressive boosters of the "American" way. Those who reject or submerge their ethnicity see themselves as classic examples of the great American Horatio Alger success story: the transition from hyphenated American to "simply" American. AfricanAmericans, on the other hand, cannot participate in this process unless their complexions allow them to "pass" for White.

While a relatively small number of AfricanAmericans have experienced upward mobility in America, their racial caste status determines and constrains their movement. Before the liberal optimistic forecast of the late Sixties and early Seventies, the number of AfricanAmericans identified as approximating middleclass status never exceeded ten percent of the nation's AfricanAmerican population. The critically conditional phrase, "approximating middleclass," indicates the caste status of AfricanAmericans and further reflects the need for a special definition of middleclass to account for the relatively minimal socioeconomic gap between those AfricanAmericans traditionally described as middleclass (professionals, teachers, nurses, small entrepreneurs, morticians, barbers, pullman porters, civil servants, and so on) and those described as lowerclass. Many AfricanAmericans have bridged this small gap in a single lifetime. This one generation shift generated the assertion and undergirds the myth that AfricanAmericans are experiencing greater and more rapid upward mobility within the Black caste. The perspective of PanAfrican communalism contends that certain EuropeanAmerican groups—by virtue of power as opposed to numbers—dominate the social/political/economic structures within this multiracial, multicultural, multiethnic society; and, this group's reality coincides with Gordon's concept of *ethclass*. On the other hand, the PanAfrican communalist model asserts that excluded, exploited, and systematically subordinated racial groups constitute an *ethcaste*.

The class organization of the dominant society is, of course, cultural, mirroring the political-economic and sociocultural values, norms and beliefs of the majority group. All people seeking to enter or assimilate into the host culture must adopt its cultural behavior and values and dissociate themselves from their original cultural heritage. Some groups experience more success than others in this assimilating process; generally because of the racial and cultural similarities between the host or majority group and themselves; for example, GermanAmericans, Scandinavian Americans, and others who represent the Teutonic or AngloSaxon, Western or Northern European Protestant lineage. Other less successful groups experience economic progress but either *choose* to remain associated with their original ethnic communities or find themselves *forced* to remain within their ethnic communities as a consequence of sociocultural exclusion; for example ItalianAmericans, IrishAmericans, JewishAmericans — note they all represent different religious persuasions from the dominant AngloSaxon Teutonic groups. For these latter groups, acceptance into the majority group's culture occurs on an individual basis. The economically successful members of these groups who choose to remain *within* their ethnic communities personify the eth*class* phenomenon as defined by Gordon.

The critical differences between *ethclass* and e*thcaste* groups are: (a) the *ethclass* group tends to be both racially and, in many respects, culturally similar to the host or majority group, with race being the critical variable; (b) *ethclass* members have the option of assimilating on a one-by-one basis should they reject or sever their ethnic cultural ties; and (c) in a caste society with race as the determining factor, *ethclass* groups enjoy the privileges which accrue to the dominant racial group although they are not able to participate as fully in the cultural and political life of the host or dominant group.

For the racially subordinated *ethcaste* groups, entrance into the host culture, *en masse* or individually proves practically impossible, although some come quite close. The only sure way to enter is to be able and willing to "pass." Society constrains and circumscribes the socioeconomic status of the racially subordinated groups by relegating them to lowercaste status. Those who experience some degree of upward economic mobility accomplish it with*in* the context of their caste. Consequently, a successful AfricanAmerican medical doctor is regarded as a successful "Black" M.D. and never as successful as h/er White counterpart, regardless of how good a doctor or how wealthy and culturally refined in Western terms s/he becomes. Caste, then, overrides and transcends socioeconomic status even in a cultural system which exalts and glorifies upward economic mobility. While we recognize the caste status of the AfricanAmerican masses (especially those referred to as the "underclass"), we sometimes find it more difficult to discern the caste status of the so-called "Black Elite." This difficulty became more pronounced in the Seventies as a consequence of the victories of the Civil Rights Movement. The often expressed claim that the AfricanAmerican middleclass expanded and experienced a dramatic increase led many theorists to conclude, quite prematurely, that AfricanAmericans had finally "arrived," altering their position in American society from that of caste (or *ethcaste*) to that of class (or *ethclass*).

William Wilson based his controversial analysis of American racial dynamics on this dramatic shift from caste to class.[3] He argues that due to the technological changes and innovations in EuropeanAmerican owned capitalist means of production and the significant changes in the legal and political status of AfricanAmericans—especially those won during the Civil Rights Movement—the class stratification within the AfricanAmerican community became more rigid. He also insisted that presently there exists an expanding, successful and socioculturally accepted Black middleclass which initiates and supports policies and strategies enhancing its recently acquired status, often at the expense of its lowerclass racial brethren. He claimed that while middleclass AfricanAmericans have succeeded through the use of traditional institutional means, they have opted to take an "out-of-sight, out-of-mind" position regarding the lower- and underclasses who are trapped in lower political and economic caste status.

Wilson's thesis suggests that the "new" AfricanAmerican middleclass has become, in the Marxian sense, of and for itself. Consistent with the liberal, and (somewhat ironically) in many ways neo-Marxian approach, Wilson does not consider the issue of racial/cultural struggle worthy of discussion. As a consequence, he erroneously implies that the so-called "new" Black middleclass possesses the economic resources to victimize poor AfricanAmericans. That is, by supporting the economic initiatives emanating from the EuropeanAmerican multinational, monopolistic capitalist elites, the "new" AfricanAmerican elite is contributing to the economic impoverishment of the Black poor and workingclass.

Wilson further argues that the class consciousness of the Black petit bourgeois exacerbates interclass hostilities, and that the Black working and underclasses now perceive the Black middleclass as their enemy. He cites the political economic advances of the Black middleclass as the primary justification for this hostility. He fails to mention that these "advances" occurred usually as a result of the AfricanAmerican middleclass often being forced to assume "caretaker" positions which requires them to "manage" the affairs of the working- and underclasses; for instance, administrators in public schools, social service workers and administrators, mayors of predominantly Black cities and towns, and so forth. These institutions affect AfricanAmericans' daily lives, ofttimes negatively. As middleclass Blacks gain control over these institutions during periods of economic decline and urban deterioration (which continued to be true in spite of the short-lived new prosperity of Reganomics), less successful AfricanAmericans shift the blame for their wretched conditions from the

White capitalist ruling elite to the Black administrative caretakers. In a sense, AfricanAmerican middleclass managers assume the role of the Black slave "driver," and the hostilities directed toward them emanate from their being the most accessible and visible representatives of the repressive system exploiting the AfricanAmerican masses. As such, the capitalist ruling elite use the Black middleclass as "frontline" troops or political "cannon fodder" in the continuing cultural struggle. From a PanAfrican communalist perspective, this dynamic amounts to a form of fratricide.

Wilson's desire to condemn the Black middleclass from a quasi-Marxist perspective causes him to omit two critical concerns: first, a discussion of the status of the Black middleclass in the broader political-economic system; and, second, an analysis of the sociocultural implications of the economic changes he identified. Had he placed the "new" AfricanAmerican middleclass within the context of the emerging *managerial* elite, his work would be a valuable contribution toward clarifying the status and role of the Black petit bourgeoisie in contemporary capitalist culture. However, to assert, as he does in *The Declining Significance of Race*, that the AfricanAmerican managerial elite *caused* the current political-economic crisis permeating the AfricanAmerican community makes his work dubious at best.

Arthur Vidich and Joseph Bensman focused on the changing political-economic composition of the EuropeanAmerican middleclass and its sociocultural implications. They argue that one of the central problems accompanying the changes in American society is the "revolution" which has occurred in the middleclass. As they describe it, a new middleclass has emerged which is composed of college-educated workers—junior executives and technical, service-oriented, managerial, and administrative professionals—white collar employees popularly referred to as "yuppies." For Vidich and Bensman, this current middleclass represents a new social phenomenon because it emerged out of the rapid increase in productivity due to automation, the continuous growth of industrialization, and the greater productivity of capital. The efforts of large, bureaucratically organized corporate giants caused this rapid increase in productivity. In their argument, the key concept is bureaucracy as a form of economic and social organization which dominates the contemporary American social structure. In this society, most of the institutional life, including the religious, educational, communications, government, and legal functions, is embedded in bureaucracies.[4]

While Vidich and Bensman attacked the Marxist class model for its inaccuracy and faulty perceptions of capitalism, they used a revisionist, quasi-Marxist approach derived from Mills' theory of the power elite to describe and explain this social phenomenon. They contend that inter-institutional cliques composed of the upper-level administrators and managers in the major corporations, government bureaucracies, and the military made the major decisions. They also attribute a great deal of influence (if not power) to the major universities and philanthropic organizations, especially the "think tanks" like the Rockefeller Foundation, Brookings Institution, and Ford Foundation. They further observed that these bureaucracies transformed the occupational structure of American society and that the new middleclass replaced in size and cultural significance both the older middleclasses and other traditional classes.

Vidich and Bensman's analyses of the changes occurring in the political-economic superstructure resembled Wilson's, but theirs included a more extensive and detailed discussion of the cultural factors accompanying the economic changes. They noted that while many analysts perceive the middleclass as the class which upholds American values, beliefs, and norms, the new version actually possesses no such tradition. It bases its lifestyles on a continuous effort to "democratize the forms, images, and stereotypes of what previously was an upper class lifestyle."

> If this process continues at its present pace, or if it should intensify, it will result in the total transformation of American social and cultural life. It would erase and destroy the character type of the hard-working, materialistic, democratic, equalitarian, Boobus Americanus who has been the epitome of American life. In short, the penetration of new forms of middle-class values — a consequence of a dissatisfaction with bureaucratization — is a major revolutionizing influence in American life.[5]

In this reformulation of Mills' and Riesman's analyses of the white collar, other-directed middleclass, Vidich and Bensman attacked the essentially emulative lifestyle of the new middleclass. They claimed this group tends to be rather smug and self-satisfied, classical psychological "parvenu" who see themselves fulfilled and justified by their behavior. In their "making it," the middleclass fail to acknowledge or appreciate the past, or to redefine the past to make it more attractive. Rather, they self-consciously create what the authors construe as an artificial culture.

Much of Vidich and Bensman's analyses appeared to be a lament against change and a reaction to the vulgarity of much of middleclass EuropeanAmerica. Still, the study held special significance for the orientation toward cultural struggle which informs my work here, particularly, their description of contemporary White middleclass culture as flawed, vulgar, emulative, and spurious because, quite ironically, this characterization was derived from descriptions of *AfricanAmerican* culture. In this analogy, they used Finestone's research on and conclusions about AfricanAmerican culture as well as other studies of the AfricanAmerican community. They shared Frazier's perception of AfricanAmerican culture as essentially emulative and a parody of EuropeanAmerican styles:

> The Negro overacts selected themes from white life to the point of satirizing them and in most cases, unlike the "cat," is not aware that he is doing so. For the lower-middle-class, middle-class, and upper-class Negro, to recognize his inadequate emulation would be too difficult to bear because such an admission would reveal the artificiality of his entire way of life and would leave no basis for living with himself.[6]

Describing White middleclass culture in many respects as pathological is compatible with the PanAfrican communalist perspective and has important implications for cultural struggle. However, many analysts challenged Frazier's pathological model of AfricanAmerican middleclass culture as biased and distorted. The elevation of the "new" Black middleclass to an *ethclass* status, similar to Wilson's position, signifies the importance of Bensman and Vidich's critical appraisal of American middleclass culture. Vidich and Bensman viewed the new African-American middleclass as a "new welfare bourgeoisie." This new bourgeoisie emerged out of the Sixties Civil Rights struggle when its members served as agitators, revolutionary statesmen, and bureaucrats. According to Vidich and Bensman, the government and philanthropic bureaucracies co-opted these former activists and militants. However, because of their past exclusion, members of new Black middleclass possess little or no knowledge of the substance behind the bureaucratic forms:

> Their attachment to form rather than substance parallels the process of emulation described by Frazier in his description of the life style of the older black bourgeoisie. Thus the new revolutionary welfare bourgeoisie acts out a form whose original forms they have never seen. The result is a visible inefficiency, mismanagement, lack of bureaucratic skill, incompetence, and insufficiency of training in the bureaucracies.[7]

From a PanAfricanist communalist perspective, I would contend that this trend and/or characteristic of the post-1954 AfricanAmerican middleclass represents one of the gravest problems confronting the AfricanAmerican community. While one could agree in part with Frazier's scathing, satirical critique of the older generation Black bourgeoisie, the objective evidence suggests that the segment of the contemporary Black middleclass to which Bensman and Vidich allude approximates Frazier's description much more closely. This group's efforts to "succeed" and acquire the appropriate materialistic "goodies" has become increasingly EuropeanAmerican; or, to use Hare's term, has made them Black-Anglo-Saxon-Protestants (BASPs or "Buppies"). The cost of its success was its loss of both AfricanAmerican cultural identity and commitment to collective, protracted struggle for the liberation of all AfricanAmericans. These individuals think they have changed in status, from an *ethcaste*-class to an *ethclass*. This self-deception on the part of the up-and-coming young "jet-setters" earning at or close to the median yearly income resulted in increased intracaste *ethclass* hostility as the dominant group manipulated this colorblind, culturally and politically naïve segment of the new Black middleclass to serve as the latter-day, "new" neocolonial elite.

While the older Black bourgeoisie or upper-middleclass traditionally maintained close ties to the AfricanAmerican community because of its dependence upon the Black masses as customers, clients, patients, and students, the new bourgeoisie owes its allegiance to the bureaucracy which often employs it to fulfill an affirmative action quota—not to say they are not fully qualified. This new bourgeoisie, often trained in elite private or public elementary, secondary, and postsecondary educational institutions, is sheltered from the AfricanAmerican urban communities. It possesses little or no knowledge of the AfricanAmerican experience and culture in America. Many, having grown up in integrated, predominantly EuropeanAmerican suburbs, become startled and shocked—often to the point of emotional trauma—if a White racist associate or colleague refers to them as "nigger." While one can sympathize with their middleclass parents' dilemma regarding the difficulties of rearing and socializing AfricanAmerican children in urban ghettoes, even the gilded ghettoes, the path many have chosen may have created more problems than solutions. For as Bensman and Vidich observed, the new Black middle-class—or more accurately, upper-middleclass individuals—have arrived in excellent positions to become the neocolonial elite administering the bureaucracies which perpetuate the new caste system:

> If present trends continue, a new caste system may replace the present
> *de facto* second-class citizenship. The new *de jure* second-class citi-
> zenship would be based on the operation of federal programs and
> budgets supported by law. Indigenous leaders and their white bureau-
> cratic masters and counterparts would manage the colonial administra-
> tors, and the net result would be a new caste position for the American
> black which surpasses the old primitive Southern caste system in its
> capacity to cope with modern organized society. Modern bureaucracy
> could create a more efficient caste system.[8]

I contend that Wilson really "meant" to refer to this phenomenon, this
bureaucratic paper-pushing and middle-level decision-making group, in
his attack on the Black middleclass. The major difficulty with his analysis
lies in his assertion that this small group acquired the power to influence
the present socioeconomic conditions of the AfricanAmerican masses.
From a PanAfrican communalist perspective, this group derives little or
no power except from its members' bureaucratic status or position. It does
not own any significant proportion of the economic means of production.
In this sense, it is similar to its predecessor. Nor does it possess significant
political power. Its members' sociocultural lifestyles closely resemble
those of their White counterparts which Bensman and Vidich so graphi-
cally described as "me"-oriented, high salaried, white collar workers with
spurious values. This "elite" Black group represents the epitome of what
one observer, Mike Thelwell, labelled the "new ignorance,"[9] or what
social critic William Strickland referred to as "the Americanization of the
race."[10]

I should add that this phenomenon is not confined to the current
generation of the Black bourgeoisie. During the period since the Civil
Rights Act of 1964, the mass media, educational institutions, and supporters of school busing have besieged the AfricanAmerican community with
integrationist propaganda as a means of achieving academic equality. The
rationale for school busing changed from one of achieving educational
equality or parity in I.Q. measures to one of bringing the races together in
order to achieve the liberal integrationist ideal or vision.[11] Programs such
as busing, affirmative action, and quotas support an underlying assumption that AfricanAmericans have no viable culture which should be
maintained and perpetuated, and that the road to Black upward mobility
requires AfricanAmericans to reject their cultural heritage and become
culturally White, that is, Black-Anglo-Saxon-Protestants. These efforts
have largely failed in their attempts to substantially change the socioeco-

nomic position of the Black masses, but succeeded in creating sociocultural confusion and chaos in the minds of AfricanAmerican youths and young adults.

The ongoing increase in the number of AfricanAmerican comedies on major television networks, the disco/"punk" mania with its "watered down" integrated soul/rock music, and the continuing emphasis of certain Black publications on the so-called "success" of Black cinema stars, professional athletes, and other celebrities all contribute to the current cultural crisis confronting AfricanAmericans. The current quiescent state of the AfricanAmerican cultural and political movements (with the exception of Reverend Jesse Jackson's Rainbow Coalition) reflects the success of these "inter-institutional elites" (Vidich and Bensman's euphemism for Mills' "power elite") program for defusing the political consciousness of the AfricanAmerican masses. The philosophical observation of Santayana that a people ignorant of its history is doomed to repeat its mistakes seems quite appropriate for the current state of affairs in the AfricanAmerican community.

The cultural orientation of the current Black bourgeoisie and its predecessors differs in that the "new" group lacks political or cultural awareness of its membership in a racial ethcaste. The Civil Rights Movement's victory over Southern Jim Crow segregation removed all the legal barriers to integration. Consequently, this generation of Black bourgeoisie (and Black youth in general) never experienced *de jure* OR *de facto* caste oppression. Prior to this period, in the AfricanAmerican community *all* socioeconomic groups (especially all segments of the AfricanAmerican middleclass) understood their caste status.

I indicated above that the traditional definition of the Black middleclass encompasses AfricanAmericans from the small entrepreneurs and rural landowners to the more educated and professional elite who earned a stable and predictable income which allowed them to accrue a relative amount of security, prestige, and status. Always small relative to the larger, more impoverished masses who earned their living doing menial, dirty, low-income dead-end jobs, the middleclass group further subdivided according to occupation, education, income, place of residence, and physical appearance.

DuBois,[12] Drake and Cayton,[13] Davis and the Gardners,[14] Myrdal,[15] and others alluded to the presence of a "Mulatto elite" as a significant element in the AfricanAmerican bourgeiosie. This subgroup was often described as Black "aristocrats," the Black *ethcaste's* equivalent of the upperclass in Warner's typology, and included a disproportionate number of descendants of free Blacks or house servants during slavery. After emancipation, many members of this group maintained and perpetuated a cultural lifestyle which kept them solidly separated from the AfricanAmerican masses. Constantly the subject of novels focusing on the theme of the tragic "Mulatto"—brilliant, educated, fair-complexioned (sometimes with blue eyes), sophisticated and cosmopolitan—this group often received its education in Europe if not at one of the elite Black private colleges created expressly for this purpose. These colleges instituted practices which attempted to keep dark complexioned "field Negroes" from being admitted. Unless they chose to pass, and some did, this "Mulatto" elite found their economic or cultural objectives circumscribed or stymied as a consequence of racial caste discrimination.[16] Culturally, many members of this group essentially imitated their EuropeanAmerican counterparts (sometimes relatives). Many belonged to White liberal, prestigious churches like the Presbyterian, Congregational, and Episcopalian. However, while they maintained a degree of sociocultural separation from the masses, they depended upon that same group for political-economic survival.

Harriet McAdoo,[17] and Andrew Billingsley[18] observed that descendants of this "Mulatto" elite group among the current AfricanAmerican middleclass still maintain their traditional Eurocentric values and practices. However, many of these descendants became active in the Civil Rights Movement and converted to PanAfrican nationalism as a consequence of their expanding racial and cultural consciousness. Culturally, these elite families tended to perpetuate extended family networks with the reciprocal obligations characteristic of such units. Although less essential to their economic survival than for lowerclass AfricanAmerican family units, they adhere to these obligations. Politically, with some notable nationalist/separatist exceptions who were followers of W.E.B. DuBois and Monroe Trotter, this elite group tends to support what Cruse[19] and Bernard[20] referred to as the integrationist strain.

This Eurocentric group maintains its *ethcaste*/class identity through its often passionate expressions of elite group membership. Those who could not or chose not to "pass" considered themselves insulted at the suggestion they may be EuropeanAmerican. Traditionally and contemporarily, the AfricanAmerican elites, as a group maintain their *ethcaste/ethclass* cultural heritage. However, even within this elite stratum, we find intracaste ethnic diversity and some hostility, especially in Midwestern and Northeastern urban areas. G. Franklin Edwards observed in his study of Black elites in the Washington, D. C. area that several of the prominent professionals migrated from one or more of the Caribbean Islands. These professionals brought with them the Caribbean tendency to identify an individual's class status according to color. During slavery the legal structure of their societies divided into three somewhat autonomous castes: White, Coloured, and Black. Of course, Blacks were on the bottom. These Caribbean professionals apparently retained this historical sensitivity to color as an indicator of class. As representatives of the "Mulatto" elite, they demonstrated contempt for those outside their status. This Caribbean-derived contempt and its "homegrown" equivalent represent another area of tension within AfricanAmerican culture.

Sensitive observers of AfricanAmerican culture, like Frazier, Drake and Cayton, identified the darker bourgeoisie as the group replacing the older "Mulatto" elite in political economic status. In their classic study of Chicago, Drake and Cayton argued that the darker bourgeoisie emerged as a consequence of the mass migration of AfricanAmericans. That mass move included a relatively small number of college graduates trained in predominantly AfricanAmerican southern colleges and universities. Many, if not most, migrated from rural southern communities to the urban northeast, midwest, and to a certain extent, far west (since the far west migration represents a more recent, post-World War II, phenomenon). Cayton and Drake further asserted that this group of entrepreneurs and professionals perceived that their political economic interests and potential could be realized through developing a Black capitalist infrastructure within AfricanAmerican urban communities. Heavily influenced by Booker T. Washington, this capitalist economic nationalism represented a major innovation among the *ethcaste*/class bourgeoisie according to Drake and Cayton.[21]

The old "Mulatto" elite in Chicago had supported itself economically by providing certain services to the EuropeanAmerican community. However, the rapid increase in White ethnic immigrants and the subsequent growth in economic competition and racial antagonism along with technological innovations and an expanding bureaucracy combined to force the "Mulatto" elite out of their traditional occupations, crafts, and professions. Their political economic status declined as they found themselves being replaced by industrial expansion and White workingclass ethnics. Many of the old elite refused to pursue economic projects geared to meeting the needs of the rapidly expanding AfricanAmerican masses and found themselves trapped in an economic vacuum. On another front, the emerging darker bourgeoisie aggressively created and developed business enterprises that did provide services to the Black masses. They were the ones who initiated "Buy Black" campaigns and appealed to racial solidarity and pride in their efforts to create alternative competitive business enterprises. However, a major change has occurred within this segment of the *ethcaste* elite.

The "vanguard" of the "new" (darker) bourgeoisie included small businessmen, entertainers and professional athletes as well as a number of "shadies" who earned their living in extralegal and illegal activities. Among those *not* included were high-salaried college- and graduate-trained professionals who were *dependent* upon White bureaucratic masters. This early "new" bourgeoisie, in spite of its capitalist orientation, attempted to become an *independent* elite, to "do for self," in the words of the Honorable Elijah Muhammed. Although essentially "mom and pop" shops, their enterprises made it possible for some AfricanAmericans to earn a living without White supervision and control. Young Blacks growing up in these communities could see AfricanAmericans owning and operating businesses independently of EuropeanAmericans. In addition, many of this bourgeois group became involved in urban machine politics and emerged as political leaders. So, while they were political integrationists, economically and socioculturally they tended to be nationalists. Their lifestyles and values overlapped extensively with that of the lower-, middle-, and workingclass Blacks. The more respectable members of this emerging bourgeoisie chose the "Mulatto" elite as their reference group and attempted to become integrated into it. When successful, they usually enhanced the economic status of the "Mulatto" elite.

One can easily discern the descendants of this earlier bourgeoisie in the Black middleclass today. Still active in Black social and fraternal associations, especially the Masons, Elks, and various Greek-letter organizations, they overlap the Black "jet set" element in sociocultural lifestyle, yet tend to be politically, economically, and culturally aware of their heritage. But, due to a desire to shelter their children from the harsh realities of the AfricanAmerican economic conditions, many descendants of the early middleclass families contribute to the loss of their children's cultural identity. This segment contains numerous "skin-color nationalists"—dark-complexioned Blacks who profess to hate Whites and "Mulattoes" passionately, yet maintain Eurocentric individualistic and opportunistic traits or sociocultural values similar to those of their culturally spurious Black and White counterparts discussed earlier.

Obviously, a great deal of Black *ethcaste* ethnic diversity also exists within this segment of the Black middleclass. Sowell,[22] discussed this diversity, often accompanied by intracaste class competition and hostility, in two articles in *The New York Times*. He noted the importance of ethnic geographical origins in identifying AfricanAmerican leaders and their analyses of problems as well as their proposed solutions. Sowell claimed that due to their ethnic origins, some Black leaders may be misleading or "hustling" AfricanAmerican people in order to receive certain privileges from White liberals. Some Caribbean groups receive better treatment and greater access to the mainstream than others. For example, Jamaicans and Barbadans appear to fare much better in this society than Haitians. Certain Jamaican or Barbadan leaders possibly pursue objectives and goals based on their own intracaste *ethclass* interests and neglect the needs of other Black ethclass groups.

Sowell also commented, along with Cruse, on the problems arising out of the cultural contact between AfricanAmericans and the large and increasing population of Caribbean immigrants in the major urban areas, especially the Northeast. Thus, within the Black *ethcaste*, there exists Black ethclass antagonism. As I noted in the earlier discussion on cultural continuities in the diaspora, cultural similarities remain much more extensive than the differences, but in a situation of oppression, the dominant group intensifies and exaggerates the differences through its ability to reward and punish. In addition, capitalist culture, the dominant system in the world, treats oppressed groups, AfricanAmericans in particular, differently when they are out of their respective colonial environments. For example, North American Blacks may receive more humane treatment while in London than in Boston, while Jamaicans experience the exact opposite.

This difference in benign tolerance versus overt subordination relates in part to the immigrant status of Jamaicans in the United States (*i.e.*, they are not one of "our" worthless, shiftless niggers) and the visiting status of AfricanAmericans in England (come to spend American dollars). It also can be attributed in part to the internal competition between nations and their racial/cultural transplants in the New World — each attempts to be more humane to the others' victims. To the sensitive and astute observer, this competition does not mask the fact that in all instances, the White dominant oppressive group exploits the Black subordinate group, nor that wherever Africans happen to be geographically, they suffer from caste oppression and exclusion. From a PanAfrican communalist perspective this is the continuation of the British "divide and conquer, divide and rule" strategy—intracaste *ethclass* antagonisms impede AfricanAmericans' ability to concentrate their collective energy on intensifying the cultural struggle and allows us to be manipulated like separate puppets in the hands of the powerful, domineering puppeteer.

Cruse referred to the ideological supporters of AfricanAmerican nationalism as the "rejected strain," or what Bernard discussed as the "externally adapted"; that is, the segment of the Black middleclass which consciously attempts to maintain and perpetuate its AfricanAmerican cultural heritage. This cultural nationalism also exists in the bourgeois segment of the Black middleclass, both historically and at present. Its members generally continue to attend religious institutions identified with the AfricanAmerican community like the African Methodist Episcopal, Baptist, A.M.E. Zion, and some Pentecostal denominations. They remain active in AfricanAmerican political and cultural organizations. Many artists and intellectuals involve themselves in promoting PanAfrican nationalism; and many veterans of the Civil Rights Movement continue to engage in some form of community organizing or work for organizations that provide services to the AfricanAmerican community.

Followers of this cultural nationalism maintain lifestyles which attempt to perpetuate the antimaterialistic communalistic values and spirituality which have been identified as the core components of AfricanAmerican culture, those norms, beliefs, and practices which sustained their/our ancestors through the horrors of capture, the Middle Passage, slavery, Jim Crow segregation, urban migration, and White backlash movements. The children of lower- and middleclass families or workingclass families along with a goodly number of upper middleclass families comprise a significant proportion of this nationalist subgroup, which also encompasses a goodly number of AfricanCaribbeanAmericans; that is, Jamaicans, Trinidadians, Barbadans, Haitians, plus continental Africans who have established permanent residence in the United States, making this group quite multiethnic also. Many acquired their educational training during the tumultuous and turbulent Sixties and early Seventies. Thus, they should be considered ideological descendants of Malcolm X, Martin Luther King, Medgar Evers, and Kwame Nkrumah. While possessing the required training and WASP cultural exposure, they consciously reject integration and choose to dedicate their lives to the

African struggle for cultural autonomy and economic equity in the U.S. and in the Diaspora.

Relatively high-salaried factory workers, (auto workers, steel workers, meat packers or processors, and so on) civil servants, and skilled blue collar workers (bus drivers, truck drivers, taxi drivers, skycaps) compose the other major segment of the contemporary AfricanAmerican middleclass. This group represents the contemporary descendants of the traditional Black middleclass as described by Drake and Cayton,[23] and Frazier.[24] Although Frazier only discussed this group in socioeconomic terms (his sociocultural analysis focused on the bourgeois element of the upper middleclass), as opposed to the studies of Scanzoni[25] and Kronus[26] which focused more on the "blue-collar" middleclass groups. This segment of the middleclass can also be divided according to sociocultural lifestyles. Such a division represents ideal types while in the "real" world, the lifestyles tend to overlap extensively.

These members, secure in their AfricanAmerican cultural identity, tend to pursue often rather conservative Black puritanical existences. They staunchly support Christian morality and safeguard their families from the evils and corruptions of this world. Obviously devoted church people, they usually belong to the Baptist, A.M.E., AM.E. Zion, Pentacostal, or Seventh Day Adventist denominations. They exhibit concern about the quality, safety and cleanliness of their neighborhoods, homes, and schools. Most of their social life revolves around the church and the affiliated organizations within the church, both locally and nationally. Some would characterize this group as the Black Calvinist "bedrock" of the AfricanAmerican community. While not always politically conscious of the racial/cultural struggle, they firmly ground their lifestyles in the rural Southern mores of traditional AfricanAmerican culture. Although one could not describe them as overt cultural nationalists, they could be considered covert nationalists and they remain very race conscious and suspicious of Whites, especially Northern urban Whites. They reflect their nationalism in their communalistic participation in churches, extended and monogamous families, music they enjoy and create, and willingness to accept their (communal) brotherly/sisterly (intraAfrican) responsibility to share their hard-earned income with those perceived as less fortunate than themselves.

The less religious element of this segment of the Black middleclass tend to be strivers and conspicuous consumers. Their lifestyle resembles that of the wealthier "jet-setters" and "sporting" crowd element of the

EuropeanAmerican upper middleclass bourgeoisie. Their social life revolves around bars, nightclubs, gambling, house parties, the latest dances and the consumption of large quantities of alcohol, although now some use "recreational" drugs. In the words of elderly retired AfricanAmericans, they are "fast livers." However, this nonreligious group also tends to be quite race conscious and sensitive. They may work with Whites but rarely "party" with them. In this sense, they display a degree of cultural consciousness although few of them would be disciplined enough to engage in prolonged political activity. Although very individualistic and opportunistic, many, within their friendship cliques, exhibit AfricanAmerican cultural communalistic values. Their lofty ambitions and efforts to keep up with the "Joneses" often keeps this group in a permanent state of indebtedness as they tend to live beyond their economic means. This group also experiences a great deal of marital instability. Yet in periods of racial crisis and turmoil, they support AfricanAmerican organizations and leaders.

From this overview of diversity of lifestyles within the AfricanAmerican *ethcaste* middleclass, we can see that this group exhibits complicated, complex, class and cultural dynamics. I am certain that a similar state of affairs exists for other racial ethcaste group, like MexicanAmerican, AsianAmericans, PuertoRican American, and NativeAmericans. In addition, the relationships between these *ethcaste* groups constitute another level of complexity. An *Ebony* magazine article by Jesse Jackson [date uncertain] revealed the presence of competition and some hostility between these *ethcaste* groups. In the late 1980s and early '90s, *The New York Times* presented several articles focusing on the rapid increase in the Spanish-speaking population, especially the illegal alien problem which also creates tension in these *ethcaste* communities.

Jackson argues quite passionately that AfricanAmericans must become increasingly aware of the socioeconomic effects of this rapid growth of the Latino population on the status of AfricanAmericans, especially its impact on the chronic high unemployment rate for AfricanAmerican males. AfricanAmerican and PuertoRican Americans have a history of ethnic tension and hostility. Much of the tension comes from economic competition and cultural insensitivity. Whatever the reason, the relationships between *ethcaste* groups often prove far from harmonious. And tension often intensifies because of the practices and policies of the federal government and the ruling elite. Yet these inter*ethcaste* difficulties seem minor in comparison to the racist oppression and subjugation victimizing each group.

Additionally, these *ethcaste* groups share numerous cultural values such as extended family networks, strong religious orientation, distinct religious practices which reflect their indigenous and often African adaptations of Christianity, music, art, food, respect for elders, and oral traditions. But as a consequence of the nature of the contact between *ethcaste* groups, contact determined by our mutual oppressor, these groups have not been able to transcend the hostilities separating them. Their ability to acquire knowledge about each other has been circumscribed. Unfortunately, the dominant group continues to encourage or initiate distrust through its promotion of stereotypical caricatures of these groups and emphasizing the relative economic success of one group in comparison to that of the others.

As noted earlier in the criticism of Wilson's thesis, the *ethcaste* groups' *ethclass* elites must provide the leadership to promote political and cultural understanding within and between their respective constituencies. In so doing, they could establish the foundation for a unified political movement which has the economic and cultural concerns of all ethcaste groups as its major agenda. The relatively successful presidential campaigns of Reverend Jesse Jackson under the inclusive umbrella of the Rainbow Coalition reflect the potential power of the *ethcaste* groups if they are able to resolve their differences and cooperate. The demographic projections suggest that our time to assume power and transform U.S. society to reflect our collective, pluralistic images has arrived. Are we ready to rise to the challenge?

CHAPTER IX

ETHCASTE
AND THE
POLITICAL ECONOMY
OF THE
AFRICANAMERICAN
MIDDLECLASS

T he concept of *ethcaste* includes the class diversity dimension of *ethclass* while simultaneously emphasizing the caste status of AfricanAmericans. Thus, the concept of *ethcaste* has an affinity with the Marxists' analysis which finds AfricanAmericans in the larger American community disproportionately *proletarian* and *lumpen proletarian* and emphasizes the racist dimension by noting that, both nationally and internationally within the world capitalist cultural proletariat and *lumpen proletariat*, AfricanAmericans occupy a caste status. The concept of *ethcaste* assumes that the exploitation of AfricanAmericans has been predicated upon their racial and cultural differences from WASPs and other EuropeanAmericans. The concept further assumes that the AfricanAmerican community possesses cultural (multiethnic) and political-economic diversity; that is, class stratification with a variety of political, cultural, and economic subgroups.

The concept of *ethcaste* is used to demonstrate that the caste/cultural status of AfricanAmericans in the United States resembles that of other Africans in the "New" World and reflects the status of African nations within the world capitalist cultural system. Therefore, we use this term *ethcaste* to discuss the historical experiences and cultural continuities indigenous to African peoples as well as their contemporary political-economic and cultural conditions. It is my argument that the concept of *ethcaste* provides AfricanAmerican social scientists with a framework which transcends the provincialism and ahistoricism characteristic of most EuropeanAmerican social scientific concepts and theory.

I have attempted to demonstrate that the dimension of PanAfrican (in the present case) cultural continuity intended by use of the term *ethcaste* has gained increasing support in scholarly use. Yet, the dimension of political-economic caste continues to be seriously questioned as a consequence of the perception of the successes of the Civil Rights movement. The heroic, self-sacrificing, collective participation of the masses of AfricanAmerican people in the struggle to *finally* break the racist political-economic caste barriers dominated the internal politics of the AfricanAmerican community during the Sixties. As the federal government passed and attempted to enforce desegregated interstate travel and hotel accommodations, passed a new law to guarantee voting rights, integrated previously segregated educational institutions and professional schools, and declared a federal "War on Poverty," it appeared that AfricanAmericans had finally forcibly opened the door to the "promised land" of the great American mainstream. Previous barriers to the acquisition of the economic and political "goodies" were eradicated — at least for some.

However, the price of these victories in both human and property terms proved very costly. The memories of mass arrests, clubbings, firehosings, dog attacks, bombings, house- and cross-burnings, the presence of National Guardsmen and armed personnel from the regular United States Army, racial murders, and "gutted" cities all attest to the tenacity with which EuropeanAmerica fought to retain its caste hegemony. As post-Watergate horrors continued to surface, we increasingly witnessed individual White citizens, trusted public figures, and legitimate law enforcement authorities (including the FBI, CIA, and state and local policemen) violate the constitutionally-guaranteed rights of AfricanAmericans and severely circumscribed them as they engaged in peaceful protest, freedom of speech, bearing of arms, enjoying the sanctity of private property, receiving due process under the law, and so forth.

The liberal political-economic elite and its intellectual apologists hailed these "new" freedoms so grudgingly granted to AfricanAmericans as re(!)affirmation for *all* Americans — as a sign that the major "black" mark on the democratic image of the United States had been eliminated. The last bastion of inequality had been conquered. The country could now "lift its head" as it demonstrated to both its liberal and socialist critics that a democracy could endure and transcend instability and potential insurrection. They proclaimed a stronger, more unified nation as a consequence of this essentially moral, conscientious, humanitarian movement.

Impatiently, Black and White social analysts rushed to demonstrate this change. Andrew Brimmer's 1969 study of the AfricanAmerican occupational structure revealed that some progress had been achieved. The study focused on the period between 1960 and 1967:

> Thus, while total employment increased by 11.5 percent, that for non-whites rose by 14 percent. Over those seven years, the rise in the number of jobs held by non-whites accounted for 12.6 percent of the expansion in total employment. The occupational distribution of employed Negroes has also changed somewhat during the current decade. Gains have been particularly striking in the professional and technical fields, in clerical work, in semi-skilled factory jobs, and in non-household service tasks. Skilled craftsmen occupations among non-whites have also increased somewhat faster than their total employment. *In contrast, the number of non-whites engaged as managers, officials, and proprietors has expanded more slowly than total non-white employment.* To a considerable extent, occupational upgrading among non-whites has paralleled an absolute decline in their employment as private household workers, as farmers and farm workers, and non-farm laborers.[1] [My emphasis.]

Brimmer also noted that the AfricanAmerican median family income had risen by five percentage points, from 54 percent in 1965 to 59 percent of White family incomes in 1967. A similar increase occurred for Blacks in the South, although at a somewhat lower income level (49 percent in 1965 to 54 percent in 1967).[2] Brimmer's statistics confirmed, in a cautiously optimistic manner, the liberal assertion that AfricanAmericans finally had begun to "change their status quite markedly in the direction of equality."[3]

While Brimmer somewhat reservedly and cautiously offered his generally optimistic analysis, Ben Wattenberg and Richard Scammon threw caution to the wind in their assessment of AfricanAmerican economic progress. In a highly controversial article in 1973, they argued that AfricanAmericans had not merely improved their relative economic position, but had finally achieved mainstream "middle class" economic status. They defined middleclass in a rather generous and arbitrary manner, as to a median family income of $8,000 in the North and $6,000 in the South. They claimed that these family incomes constituted the bottom of the middleclass as defined in Warner's scheme, but that families with these income levels could obtain adequate food, clothing, and safe, sanitary housing.

Based on this definition of middleclass, they placed 52 percent of African American families in the middleclass.[4] For the first time in AfricanAmerican history, a majority of AfricanAmerican families had achieved a standard of living above the poverty line—a true economic revolution. However, these theorists found even more about which to be elated. A significant proportion of AfricanAmerican husband-wife families outside the South and under the age of thirty-five had achieved income parity with similarly situated EuropeanAmerican families. Better yet, in those AfricanAmerican families where the wife also worked, parity had been achieved and some even surpassed their EuropeanAmerican counterparts. Thus, Wattenberg and Scammon applauded Black leaders and their White liberal legislative supporters for the success of the Sixties.

To many observers, AfricanAmericans had not only transcended certain socioeconomic barriers, they also had established a new political presence as a consequence of the voting rights legislation passed in the Sixties. Many heralded this new AfricanAmerican political presence as the second Reconstruction. Martin Kilson observed that the increase in the number of Black elected officials represented the institutionalization of the politics of AfricanAmerican ethnicity:

> There are now about 1,500 elected Negro politicians or officials, 62 percent of them outside the South, representing overwhelmingly city constituencies. They are located in 41 of the 50 states, and include, among others, 12 Congressmen, 168 state legislators, 48 mayors, 575 other city officials, 362 school members, and 114 judges and magistrates.[5]

Kilson noted further that the institutionalization of Black ethnicity reflected a leadership change in the AfricanAmerican community. During the Sixties, two styles of leadership competing with each other for the allegiance of the AfricanAmerican urban masses surfaced. One was highly ideological and militantly articulated Black ethnicity as a matter of principle and commitment. The other, also militant but more pragmatic, articulated Black ethnicity as a matter of political necessity. Kilson attributed the new AfricanAmerican political presence to the triumph of the latter style which resulted in the election of Black politicians who had the discipline and organizing ability to create a Black ethnic political machine. Unlike the undisciplined, flamboyant, militant ideologues (who attracted a great deal of AfricanAmerican lower- and working class supporters), he found the new ethnic politicians capable of developing the kind of ethnic political organizations which proved so successful in achieving cultural, political, and economic acceptance and mobility for EuropeanAmerican ethnics. Therefore, the emergence of Black ethnic politics indicated that AfricanAmericans were using the traditional American ethnic strategy for cultural acceptance and socioeconomic mobility.

Although Kilson appeared to favor this change, he made a critical observation germane to this analysis. He observed that the 'impractically' ideological militant leaders tended to come from lower-strata backgrounds with a special claim to having spearheaded the militant style common to much of "Negro" leadership. On the other hand, although a good portion of the second leadership group—the pragmatics—appeared to be first-generation middleclass, they "currently" (*i.e.*, in 1971) were "leading the Black bourgeoisie's efforts to seize a dominant role in the emerging politics of black ethnicity."[6] The significance of this observation will emerge in subsequent discussions of the Black middleclass. I will simply say at this point that Kilson's observation generated an impressive body of literature critically assessing both the Civil Rights Movement and the role of the Black bourgeoisie.

In addition to this optimistic analysis of AfricanAmerican progress, the mass media, especially movies and television, also "discovered" the AfricanAmerican experience. Clean cut, neatly dressed with coiffured "Afro" hairstyles, up-and-coming young Black men and women began to appear in television commercials, playing leading roles in serials like *The Mod Squad, Mission: Impossible, Room 222, I Spy,* and others. AfricanAmericans became so "integrated" into the mainstream that they began to appear in daytime soap operas, expanding the number soap opera "junkies" among AfricanAmericans of all ages. Black personalities hosted talk shows, presented the evening news, and interviewed newsworthy AfricanAmerican and EuropeanAmerican public figures.

If you believe White Supremacist rhetoric, the most "dangerous" topic separating Blacks and Whites because of its association with lynching, immolation, and emasculation, became a theme for one of the most popular movies of the decade and catapulted noted AfricanAmerican actor Sidney Poitier to the pinnacle of fame. I refer to the issue of AfricanAmerican/EuropeanAmerican marriages and sexual relations, the heart of the tension in the film *Guess Who's Coming to Dinner?*

Television comedies such as *The Flip Wilson Show, Sanford and Son,* and *Good Times* also exposed some stereotypical aspects of AfricanAmerican culture to the larger American society. The pervasive influence of television caused Wade Nobles to contend that it had damaged and threatened to disintegrate the structure of the AfricanAmerican family:

> ... we contend that the structural damage to the Black family is very recent (reaching its most intense form with the television explosion of the 1950's) and that the process of "shifting" which ultimately will affect the functional character of the family unit, has not completed itself. That is, even though the historical definition of the Black family is undergoing a change which is similar to the unit's transformations occurring in all post-technological societies, the "shift" has not been completed nor (and more importantly) if allowed to complete itself, will its effects be similar for Black people as it is for non-Black peoples. For instance, not only will the consequence of this shift be the disintegration of the structural and functional character of the Black family, but it will also be the elimination of the protective buffer (which the family affords its members) against a hostile and racist society which by its nature particularly dehumanizes Black people.[7]

The current debates and tensions surrounding discussions about the "breakdown" of the AfricanAmerican family, especially in the so-called underclass, attest to the accuracy of Nobles' assessment and prophetic vision. This politically orchestrated effort to convince the AfricanAmerican community that it had gained acceptance was further reinforced by plays written by, directed by, and starring AfricanAmericans appeared on Broadway. Indeed, in the aesthetic world, AfricanAmerican artists received the popular recognition and financial rewards more nearly commensurate with their accomplishments and contributions than any time since the Harlem Renaissance.

Yet, in the midst of this myth of the long-sought-after, finally-achieved integration or assimilation (of sorts), certain persistent and basic socio-economic conditions continued to exist, conditions endemic to the AfricanAmerican community since slavery and emancipation. I am reminded of how fond Black folk are of the old saying, "all that glitters ain't gold," in their own idiom. Several Black and White economic analysts began to critically examine the 1970 census data on the socioeconomic conditions of AfricanAmericans. A familiar pattern began to emerge, a pattern Andrea Rushing referred to in another context as "the changing same."[8]

Lloyd Hogan critiqued this phenomenon in an article severely criticizing the liberal, optimistic "mirage." He cited evidence indicating that, without taking drastic measures during the 1970s, the plight of AfricanAmericans could well approach catastrophe. Using the number of Black-owned businesses or those hiring Black workers as one indicator of economic scarcity and/or prosperity, Hogan presented data from a then-recent census survey which estimated that not more than 4,000 AfricanAmerican families, consisting of some 15,000 individuals, owned commercial or business firms and whose main sources of livelihood derived from profits, interest, dividends, and rents. Hogan further noted that:

> It is also estimated that not more than 200,000 Black families, consisting of some 650,000 individuals, are self-employed in small and marginal farms and businesses. For these families, the income derived from these businesses consists primarily of wages for their own labor. They employ little, if any, paid labor outside their own families.[9]

That the families to which Hogan referred constituted only four percent of the total number of AfricanAmerican families reflects, by implication, the overwhelmingly proletarian character of the AfricanAmerican community. The four percent constituted, for all intents and purposes, the Black "capitalist" class. One uses "capitalist" in a qualified sense because all of their profits combined would not account for ONE percent of America's net corporate profits, meaning that 96 percent of AfricanAmerican families earn their livelihood from the sale of their labor—an estimated 21.7 million individuals at that time. Hogan proceeded to present evidence which affirms Ogbu's concept of the *caste line* in the American occupational structure. He indicated that there are definite racist tendencies within the American occupational structure:

> Some jobs are strictly reserved for Blacks; some are strictly reserved for whites; and a third category is racially indifferent. In general, the white collar (other than clerical) and highly skilled crafts occupations, are reserved for whites; the semiskilled crafts, unskilled laborers, and service occupations are reserved for Blacks. In recent years, clerical jobs have become almost racially indifferent, although there is still a slight bias in favor of whites.[10]

A more refined classification of jobs or occupations illustrates even more visibly the racist bias in the American occupational structure (or the caste line). Hogan demonstrated that while AfricanAmericans constituted 9.5 percent of the total labor force, they comprised 38 percent of the private household workers and 19 percent of the nonfarm laborers, the bottom end of the occupational structure. In contrast, AfricanAmericans constituted only 3 percent of the sales workers and only 3 percent of the managers and administrators (the upper end of the occupational structure). If one adds to this rather gloomy portrait the disproportionate representation of AfricanAmericans among families on public welfare or social security, the unemployed and those omitted from official government statistics (that is, the unemployables and the sporadic or underemployed), the caste position of AfricanAmericans within the predominantly White labor force becomes even more obvious. These statistics reveal that even during a so-called period of prosperity and expanding economy, AfricanAmericans experienced an unemployment rate of Depression magnitude: "The official statistics for the 1960s and the early years of the 1970s is an almost constant 10 percent, twice the official rate for whites." Hogan's PanAfrican communalist interpretation of these statistics clearly reflects why AfricanAmericans have always constituted a political-economic *ethcaste* in America:

> Blacks have no direct role in determining the level of economic activity. Decisions about war and peace and the determination of the strategic economic generators are not within the capability of the Black population. Large-scale public and private investment decisions, changes in the money supply, public taxing and expenditure policy, wage and price determination — all these are in the hands of government and large-scale business and financial institutions.[11]

In a similar vein, John Ogbu's work on minority education and caste also documents the occupational ethcaste status of AfricanAmericans and other *ethcaste* groups and examines its consequences for their educational preparation in America. He presents several characteristics useful for distinguishing between caste groups on one hand, and autonomous, immigrant minorities on the other. Autonomous minorities are not totally subordinated economically or politically, but possess a distinctive racial, ethnic, or religious identity. They may occupy and control their own geographical turf. They may be subject to some prejudice and discrimination but not rigid stratification. And, they may be victims of an ideology, like anti-Semitism, which perceives them as innately inferior.[12] Ogbu described immigrant minorities, such as the Chinese and Japanese in America, as (1) operating outside the beliefs of the host society's system of social hierarchy; (2) not being deeply affected by the inferiority-superiority ideology inherent in such a host system; and (3) having the options of remaining in the host society or leaving if their position becomes unbearable.

In contrast to the rather flexible, elastic, voluntary relations which both autonomous and immigrant minorities enjoy with the dominant society, caste groups suffer domination/subordination in a most rigid, inelastic manner. Indeed, as the characterization "caste" indicates, they can be compared with "pariah" groups in the classical Hindu system: (1) regarded as inherently inferior in all respects; (2) considered to be intrinsically polluted, stigmatized and excluded; (3) assigned sharply defined economic rituals and political roles; (4) compelled to the dirtiest, most demeaning and unpleasant work; (5) not allowed to compete for the most desirable roles on the basis of their individual training and ability; and, (6) forced to play roles that the society generally perceives as a confirmation of their innate inferiority or their "natural" position in the society. For caste groups, "political subordination is reinforced by economic subordination,"[13] a point I have emphasized with respect to *ethcaste* groups.

Ogbu presents census data on AfricanAmerican participation in the American occupational structure for both the North and the South over a period of three decades. His findings paralleled Hogan's, clearly demonstrating AfricanAmericans' minimal representation in the upper echelons of the occupational structure in categories like professional, technical, and kindred workers; farmers and farm managers; managers and administrators except farm; clerical, sales, and kindred workers; craftsmen and foremen, reflecting racist practices and policies. Both found African Americans overrepresented among the lower echelons in categories like operatives and kindred workers; domestic servants; service workers except domestic; farm laborers and foremen; and laborers except farm laborers.

For the vast majority of AfricanAmerican people, the occupational caste ceiling ends at the level of "operators and kindred workers," the only exception being the relatively large increase in the number of Blacks employed in the "racially neutral" (Hogan's terminology) clerical and sales category. Ogbu presents compelling evidence supporting the thesis that through systematic miseducation, the educational system in the United States reinforces and supports this caste ceiling by preparing AfricanAmericans to perform within their restricted occupational status and not preparing them to occupy positions above this caste ceiling.

Ogbu further noted that even when a few AfricanAmericans break through this occupational caste barrier, their ascriptive racial background still constrains their professional pursuits:

> Black employees are not given responsibilities commensurate with their training and abilities, and they have less opportunity for advancement than their white peers. The job ceiling has been raised significantly since 1961, but the new black representation in the high-status jobs is not yet accompanied by an equal share of the responsibilities that go with such jobs.[14]

Ogbu found this to be the case even among those AfricanAmericans who had managed to achieve a "high quality" education. He concluded that improvements in Blacks' occupational status do not necessarily follow improvements in Black academic achievement as they do for Whites.

Ogbu's analysis reinforced an earlier but similar observation by Siegel who analyzed AfricanAmerican versus EuropeanAmerican income differentials according to education and occupation. Based on an analysis of 1960 census data, Siegel found that generally income tended to increase more rapidly with more education; that income increased more rapidly with increasing education for some occupations as opposed to others; and, in the observation germane to this discussion, the White versus non-White income differential *increased* with increases in education. Siegel observed further that if one perceived education as an investment, with the greatest return on this investment occurring in the upper echelons of the occupational structure, Blacks who manage to upgrade themselves educationally will often find that the occupational door closes before them at the very levels which would have enabled them to realize their investment.[15]

As Ogbu and others have noted, lowerclass Blacks' ambivalence about attaining higher education and continuing to advanced degrees and the professions appears quite rational, given that caste barriers will prevent them from ever realizing the full benefits accruing to their White counterparts. This situation reflects what Robert Blauner and others have called the system of racial privileges inherent in both classical and domestic colonial situations.

Herrington J. Bryce's critical response to Wattenberg and Scammon demonstrated another indication of the persistence of AfricanAmericans political-economic *ethcaste* status. Bryce found that the under-35, husband-wife AfricanAmerican family residing outside the South represented only 16 percent of such families in the United States, and, more importantly, they represent only 10 percent of all AfricanAmerican families.[16] Therefore, while this small percentage of AfricanAmerican families *may have reached parity* with their White counterparts, the vast majority of AfricanAmerican families (90 percent) still lag behind. As a matter of fact, he noted that the absolute gap between Black and White family incomes had *increased* from roughly $2,500 in 1947 to just over $4,000 in 1971.[17] A strange contradiction: we managed to achieve parity as we fell further behind. Note the elusive, shifting caste line.

David Swinton's article highlighted the deterioration of Black income gains in the late Sixties and early Seventies. He presented data which indicated that the Black-to-White median income ratio reached its highest point in 1969 and 1970. He further observed that the rapid increase in Black median family income only marginally related to the Civil Rights Movement. Principally, the cyclical behavior of the economy during the Viet Nam War induced boom caused the increase:

> The behavior of median black family income relative to median white family income in the late 1960's was very similar to the swing in the index during the economic boom of the early fifties — the Korean War period — when the relative nonwhite to white income also shot up four percentage points — only to return to pre-boom levels in the recession of the late fifties. Such cyclical changes do not presage a basic change in the relative position of blacks but merely indicate the well-known fact that in times of frenetic economic activity even the disadvantaged are pressed into service. These full-employment periods give marginal blacks an opportunity to find employment, and give many other blacks the opportunity to move from the category of sub-employed to fully employed.[18]

The current high unemployment rate among AfricanAmericans attests to the accuracy of Swinton's predictions.

To return briefly to Bryce's criticisms of Wattenberg and Scammon, it should be noted that he presented evidence which totally contradicted their optimistic projections, evidence which they chose to ignore in their haste to convince Black and White Americans that the capitalist culture's "promised land" had dawned for AfricanAmericans. Bryce found AfricanAmericans underrepresented in professional occupations by 35 percent, in managerial occupations by 70 percent, in crafts by 30 percent, and in clerical occupations by about 21 percent.[19] In addition, the difference between AfricanAmerican and White life expectancy was increasing. In 1960, a Black 25 years old was expected to live 5.2 fewer years than his White counterpart. By 1970, a Black was expected to live 6 years less. Bryce further discovered maternal and infant mortality rates for Blacks three times those of Whites. In addition, the suicide rate among

Blacks between the ages of 15 and 24 years doubled between 1960 and 1969. And, as the economy began a downturn, the number of Blacks on AFDC (Aid to Families With Dependent Children) increases.

The clash of the optimistic versus pessimistic interpretations of Black economic progress during the Sixties and early Seventies was reflected in two contradictory quantitative economic analyses. While Sar Levitan, and others, appropriately entitled their volume *Still a Dream* (reflecting their cautious interpretation of this so-called progress), Richard B. Freeman offered a more optimistic analysis similar to, though somewhat more cautious than, that of Wattenberg and Scammon. Freeman perceived AfricanAmerican increases in the upper levels of America's occupational structure as nothing short of "revolutionary:"

> The demand for black college graduates increased enormously, with consequent improvements in job opportunities and salaries. For the first time, national corporations began to recruit black men and women for managerial and professional jobs, seeking employees at southern black colleges that had previously never seen white recruiters. Increasing numbers of black college men entered managerial and business-oriented professions, such as accounting and law rather than the traditional teaching field. The income of black college graduates rose sharply relative to that of white graduates, ending the historic pattern of increasing racial income differentials with the level of education. The starting salaries of black college graduates reached parity with those of whites. The educational position of blacks improved substantially as colleges and universities began recruiting black students and faculty. Black college enrollments skyrocketed, particularly in traditionally white institutions. In short, there was a *dramatic collapse in traditionally discriminatory patterns in the market for highly qualified black Americans.*[20]

When forced to confront the fact that his study revealed AfricanAmericans generally concentrated in professions where the "average levels of education and income were low, where government was important," Freeman's optimism diminished somewhat. He also discovered that while some AfricanAmericans made this fantastic leap into the upper level occupations, persons from the higher socioeconomic levels made the greatest improvement, thereby creating larger "class" cleavages in the AfricanAmerican community.[21] Freeman's portrait of AfricanAmerican economic progress clearly reflects the liberal, gradualistic approach — "You are making progress because whereas ten years ago, five of the managers were black, today, after all the bloodshed and turmoil of the Civil Rights Movements, eight of you are." One cannot help wondering what price we must pay to have fifteen more!

Levitan's study conforms more consistently to "the changing same" analyses of Hogan, Bryce, Ogbu, and others. They all documented AfricanAmericans having made some gains in income and higher-level occupations. Yet they also found these gains at the upper levels, accompanied by the contradictory phenomenon of increases in the number of AfricanAmericans in poverty:

> Despite income gains which affected most blacks during the decade of the 1960's, a total of 7.7 million blacks still lived in what the census defined as poverty in 1972 [income less than $2,275 for a nonfarm family of four]. Another 2 million were classified near-poor with incomes less than 25 percent above the poverty threshold.... Together, the poor and near-poor represented a staggering 42 percent of all blacks, and blacks were three times as likely to be poor as whites. Black poverty declined in the 1960's but less than whites, so that blacks increased from 25.1 percent of the poor in 1959 to 31.2 percent in 1972.[22]

The data presented by Levitan and others, also demonstrated the underrepresentation of AfricanAmericans in the most prestigious occupations and their overrepresentation in the lower, undesirable categories. They further informed those lauding AfricanAmericans' dramatic shift out of menial jobs that the occupations in which most new jobs opened for AfricanAmericans during the decade were "janitors and sextons."[23] In addition, they presented data which challenged and contradicted the liberal assertions regarding the rapid increase in the number of AfricanAmericans at the upper levels of the federal bureaucracies. AfricanAmericans constituted just 3 percent of those at GS12 level ($17,500/year), only 2.3 percent of those above the GS16 or "supergraders," but 19 percent of the federal workers below grade 6 ($9,000/year).[24] In essence, AfricanAmericans employed by the federal government continue to occupy the same status as those in the private sector: Black workers (slaves) taking orders from White managers (overseers and/or bosses).

The same study's data also contradicted Freeman's observation regarding an emerging exclusive, college-educated and professional middle class. They found that almost half of the Black men earning $10,000 and above were employed in occupations such as operatives, laborers, clerical, or service workers. They further illustrated their point by noting that of the 324,000 Black males who earned more than $10,000 in 1970, "3 percent were engineers, 5 percent were teachers, and 2 percent were physicians or dentists."[25] In a brief explanatory comment on the implications of this phenomenon for studies of the AfricanAmerican middleclass, the authors observed that while these occupations correspond to the more conventional image of success, they found more Black male construction workers than teachers, more mechanics than engineers, and more truck drivers than physicians and dentists: "So far, at least, the emerging Black middleclass is not composed exclusively of a white-collar elite, but of a relatively broad cross-section of well-paid workers in all occupations."[26] While a similar trend might occur in the EuropeanAmerican community, precious few occupation and class analysts would include truck drivers, mechanics, and construction workers in the White middleclass.

In a more recent study designed to test the validity of the conflicting views current in the racial progress controversy, Reynolds Farley empirically documented the persistent economic dialectic characteristic of the AfricanAmerican experience in America. He used several sophisticated statistical techniques to determine the accuracy of the four major arguments regarding AfricanAmerican progress. The first argument tested the assertion that racial progress was occurring rapidly; thus, Blacks are "catching up" with Whites. The second position tested the converse: little racial progress was made in the Seventies. After a rather extensive re-examination of the pertinent census data, Farley summarized his results on these issues as follows:

> On the important indicators — educational attainment of the young, occupations of the employed, and earnings of workers — there is unambiguous evidence that racial differences narrowed in the 1970's just as they did in the 1960's. Despite the clear and substantial improvements, however, racial differences remain. The proportion of young people who are college graduates, for instance, is about twice as great for whites as for blacks and the proportion of black men who now hold white collar jobs is smaller than the comparable proportion of white men 1950.[27]

Farley's re-examination of unemployment rates among African- and EuropeanAmericans indicated little evidence of gains in the relative income of AfricanAmerican families or the proportion impoverished. "Indeed, the number of black poor has grown and the gap which separates the income of the typical black family from that of the typical white family has grown larger."[28]

The third and fourth conflicting arguments focused on the controversial assertion of increased class disparity among AfricanAmericans. As noted, AfricanAmericans achieved great economic gains in the past two decades, and the less-educated and semi-skilled (the William J. Wilson thesis) experienced small or nonexistent gain. Farley's analysis of the census data on the earnings of employed workers found no substantive support for this position:

> Labor market discrimination — as assessed by racial differences in earnings for those who have ostensibly similar characteristics — declined for all groups of blacks. To be certain, the gains were generally larger for young blacks than for older blacks and larger for the highly educated than for those who spent only a few years in school. However, we can be quite certain that in all regions, in all educational groups, in all major industries, and at all age levels, black workers now report earnings which are closer to those of comparable white workers than black workers did in 1970 or 1960. It is misleading, if not erroneous, to state that the recent gains are concentrated among the black elite.[29]

Farley observed the distribution of these gains across socioeconomic levels noting that the racial gap nonetheless remained indicating continued labor market discrimination.

As a final demonstration of the inaccuracy of the theory of increasing class cleavage, Farley argued that the quantitative measures of inequities in the distribution of family income and educational attainment suggest that the so-called "growing gulf" is not occurring: "The array of black families by income has hardly changed and cohorts of young people are now more homogeneous in educational attainment — rather than less — than were previous cohorts."[30]

Farley's study of AfricanAmerican progress concluded on much the same note as the optimists and pessimists discussed above; that is, the more the AfricanAmerican community gains or progresses, the more it declines and deteriorates when compared with Whites. These contradictory processes occur simultaneously, verifying the observation made earlier regarding the political-economic position of Blacks in American society, "the more things change, the more they remain the same" or "the changing same."

Farley's refined application of statistical techniques essentially confirmed the Wattenberg and Scammon thesis although he resisted the temptation to present his results in their optimistic language. The major strength of his study involved the balanced presentation of the results. His failure or, perhaps, inability to present or discuss theoretical models which have attempted to explain or account for this peculiar racial dynamic—for example, the internal or domestic colonial model—revealed his major weakness. Consequently, he implied (or his interpretation of the data suggested) that the root cause of these contradictory socioeconomic trends reside in changes occurring in the structure of the AfricanAmerican family (back yet again to the infamous Moynihan thesis). If more AfricanAmerican families remained intact, that is, monogamous nuclear units, AfricanAmericans would approach socioeconomic parity at a much faster rate. However, AfricanAmerican families are becoming female-headed units at a more rapid rate than Whites, which prevents or impedes upward mobility and socio-economic equality. The previous works of several students of AfricanAmerican family life had already revealed the flaws in this position.

These analyses of the AfricanAmerican "elite" consistently fit the traditional descriptions of this group appearing in the earlier works (of DuBois, Drake and Cayton, and Frazier) presented in the preceding chapters. However, the presence of these sometimes parallel, sometimes contradictory trends emerging out of the literature has created a new intellectual interest in the AfricanAmerican middleclass.

CHAPTER X

CONCLUSION

Although I considered many possible conclusions, I finally decided to end with a summary analysis and discussion of anthropologist Charles Keil's monograph *Urban Blues*. I have said throughout that the future of AfricanAmericans in this country and the world depends upon our becoming increasingly conscious of our culture: the way of life which serves our interests, reflects our sensibility, our spiritual, emotional, intellectual, political-economic "being." Keil's analysis of the concept of "soul" presents many of the cultural values to which I have alluded, values which should serve as the ideological bases for our continuing struggle for freedom. During the struggles of the Sixties, AfricanAmericans shifted the emphasis from one of integrationism to affirmative nationalism (including the desire to create a separate Black state). Keil considered this shift as one which reflected the cultural definition of "soul." He presented several broad assumptions to justify his assertions:

> American society is in the midst of a revolution, and the crisis is forcing basic cultural readjustments on the part of both blacks and whites; the black masses have only very recently been emotionally affected by the current "revolution"; most of those in the ghettoes, though they read or hear about it, have yet to receive any concrete benefits from this revolution; Negro men [and women] are especially disadvantaged, from almost any point of view, and at the very bottom of the American socio-economic heap; the spokesmen for these people—bluesmen, ministers, comedians, disc-jockeys—are much more interested in freedom and self-respect than in integration *per se* and, perhaps because of their vested ethnic interests even a little afraid, consciously or unconsciously, of absorption or disappearance in the white mainstream. If assertions of this sort have validity, then the soul movement readily takes on a strong nativistic and revitalizing tone. The concept of nativism implies...a reaction, an affirmation of the old values in

191

response to new stresses and conflicts. It may well be that the soul movement represents a retrenchment or retreat, corresponding in some respects to what is called the white backlash.... There is this nativistic aspect to soul, and it may be dominant at present; but the related concept of revitalization, with its emphasis on sweeping reform and establishment of a new order based, in part at least, on the old values, is becoming more applicable to the soul movement with every passing day.[1]

As Keil suggests, I am urging AfricanAmericans to look to the past for the cultural responses and resources to fortify ourselves for the protracted struggle required for the resurrection, redemption, and rebirth of AfricanAmerican peoples and cultures.

In discussing AfricanAmerican culture, Keil noted that it reflects the unique reality of Black people:

... a different culture with which to master that reality, and a unique perspective by incongruity on American society that may be this nation's outstanding and redeeming virtue.[2]

However, Keil was not merely content with documenting the presence of AfricanAmerican culture, he also presented an excellent summary of the "gifts" that AfricanAmerican culture can bestow upon its wayward WASP cohabitants in the physical space called America:

The urban Negro male today may be Everyman's tomorrow. He has learned to live with the threat of irrational violence; and we too must develop a life-preserving stance toward the vast, impersonal and constantly growing forces of annihilation that hover over us. He is "fatherless;" and as the pace of our unplanned, unchecked techno-logical "progress" accelerates, our "fathers" can no longer provide adequate models of what it means to be a man either—each succeeding generation will find itself in a radically changed envi-ronment. The Negro is useless and expendable in terms of the economic system. Now we can foresee the day when an elite staff of engineers and laboratory technicians will create and nurse the machines that supply all our material needs while the rest of humanity stands idly by, bored and unproductive. Alternatively, we must learn to entertain each other. The Negro lives in a state of compressed humanity: the ghetto; as the population continues to expand, if not explode, our living space must become similarly constricted. The Negro has had to come to terms somehow with a hostile majority of a different color that surrounds him; we are rapidly coming face to face with the same situation. The Negro in America is learning to combat and solve these problems. The solutions that he finds will perhaps be those the American in the world must borrow for himself, in the not too distant future.[3]

Given the current state of urban America, one must acknowledge that Keil was very visionary. His observations are more accurate today than when he published his study. Yet, he focused on the negative, stress reduction components of AfricanAmerican culture. He apparently thinks that AfricanAmericans are the experts to consult when the rest of the country becomes an impoverished, crime infested ghetto. While I can appreciate the fantastic creativity AfricanAmericans have demonstrated while coping with one of the most vicious political-economic systems known, I do not share his pessimistic forecast for the future of the country or for Black people.

Keil obviously fell in love with the blues creators and the cultural environment which nurtured them. However, he failed to see the political-economic possibilities contained within the cultural values. In so doing, he makes the same mistake that conservative racists social scientists make when studying AfricanAmerican culture. It is clear to the sensitive observer that AfricanAmerican life revolves around strong group support and cooperation. AfricanAmericans like to entertain each other in groups, work together as a group, worship together and call on the "Spirit" as a group. The obvious economic principle within the culture is one which expresses these shared values; communal, cooperative, collective. If and when enlightened EuropeanAmericans can appreciate and internalize these values, viable coalitions can be formed and a movement launched to transform America so that it reflects and affirms the more humane AfricanAmerican cultural values.

The mistake that most observers of the AfricanAmerican community make is that of ignoring the political-economic principles and values embedded in AfricanAmerican culture. One of the reasons some Blacks have found the Marxist socialist vision attractive is that it advocates cooperative economics as well as a just, equitable distribution of the world's wealth. In this sense, Keil was correct when he alluded to the revolutionary dimension of AfricanAmerican culture. The radical change would not or need not be one of EuropeanAmericans learning to maintain their humanity while coping with racist violence, economic violence, and political violence. Rather, from a PanAfrican communalism perspective, EuropeanAmericans must embrace the AfricanAmerican vision for a transformed America as a means to eliminate the conditions culturally and economically strangling both people.

Keil, and other romantic interpreters of AfricanAmerican lowerclass culture and the pathology associated with it, appear to believe that there is something virtuous about living in poverty just because those who survive it create powerful, soothing, self-affirming music and poetry, athletes, dancers, storytellers, ministers, teachers, mothers, fathers, and so forth. The vision of America contained within AfricanAmerican culture is not one grounded in reproducing Black misery but one which allows AfricanAmericans to express their creativity in a friendly, warm, supportive, empowering environment; something Blacks have never experienced in this country. The "gifts" which Keil believes AfricanAmericans could offer America pale in the light of the "gifts" AfricanAmericans will offer once this space we share is renegotiated such that we have an opportunity to pursue our cultural practices and express our values openly, freely. In this sense, Keil is guilty of that famous T.S. Eliot observation, "having an experience but missing the meaning."

The PanAfrican communalism perspective points to the need for sensitive, perceptive analyses of the AfricanAmerican community which move beyond the obvious; which transcend both the social scientific pathological theories as well as the overt pathology of our urban and rural communities. Scholars must ask the essential questions: How have AfricanAmericans survived given the power, sophistication, efficiency, and ruthlessness of the oppression imposed by liberal democratic capitalism? Where did AfricanAmerican people obtain the physical, spiritual, and emotional resources to sustain us in this four hundred years of struggle?

Many of the answers lie in our African derived, rural southern-nurtured cultural heritage. As Lawrence Levine in *Black Culture and Black Consciousness,* John Gwaltney in *Drylongso,* Eugene Genovese in *Roll, Jordan, Roll,* Vincent Harding in *There is a River,* and others have demonstrated, southern AfricanAmericans fashioned the social institutions, behavioral values, norms, expectations, and rituals which form the core of AfricanAmerican culture. That core includes the maintenance in modified form of the African extended family and the values of communal economic and social support associated with it; the Black church which kept the African spiritual practices alive in the "shouting," dancing, singing, speaking-in-tongues worship services;

the African medicinal practices which combined appealing to the Supreme Spirit with the use of herbal remedies; the child rearing practices which reflected the African belief that children are sacred and should be loved, held in adults' arms, objects of family adoration and affection; the African belief that the Supreme Spirit is a part of each individual and can be called upon to work miracles, to transform apparent losses into victories, to "make a way out of no way; and, the rich African tradition of folk tales and stories which contain communally held values and behavioral expectations.

The South was and continues to be PanAfrican in that AfricanAmericans are biological and cultural mixtures of all the African peoples transported to these United States. The unique, distinct life-styles associated with Blacks in America is an African legacy and "gift" to this country. Wade Nobles' summary description of the roots of AfricanAmerican family values highlights the aforementioned cultural attributes:

> In families functioning in accordance with the African world view, a totally different emphasis on self-identity is found.... Here the orientation is to conceive of the self as coming into being as a consequence of the group's being. In African (Black) families, self-conception is created by instilling in its members the principle: *I* am because *we* are and because *we* are, therefore, *I* am.... In so doing, the Black family unit psychologically sets its members to perceive no real distinction between the personal self and other members of the family. They are, in a sense, one and the same. One's being is the group's or family's being. One's self is the "self of one's people." One's being is the "we" instead of the "I." One's self-identity is, therefore, always a people identity or what could be called an *extended identity* or extended self.[4]

I contend that this cultural orientation constitutes *the* source of AfricanAmericans' survival and prosperity (for some) in the midst of domestic neocolonial *ethcaste* oppression. In addition, this orientation remains just as "alive" in certain segments of the *ethcaste* elite as it is amongst the rural southern plantation dwellers. Therefore, for any segment of the so-called Black middleclass to misuse this orientation for its personal or collective economic aggrandizement at the expense of its less fortunate brothers and sisters represents the quintessential success of WASP liberalism and reflects a form of Black capitalism on the top that degrades and denies the organized group life among the lower- and underclasses.

The other central source of AfricanAmerican resilience lies in its peculiar, distinct, Christianity or African-centered religion. For African Americans, especially the Pentecostal, "shouting" Baptists, and Methodists, God is not as an external, remote, spiritual Being Whom the believer can only "know" that he or she "pleases" through the successful acquisition of material wealth (*à la* Weber's "Protestant ethic"). On the contrary, for AfricanAmerican Christians, God is a living Being. S/He lives within us and we feel H/er presence through the power of the Holy Ghost. (Shouting!! 'Cause you feel so *good*!!) S/He is a God of the righteous, those who treat fellow Christian brothers as family (brothers and sisters)—again reinforcing the notion of the African extended self.

Consequently, when AfricanAmerican church folk say that they need to go into a quiet, solitary "spot" and "have a little talk with Jesus," they express their belief in the Supreme Being's power of protection, redemption, transcendence over earthly problems and situations, including EuropeanAmerican capitalism and racism. The fact that AfricanAmerican Christians' churches continue to provide for the physical, emotional, and spiritual needs of their members is often lost in the academic debates on Black religion as an "opiate" to its constituency. Black religion is a far better opiate to its followers than Valium, Prozac, alcohol, "speed," "crack," heroin, wife-swapping, family psychiatrist or any other drug and/or emotional support practitioners.

As the masses of AfricanAmericans move to create their vision of America (cultural pluralism with a communalist economic base), the AfricanAmerican middleclass and elite must decide to whom and what they will commit themselves. While I would like to assert optimistically that they have only one "true" choice, I am cynical enough to recognize that they see many alternatives, with the number increasing almost daily. If and when the culturally, politically conscious AfricanAmerican freedom fighters move to take America to "higher ground," these "liberal" Blacks will be perceived as the enemy; their enemy status manifested in their lack of commitment to and comprehension of AfricanAmerican culture.

Many will challenge this model due to its emphasis on cultural struggle and conflict because it appears to place less importance or significance on the economic dimension. I have chosen not to place economics in the forefront of this argument because I believe the problems confronting AfricanAmericans in the United States and the Diaspora cannot be confined merely to economics. We have no economic problems beyond solution. And the ones we have stem from our status as a domestic neocolonial caste. Further, an increase in jobs, money, and economic development will not necessarily improve our situation. One thing we have learned from the plight of the dominant group's working- and middleclasses is that more jobs, more money, and more fringe benefits do not alter fundamental class relations or positions; they merely perpetuate the *illusion* of change, while continuing inflation and continually increasing taxes nullify and negate the highly-publicized economic "progress."

In addition, constant economic expansion and technological acceleration are destroying America's (and the world's) natural resources at an ever-increasing rate and imperil the future for our children. So, we do not need only economic development. We need economic *control*; that is, we must struggle along with other progressive forces to gain control over the exploitive economic institutions of the international capitalist cultural elite. Realizing at all times, to paraphrase Brother Malcolm X, that we have no permanent friends and no permanent enemies; just permanent interests, we must gain greater control over as well as transform the institutions and individuals impinging upon, constraining, and determining our lives.

In initiating a new stage of struggle, we must be guided by imperatives generic to our cultural values and heritage. Needless to say, this sociocultural vision and political-economic alternative must be anti-materialistic, anti-individualistic, anti-militaristic, anti-capitalistic, and anti-sexist. It must emphasize the need for all people to become culturally aware and secure, thus able to appreciate cultural and racial differences. It would emphasize the need for greater spirituality and morality in the affairs of humans. As a people with a cultural heritage rich in these values, AfricanAmericans have much to contribute to the humanization of a society currently led by an elite that is increasingly spiritually bankrupt, amoral, and suicidal.

One of the major themes of several national AfricanAmerican conferences has been the fact that AfricanAmericans have never been motivated to act, to struggle out of mere economic necessity. If one analyzes the Civil Rights Movement, one will see that Blacks — especially Southern AfricanAmericans—were risking their lives for human dignity and racial/cultural integrity, not *just* economic democracy. Indeed the coupling of economic parity along with equal justice and true democracy is often cited as the cause for Dr. King's assassination as he worked to organize the Poor People's campaign and assist the Memphis garbage workers in their efforts to acquire higher wages and better working conditions.

Clearly this next round of struggle must be grounded in the need for an alternative economic system which meets the economic needs of AfricanAmericans and other people of color both domestically and internationally. However, in order to launch and sustain this most dangerous political initiative, the spirit of the Southern Movement must be revitalized and invoked in order to attain what Billingsley has termed "AfricanAmerican peoplehood": collective sharing, sacrifice, worship, suffering, and determination. That this spiritually-inspired and moral movement derived its strength, resilience, energy, and commitment from the AfricanAmerican church in particular and AfricanAmerican spirituality generally is testimony to the roles these institutions and practices play in our cultural life.

The Civil Rights movement seriously challenged the cultural values and practices of mainstream America and, in part, succeeded in modifying them. However, the struggle is far from over. AfricanAmericans must again reach into this rich cultural reservoir and initiate a new movement in our persistent efforts to create a new America: an America which accepts and appreciates its multicultural constituency while altering its economic system to function in the interests and needs of the masses of both America and the world as opposed to the accumulation of profits by the capitalist elite. AfricanAmericans and other *ethcaste* groups have no choice in the pursuit of these objectives, unless one considers gradual death to be superior to instant death. In either case, the end result is the same.

The challenge confronting AfricanAmericans of all classes and ethnic origins is summarized eloquently (and spiritually) in the following song/poem by Gil Scott-Heron, Brian Jackson and the Midnight Band entitled "Western Sunrise":

> *The world is dark, we look to the horizon;*
> *reflections of the sunset yesterday*
> *Man is in a state of loss, subjected to an evil force.*
> *It hurt so bad the sun has to stopped to pray.*
> *An old man in another land is crying,*
> *to see his soul reborn in misery:*

Where wrong is made to seem all right,
where peaceful man is forced to fight.
Where mirrors are the source of light to see
a sunrise in the Western sky: Good Morning!
A miracle before your eyes unfurls.
A sunrise in the western skies, the seventh angel
loudly cries and we begin to visualize new worlds.
Sunrise in the rain.
Sunrise in the rain.[5]

AfricanAmericans and those who share this vision must initiate a "western sunrise" if we are ever to realize our full humanity. America must welcome this "western sunrise" if it is to survive.

ONE LOVE

CHAPTER NOTES

NOTES FOR CHAPTER I

The Problem

1. Nathan Hare, "What Black Intellectuals Misunderstand About the Black Family," *Black World*, vol. 25 (March, 1976), pp. 4–15. See also Robert Hill, *The Strengths of Black Families*, (New York: Emerson Hall Publishers, 1972); Andrew Billingsley, *Black Families in White America*, (Englewood Cliffs, NJ: Prentice-Hall, 1968); Harriette P. McAdoo (ed.), *Black Families*, (Beverly Hills, CA: Sage Publications, 1981); Joyce Ladner, *The Death of White Sociology*, (New York: Random House, 1973); and Robert Staples, *The Black Family: Essays and Studies*, (Belmont, CA: Wadsworth, 1971).
2. William J. Wilson, *Power, Racism, and Privilege: Race Relations in Theoretical and Socio-Historical Perspectives* (Glencoe, IL: Free Press, 1976); Talcott Parsons, *The Social System*, (New York: Free Press, 1964).
3. Mina Davis Caulfield, "Culture and Imperialism: Proposing a New Dialectic," in *Reinventing Anthropology*, Dell Hymes (ed.) (New York: Random House, 1969), pp. 197–198.
4. Melville Herskovits, *The Myth of the Negro Past*, (Boston: Beacon Press, 1958).
5. John F. Szwed, "An Anthropological Dilemma: The Politics of Afro-American Culture," in *Reinventing Anthropology*, p. 158.
6. Mina Caulfield, "Culture and Imperialism: Proposing a New Dialectic," p. 189.
7. Ibid., p. 193.
8. John F. Szwed, Op. cit., p. 160. ("An American Anthropological

Dilemma: The Politics of Afro-American Culture.")

9. Lee Rainwater (ed.), *Soul*, (Chicago: Aldine Publishing Co., 1970); Elliot Liebow, *Tally's Corner: A Study of Negro Streetcorner Men*, (Boston: Little, Brown, 1967); and Kenneth Clark, *Dark Ghetto: Dilemmas of Social Power*, (New York: Harper and Row, 1965).

10. John F. Szwed, "An American Anthropological Dilemma ...," p. 166.

11. W. E. B. DuBois, *The Philadelphia Negro: A Social Study*, (New York: Schocken Books,1968); E. F. Frazier, "Durham: Capital of the Black Middle Class," in *The New Negro*, Alain Locke (ed.), (New York: Arno Press, 1968); W. E. B. DuBois, *Some Efforts of the American Negroes for Their Own Betterment*, (Atlanta, GA: Atlanta University Press, 1898); St. Clair Drake and Horace Cayton, *Black Metropolis*, (New York: Harcourt, Brace, and Jovanovich, 1970); Gunnar Myrdal, *An American Dilemma: The Negro Problem in Modern Democracy*, (New York: Harper, 1944); William Muraskin, *Middle-Class Blacks in White Society*, (Berkeley: University of California Press, 1975); John Scanzoni, *The Black Family in Modern Society*, (Boston: Allyn and Bacon, 1971); and Sidney Kronus, *The Black Middle Class*, (Columbus, OH: Charles Merrill, 1971).

12. Max Weber, *The Protestant Ethic and the Spirit of Capitalism*, (New York: Charles Scribner's Sons, 1958).

NOTES FOR CHAPTER II

Analysis of Controversial Issues Surrounding The Black Ethcaste Elite

1. Robert Blauner, *Racial Oppression in America*, (New York: Harper and Row, 1972); *Alienation and Freedom: The Factory Worker and His Industry*, (Chicago: University of Chicago Press, 1964).

2. Charles Valentine, "Deficit, Difference, and Bicultural Models of Afro-American Behavior," *Harvard Educational Review*, vol. 41 (May, 1971), p. 140.

3. Harold Cruse, *The Crisis of the Negro Intellectual*, (New York: William Morrow, 1967).

4. Jesse Bernard, *Marriage and Family Among Negroes*, (Englewood Cliffs, NJ: Prentice-Hall, 1966); St. Clair Drake and Horace Cayton,

Black Metropolis, (New York: Harcourt, Brace, and Jovanovich, 1970); W. E. B. DuBois, *The Philadelphia Negro: A Social Study* (New York: Schocken Books, 1968, reprint of 1899 edition).

5. St. Clair Drake and Horace Cayton, *Black Metropolis*.

6. Herbert Blumer, *Symbolic Interactionism: Perspective and Method*, (Englewood Cliffs, NJ: Prentice-Hall, 1969).

7. August Meier and David Lewis, "History of the Negro Upper-Class in Atlanta, Georgia, 1890-1958," *Journal of Negro Education*, vol. 28 (Spring, 1959), pp. 128-139.

8. Meier, "Negro Class Structure and Ideology in the Age of Booker T. Washington," *Phylon*, vol. 23 (Fall, 1962), p. 266.

9. Harold Cruse, *The Crisis of the Negro Intellectual*.

10. Oliver Cox, "The Leadership of Booker T. Washington," *Social Forces*, vol. 30 (October, 1951), p. 93.

11. E. Franklin Frazier, *Black Bourgeoisie: The Rise of a New Middle Class in the United States*, (New York: Macmillan, 1962).

12. E. F. Frazier, "Durham: Capital of the Black Middle Class," in *The New Negro*, Alain Locke (ed.), (New York: Arno Press, 1968).

13. E. F. Frazier, "The Negro Community, A Cultural Phenomenon," Social Forces, vol. 7 (March, 1929), pp. 415-420; *The Negro Family in the United States, 1894-1962*, (Chicago: University of Chicago Press, 1966).

14. Melville Herskovits, *The Myth of the Negro Past*, (Boston: Beacon Press, 1958).

15. William A. Muraskin, *Middle-Class Blacks in White Society*, (Berkeley: University of California Press, 1975), p. 5.

16. C. Wright Mills, *The Power Elite*, (New York: Oxford University Press, 1956).

17. *Ibid.*, p. 59.

18. Muraskin, *Op. cit.*, p. 66.

19. Albert Memmi, *The Colonizer and the Colonized*, (New York: The Orion Press, 1975).

20. *Ibid.*, pp. 83-84.

21. C. J. Mumford, "Social Structure and Black Revolution," *Black Scholar*, vol. 4 (November-December, 1972), pp. 11-23.

22. Robert Allen, *Black Awakening in Capitalist America*, (Garden City, NY: Doubleday, 1969).

23. Martin Kilson, "Black Politics: A New Power," *Dissent*, vol. 18 (August, 1971), pp. 333-345.

24. Will D. Tate, *The New Black Urban Elite*, (San Francisco: R and D Research Associates, 1976).
25. Robert Staples, *Introduction to Black Sociology*, (New York: McGraw-Hill, 1976).
26. Eugene Genovese, *Roll, Jordan, Roll: The World the Slaves the Made*, (New York: Pantheon Books, 1974); John Blassingame, *The Slave Community: Plantation Life in the Antebellum South*, (New York: Oxford University Press, 1972).
27. Carol Stack, *All Our Kin: Strategies for Survival in a Black Community*, (New York: Harper and Row, 1974).
28. Robert Hill, *The Strengths of Black Families*, (New York: Emerson Hall Publishers, 1972); Andrew Billingsley, Black Families in White America, (Englewood Cliffs, NJ: Prentice-Hall, 1968); Harriette McAdoo (ed.), *Black Families*, (Beverly Hills, CA: Sage Publications, 1981).
29. E. F. Frazier, "The Negro Middle-Class and Desegregation," *Social Forces*, vol. 4 (April, 1957), p. 301.

NOTES FOR CHAPTER III

Critical Review of Selected Sociological Class Theories 1: Karl Marx and Racial Cultural Struggle

1. Harold Cruse, *The Crisis of the Negro Intellectual*, (New York: William Morrow, 1967).
2. Herbert Blumer, *Symbolic Interactionism: Perspective and Method*, (Englewood Cliffs, NJ: Prentice-Hall, 1969).
3. See Charles Anderson, *The Political Economy of Social Classes*, (Englewood Cliffs, NJ.: Prentice-Hall, 1974).
4. Richard Lichtman, "Symbolic Interactionism and Social Reality: Some Marxist Queries," *Berkeley Journal of Sociology*, vol. 15 (1970), pp. 76-77.
5. Marvin Harris, *The Rise of Anthropological Theory*, (New York: Thomas Crowell Co., 1968).
6. *Ibid.*, p. 64.
7. *Ibid.*, p. 97.
8. Robert Blauner, "Marxist Theory, Nationality, and Colonialism,"

(unpublished paper at the time of this writing).

9. *Ibid.*, p. 1.

10. Charles Anderson, *The Political Economy of Social Classes.*

11. *Ibid.*, p. 42.

12. *Ibid.*, p. 43.

13. George Orwell, *Down and Out in Paris and London*, (New York: Harper, 1933).

14. Robert Blauner, *Alienation and Freedom: The Factory Worker and His Industry*, (Chicago: University of Chicago Press, 1964).

15. Lloyd Hogan, *The Principles of Black Political Economy*, (Boston: Routledge and Kegan Paul, 1977).

16. Charles Anderson, *The Political Economy of Social Classes*, p. 56.

17. *Ibid.*, p. 52.

18. *Ibid.*, p. 57.

19. *Ibid.*, p. 60.

20. Peter Schrag, *The Decline of the WASP*, (New York: Simon and Schuster, 1971).

21. Lewis Corey, "The Middle Class," in *Class, Status, and Power*, Reinhard Bendix and Seymour M. Lipset (eds.), (Glencoe, IL: The Free Press, 1953), p. 380.

NOTES FOR CHAPTER IV

Critical Review of Selected Sociological Class Theories 2: Max Weber

1. This review will include an analysis of several of Weber's primary writings as well as secondary works written by acclaimed theoreticians, such as: H.H. Gerth and C. Wright Mills (editors and translators), *From Max Weber: Essays in Sociology*, (New York: Oxford University Press, 1946); Max Weber, *The Protestant Ethic and the Spirit of Capitalism*, (New York: Charles Scribner's Sons, 1958); Robert W. Green (ed.), *Protestantism and Capitalism*, (New York: D. C. Heath and Co., 1959); Reinhard Bendix and Seymour M. Lipset, *Class, Status, and Power*, (New York: The Free Press, 1966), see especially Part I, "Theories of Class Structure."

2. Hans Gerth and C. Wright Mills, *From Max Weber: Essays in Sociology.*

3. Régis Debray, *Revolution in the Revolution*, (New York: Grove Press, 1967).

4. Weber, *The Protestant Ethic and the Spirit of Capitalism*.

5. William A. Muraskin, *Middle Class Blacks in White Society*, (Berkeley: University of California Press, 1975).

6. Harold Cruse, *Crisis of the Negro Intellectual*, (New York: William Morrow, 1967).

7. Charles Anderson, *The Political Economy of Social Classes*, (Englewood Cliffs, NJ: Prentice-Hall, 1974).

8. Anthony Giddens, *Class Structure of Advanced Societies*, (New York: Harper and Row, 1973).

9. Weber, "Class, Status, and Party," in R. Bendix and S. M. Lipset (eds.), *Class, Status, and Power*, p. 21.

10. Weber, "Class, Status, and Party," in H. Gerth and C. W. Mills (eds.), *Max Weber: Essays in Sociology*, pp. 180-195.

11. Lewis Coser, *The Functions of Social Conflict*, (Glencoe, Ill.: The Free Press, 1956).

12. Robert Nisbet, *Sociology as an Art Form*, (New York: Oxford University Press, 1976), p. 113.

13. Robert Blauner, "Marxist Theory, Nationality and Colonialism," (unpublished paper at time of writing), p. 10.

14. Milton Gordon, *Social Class in American Sociology*, (Durham, NC.: Duke University Press, 1968).

15. Anderson, *The Political Economy of Social Classes*, p. 121.

16. Ralf Dahrendorf, *Class and Class Conflict in Industrial Society*, (Stanford, CA: Stanford University Press, 1969).

17. This school of thought is represented by the following works: David Reisman, *The Lonely Crowd*, (New York: Doubleday, 1953); Robert Dahl, *Who Governs*, (New Haven: Yale University Press, 1961); David Truman, *The Government Process: Political Interest and Public Opinion*, (New York: Knopf, 1951); Edward Banfield, *The Unheavenly City: The Nature and the Future of Our Urban Crisis*, (Boston: Little Brown, 1970).

18. Representative works of the elite school of thought include: C.W. Mills, *The Power Elite*, (New York: Oxford University Press, 1966); Floyd Hunter, *Community Power Structure*, (Chapel Hill, NC.: University of North Carolina Press, 1953); Robert S. and Helen M. Lynd, *Middletown*, (New York: Harcourt Brace, 1929); G. William Domhoff, *Who Rules America*, (Englewood Cliffs, NJ.: Prentice-

Hall, 1967).

19. Charles H. Page, "Social Class and American Sociology," in R. Bendix and S. M. Lipset (eds), *Class, Status, and Power*, pp. 45-48.

20. Thorsten Veblen, *The Theory of the Leisure Class*, (New York: Huebsch, 1919).

21. C. W. Mills, *White Collar*, (New York: Oxford University Press, 1951).

22. William Kornhauser, *The Politics of Mass Society*, (Glencoe, IL: The Free Press, 1969).

NOTES FOR CHAPTER V

American Sociological Class Theory and Democratic Capitalist Culture

1. Abdul Alkalimat (a.k.a. Gerald McWorter), "The Ideology of Black Social Science," *The Black Scholar*, vol. 1, (1968), pp. 28-35.

2. Howard Jensen, "Introduction," to Milton Gordon's (ed.), *Social Class in American Sociology*, (Durham, NC: Duke University Press, 1968), p. 58.

3. Floyd House, *The Development of Sociology*, (New York: McGraw-Hill, 1936).

4. Thomas F. Gossett, *Race: The History of an Idea in America*, (New York: Schocken Books, 1963), p. 174.

5. House, *The Development of Sociology*, p. 231.

6. Thomas F. Gossett, *Race: The History of an Idea in America*, p. 175.

7. Jensen, "Introduction," to Milton Gordon's (ed.) *Social Class in American Sociology*, pp. iv, 3, 4.

8. *Ibid.*, p. v.

9. Ruth Kornhauser, "The Warner Approach to Social Stratification," in R. Bendix and S.M. Lipset (eds.), *Class, Status, and Power*, p. 226.

10. *Ibid.*.

11. Gordon (ed.), *Social Class in American Sociology*, pp. 121-122.

12. Walter Goldschmidt, "Social Class in America," *American Anthropologist*, vol. 52 (1960), p. 486.

13. *Ibid.*, pp. 487-488.

14. Kurt Mayer, "The Theory of Social Classes," *Harvard Educational Review*, vol. 23 (Summer, 1963), p. 158.

15. Kingsley Davis and Wilbert Moore, "Some Principles of Stratification," in *Class, Status, and Power*, p. 48.
16. *Ibid.*, p.48.
17. *Ibid.*, p.49.
18. *Ibid.*
19. Robert Nisbet, "The Decline and Fall of Social Class," *Pacific Sociological Review*, (Spring, 1958), p. 11.
20. Arnold Rose, "The Concept of Class and American Sociology," *Social Research*, vol. 25 (Spring, 1958), pp. 53-69.
21. *Ibid.*.
22. Talcott Parsons, "Equality and Inequality in Modern Society, or Social Stratification Revisited." *Sociological Inquiry*, vol. 40 (Spring, 1970), p. 14.
23. *Ibid.*, p. 18.
24. *Ibid.*, p. 21.
25. *Ibid.*, p. 21.
26. Anderson, *The Political Economy of Social Classes*.
27. Talcott Parsons, "Equality and Inequality in Modern Society...," *Sociological Inquiry*, vol. 40, p. 24.
28. Gordon, *Social Class in American Sociology*, p. 236.
29. *Ibid.*, p. 249.
30. Excellent discussions of this school can be found in Milton Gordon's *Social Class in American Sociology* and Charles Anderson's *The Political Economy of Social Classes*.
31. C. W. Mills, *The Sociological Imagination*, (New York: Oxford University Press, 1959), p. 20.
32. Gordon, *Social Class in American Sociology*, p. 17.
33. Kurt Mayer, "The Theory of Social Classes," *Harvard Educational Review*, vol. 23, pp. 152-153.
34. Thorsten Veblen was the author of several articles and books critical of American institutions. Among them were *Vested Interests and the Common Man*, (New York: Capricorn Books, 1969); *The Higher Learning in America*, (New York: Augustus M. Kelley Publishers, 1918); and *Theory of the Leisure Class*, (New York: Funk and Wagnalls, 1967).
35. Arnold Rose, "The Concept of Class and American Sociology," *Social Research*, vol. 25, p. 63.
36. Mills' noted works include *The Power Elite*, (New York: Oxford University Press, 1956); *White Collar*, (New York: Oxford Univer-

sity Press, 1951); and *The Sociological Imagination*, (New York: Oxford University Press, 1959).

37. E. Digby Baltzell, *The Protestant Establishment: Aristocracy and Caste in America*, (New York: Random House, 1964).

38. Floyd Hunter, *Community Power Structure*, (Chapel Hill, NC: University of North Carolina Press, 1953).

39. Although Veblen and Mills never identified themselves explicitly as Marxists, I would agree with Floyd House's position that in a broad classification, they could be placed in the Marxian tradition vis-a-vis their critical dissection of American culture. See House's *The Development of Sociology*.

40. Robert S. and Helen M. Lynd, *Middletown*, (New York: Harcourt, Brace and Jovanovich, 1959).

41. Robert Presthus, *Men at the Top: A Study in Community Power*, (New York: Oxford University Press, 1964).

42. G. William Domhoff, *Who Rules America?*, (Englewood Cliffs, NJ: Prentice-Hall, 1967).

43. Prominent works on this current era include Daniel Bell's *The End of Ideology*, (Glencoe, IL.: Free Press, 1960); Ralf Dahrendorf's *Class and Class Conflict in Industrial Society*, (Stanford, CA: Stanford University Press, 1969); and William J. Wilson's *The Declining Significance of Race*, (Chicago: University of Chicago Press, 1978).

NOTES FOR CHAPTER VI

Class, Caste, and Race: Toward An Alternative Perspective

1. Thomas Gossett, *Race: The History of an Idea in America*, (New York: Schocken Books, 1965).

2. The description of southern culture as an example of new world European feudalism is found in Gunnar Myrdal's *An American Dilemma: The Negro Problem and Modern Democracy*, (New York: Harper and Bros., 1944); Eugene Genovese's *The Political Economy of Slavery*, (New York: Pantheon Books, 1965), and *Roll, Jordan, Roll: The World the Slaves Made*, (New York: Pantheon Books, 1974).

3. Max Weber, "Class, Status, and Party," in R. Bendix and S. M. Lipset

(eds.), *Class, Status, and Power*, (New York: Free Press, 1966), p. 25.

4. Arnold Rose, "The Concept of Class in American Sociology," *Social Research*, vol. 25 (Spring, 1958), p. 64.

5. W. Lloyd Warner and Paul Lunt, *The Social Life of a Modern Community*, (New Haven: Yale University Press, 1942); and Warner, et. al., *Social Class in America*, (Chicago: Science Research Associates, 1949).

6. Milton Gordon, *Social Class in American Sociology*, (Durham, NC: Duke University Press, 1958), p. 119.

7. Gunnar Myrdal, *An American Dilemma*, (cited above).

8. Robert Park, *Race and Culture*, (Glencoe, IL.: Free Press, 1950), and R. E. Park and Ernest Burgess, *The City*, (Chicago: University of Chicago Press, 1925); E. F. Frazier, *The Negro Family in the United States, 1894-1962*, (Chicago: University of Chicago Press, 1966); Charles Johnson, *The Shadow of the Plantation*, (Chicago: University of Chicago Press, 1934); St. Clair Drake and Horace Cayton, *Black Metropolis*, (New York: Harcourt, Brace, Jovanovich, 1970).

9. Gunnar Myrdal, *An American Dilemma*.

10. Oliver Cox, "Race and Caste: A Distinction," *American Journal of Sociology*, vol. 50 (March, 1945), p. 360.

11. *Ibid.*, p. 360.

12. *Ibid.*, p. 360.

13. *Ibid.*, pp. 360-361.

14. His classic work on these topics remains essential reading for those interested in this subject area: *Caste, Class, and Race*, (New York: Monthly Review Press, 1959).

15. Frantz Fanon, *Black Skin, White Masks*, (New York: Grove Press, 1967); *The Wretched of the Earth*, (New York: Grove Press, 1966).

16. Cox's position on caste is even more ambiguous and confusing when one reads his excellent analysis of lynching and his perceptive, provocative critique of Nathan Hare's *Black Anglo-Saxons*, (New York: Marzani and Munsell, 1965). Thus, his analysis of concrete situations appears to contradict his theoretical framework. His work reflects an inner tension between his Marxian-oriented tendencies and his racial (or almost nationalistic) interpretations of certain phenomena.

17. Gerald Berreman, "Caste in India and the United States," *American Journal of Sociology*, vol. 66 (September, 1960), p. 122.

18. Herbert Blumer, "Race Relations as a Sense of Group Position," *Pacific Sociological Review*, vol. 1, (1958), pp. 3-7.
19. Lucio Mendieta y Nunez, "The Social Classes," *American Sociological Review*, vol. 11 (April, 1946), p. 170.
20. *Ibid.*, p. 172.
21. *Ibid.*.
22. *Ibid.*, p. 173.
23. *Ibid.*, p. 175.
24. Harold Cruse, *The Crisis of the Negro Intellectual*, (New York: William Morrow, 1967); James and Grace L. Boggs, *Racism and Class Struggle*, (New York: Monthly Review Press, 1970); C. W. Mills, *Power, Politics, and People*, (New York: Oxford University Press, 1963).
25. Cruse, *Ibid.*; Mills, *Ibid.*; and Charles Anderson, *The Political Economy of Social Classes*, (Englewood Cliffs, NJ: Prentice-Hall, 1974).
26. W. E. B. DuBois, *The Philadelphia Negro*, (New York: Schocken Books, 1967), p. 317. (book originally published in 1899)
27. Immanuel Wallerstein, "The Rise and Future Demise of the World Capitalist System: Concepts for Comparative Analysis," *Comparative Studies in Society and History*, vol. 16 (September, 1974), pp. 387-415; and *The Modern World System: Capitalist Agriculture and the Origins of the European World Economy in the Sixteenth Century*, (New York: Academic Press, 1974).

NOTES FOR CHAPTER VII

Internal Colonialism and Black Culture — The PanAfrican Continuum

1. Robert Blauner, "Internal Colonialism and Ghetto Revolt," *Social Problems*, vol. 16 (Spring, 1969), pp. 393–408.
2. Milton Gordon, *Assimilation in American Life: The Role of Race, Religion, and National Origins*, (New York: Oxford University Press, 1964).
3. Charles Hamilton and Stokely Carmichael, *Black Power*, (New York: Random House, 1967).
4. Robert Staples, "Race and Colonialism: The Domestic Case in

Theory and Practice," *The Black Scholar*, vol. 7 (June, 1976), pp. 37–38.

5. James Turner and W. Eric Perkins, "Toward a Critique of Social Science," *The Black Scholar*, vol. 7 (April, 1976), pp. 2–11. Several other AfricanAmerican scholars have engaged in debate on these questions and issues including Mack H. Jones, "Scientific Methods as a Tool for Improving the Quality of Value Judgments with Particular Concern for the Black Predicament in the United States," *Review of Black Political Economy*, vol. 7 (Fall, 1976), pp. 7–21; William Strickland, "Black Intellectuals and the American Scene," *Black World*, vol. 25 (November, 1975); Harold Cruse, *The Crisis of the Negro Intellectual*, (New York: William Morrow, 1967).

6. Chinweizu, *The West and the Rest of Us*, (New York: Random House, 1975).

7. E. Franklin Frazier, *Race and Cultural Contacts in the Modern World*, (Boston: Beacon Press, 1965).

8. Immanuel Wallerstein, "American Slavery and the Capitalist World Economy," *American Journal of Sociology*, vol. 81 (March, 1976), pp. 1199–1213. The article is a review and critique of the works of Genovese, and Fogel and Engerman, three authors whose studies and writing also grapples with these questions.

9. William J. Wilson, *Power, Racism, and Privilege: Race Relations in Theoretical and Socio-Historical Perspectives*, (New York: Free Press, 1973).

10. Sydney Mintz, "Macro-Batics: A Review Essay on Wallerstein's *The Modern World System*,"(unpublished paper at the time of this writing).

11. Robert Blauner, "Black Culture," in his *Racial Oppression in America*, (New York: Harper and Row, 1972).

12. Douglas V. Davidson, "Black Culture and Liberal Sociology," *Berkeley Journal of Sociology*, vol. 6 (Summer, 1969), pp. 420–437.

13. Robert Blauner, *Racial Oppression in America*, p. 135.

14. John Henrik Clarke's essay on his search for identity reveals in a very sensitive and moving manner the consequences of this denial. See "A Search for Identity," *Social Casework*, vol. 51 (May, 1970), pp. 259–264. Also, the popularity of Alex Haley's literary account of his "roots" reflects the extent to which AfricanAmericans are interested in acquiring greater knowledge of their past and how we got to be where we are presently. See *Roots*, (New York: Doubleday, 1976).

15. Lucile Duberman, *Social Inequality: Class and Caste in America*, (Philadelphia: Lippincott, 1976).
16. James A. Geschwender, *Racial Stratification in America*, (New York: William C. Brown, 1978).
17. It could be argued that AsianAmericans (Japanese-, Chinese-, and KoreanAmericans) are exceptions to this phenomenon in that they are not perceived as cultureless: *they are perceived as being both racially and culturally different.* Race, in this context, can be analytically distinguished from ethnicity. While this distinction may be useful in certain analytical contexts, it does not alter the thesis that *African-Americans are perceived as just a race* in the popular mind (and much of the social scientific literature).
18. Sydney W. Mintz and Richard Price, *An Anthropological Approach to the Afro-American Past: A Caribbean Perspective*, (Philadelphia: Institute for the Study of Human Issues, 1976), p. 1.
19. *Ibid.*, p. 3.
20. *Ibid.*, p. 4.
21. *Ibid.*, p. 5.
22. *Ibid.*, p. 5.
23. *Ibid.*, p. 6.
24. *Ibid.*, pp. 13.
25. *Ibid.*, pp. 16.
26. Eugene Genovese, *Roll, Jordan, Roll: The World the Slaves Made*, (New York: Random House, 1972), p. 3.
27. *Ibid.*, p. 4.
28. *Ibid.*, p. 5.
29. *Ibid.*, p. 5.
30. Alex Haley's description of this process in *Roots* is the result of extensive research which supports this thesis. (Haley was a part of African-American research group conducting studies of African history and culture). Also Walter Rodney"s *How Europe Underdeveloped Africa*, (Washington, DC: Howard University Press, 1974) and W. E. B. DuBois' *The World and Africa*, (New York: International Publishers, 1965) document this practice.
31. Sydney Mintz and Richard Price, *An Anthropological Approach to the Afro-American Past...*, p. 16.
32. See, for example, Norm Whitten and John Szwed (eds.), *Afro-American Anthropology*, (New York: Free Press, 1971); Rhoda Goldstein (ed.), *Black Life and Culture in the United States*, (New

York: Thomas Y. Crowell, 1971); J. L. Dillard, *Black English: Its History and Usage in the United States*, (New York: Random House, 1972); Andrew Billingsley, *Black Families in White America*, (Englewood Cliffs, NJ: Prentice-Hall, 1968); Lawrence Levine, *Black Culture and Black Consciousness*, (New York: Oxford University Press, 1977); Wade W. Nobles, "African Root and American Fruit: The Black Family," *Journal of Social and Behavioral Sciences*, (Spring, 1974) pp. 53–64.

33. Will Herberg, *Protestant, Catholic, Jew: An Essay in American Religious Sociology*, (Garden City, NY: Anchor Books, 1960).
34. Milton Gordon, *Assimilation in American Life: The Role of Race, Religion, and National Origins*.
35. Sydney Mintz and Richard Price, *An Anthropological Approach to the Afro-American Past*, p. 26.
36. Wade W. Nobles, "African Root and American Fruit," *Journal of Social and Behavioral Sciences*.
37. *Ibid.*, pp. 54–55.
38. Sydney Mintz and Richard Price, *An Anthropological Approach to the Afro-American Past*, pp. 34–35.

NOTES FOR CHAPTER VIII

Ethcaste and Sociocultural Diversity among the Black Middleclass

1. Milton Gordon, *Assimilation in American Life: The Role of Race, Religion, and National Origins*, (New York: Oxford University Press, 1964).
2. James A. Geschwender, *Racial Stratification in America*, (New York: William C. Brown, 1978).
3. William J. Wilson, *The Declining Significance of Race*, (Chicago: University of Chicago Press, 1978).
4. Joseph Bensman and Arthur Vidich, *The New American Society: The Revolution of the Middle Class*, (Chicago: Quadrangle Books, 1971).
5. *Ibid.*, p. 29.
6. *Ibid.*, p. 120.
7. *Ibid.*, p. 228.
8. *Ibid.*, p. 235.

9. Michael Thelwell, writer and professor of literature in the W. E. B. DuBois Department of Afro-American Studies, University of Massachusetts, Amherst in a personal conversation.

10. William Strickland, "The Rise and Fall of Black Political Culture: Or How Blacks Became a Minority," *Monthly Report*, (May/June, 1979), (Atlanta: The Institute of the Black World).

11. Douglas V. Davidson, "Reflections on the Myth of Busing for 'Quality' Integrated Education," *Annual Report*, (October, 1974), (Atlanta: The Institute of the Black World).

12. W. E. B. DuBois, *The Philadelphia Negro: A Social Study*, (New York: Schocken Books, 1968). Reprinted from the 1899 edition.

13. St. Clair Drake and Horace Cayton, *Black Metropolis*, (New York: Harcourt, Brace, Jovanovich, 1970).

14. Allison Davis, Burleigh B. Gardner and Mary Gardner, *Deep South*, (Chicago: University of Chicago Press, 1941).

15. Gunnar Myrdal, *An American Dilemma: The Negro Problem and Modern Democracy*, (New York: Harper and Bros., 1944).

16. James Weldon Johnson's *The Autobiography of an Ex-Coloured Man* (New York: Knopf, 1937); and the novels and short stories of Charles Chestnutt are excellent examples of this theme.

17. Harriette McAdoo, "Black Kinship," *Psychology Today*, (May, 1979), p. 67ff.

18. Andrew Billingsley, *Black Families in White America*, (Englewood Cliffs, NJ: Prentice-Hall, 1968).

19. Harold Cruse, *Crisis of the Negro Intellectual*, (New York: William Morrow, 1967).

20. Jesse S. Bernard, *Marriage and Family Among Negroes*, (Englewood Cliffs, NJ: Prentice-Hall, 1966).

21. G. Franklin Edwards, *The Negro Professional Class*, (Glencoe, IL: Free Press, 1959).

22. Although Drake and Cayton's observations were confined to Black Chicago, Osofsky noted a similar trend in Harlem. See Gilbert Osofsky, *Harlem: The Making of a Ghetto*, (New York: Harper and Row, 1965).

23. Thomas Sowell, "Leaders — or, 'Leaders'?" *The New York Times*, (April 12, 1979); "Led, and Misled," *The New York Times*, (April 13, 1979).

24. St. Clair Drake and Horace Cayton, *Black Metropolis*. (cited above).

25. E. F. Frazier, *Black Bourgeoisie: The Rise of a New Middle Class in*

the United States, (New York: Macmillan, 1962).

26. John Scanzoni, *The Black Family in Modern Society*, (Boston: Allyn and Bacon, 1971).

27. Sidney Kronus, *The Black Middle Class*, (Columbus, OH: Charles Merrill, 1971).

NOTES FOR CHAPTER IX

Ethcaste and the Political Economy of the AfricanAmerican Middleclass

1. Andrew Brimmer, "The Black Revolution and the Economic Future of Negroes in the United States," *The American Scholar*, vol. 38 (Autumn, 1969), pp. 630–631.

2. *Ibid.*, p. 632.

3. Talcott Parsons, "Equality and Inequality in Modern Society, or Social Stratification Revisited," *Sociological Inquiry*, vol. 40 (Spring, 1979), p. 14.

4. Ben J. Wattenberg and Richard M. Scammon, "Black Progress and Liberal Rhetoric," *Commentary*, vol. 55 (April, 1973), pp. 35–44.

5. Martin Kilson, "Black Politics: A New Power," *Dissent*, vol. 18 (August, 1971), p. 340.

6. *Ibid.*, p. 337.

7. Wade Nobles, "African Root and American Fruit: The Black Family," *Journal of Social and Behavioral Sciences*, (Spring, 1974), p. 58.

8. Andrea B. Rushing, "The Changing Same: Images of Black Women in Afro-American Poetry," *Black World*, vol. 18 (September, 1975).

9. Lloyd Hogan, "Blacks and the American Economy," *Current History*, vol. 67 (November, 1974), p. 222.

10. *Ibid.*, p. 222.

11. *Ibid.*, p. 223.

12. John U. Ogbu, *Minority Education and Caste*, (New York: Academic Press, 1978), p. 23.

13. *Ibid.*, pp. 150–152.

14. *Ibid.*, p. 172.

15. Paul M. Siegel, "On the Cost of Being a Negro," *Sociological Inquiry*, vol. 35 (Winter, 1965), p. 51–52.

16. Herrington J. Bryce, "Are Most Black Families in the Middle Class?" *The Black Scholar*, vol. 5 (February, 1974), pp. 32–37.

17. *Ibid.*, p. 33.

18. David Swinton, "The Black-White Income Gap: New Trend for the Worse," *Business and Society Review*, vol. 13 (Spring, 1975), pp. 72–75.

19. Herrington Bryce, "Are Most Black Families in the Middle Class?" *The Black Scholar*, vol. 5 (February, 1974), p. 34–35.

20. Richard Freeman, *Black Elite: The New Market for the Highly Educated Black Americans*, (New York: McGraw-Hill, 1976), p. xxx.

21. *Ibid.*, p. 16.

22. Sar Levitan, et. al., *Still a Dream: The Changing Status of Blacks Since 1960*, (Cambridge, MA: Harvard University Press, 1975), p. 32–33.

23. *Ibid.*, p. 53.

24. *Ibid.*, p. 164–165.

25. *Ibid.*, p. 191.

26. *Ibid.*, p. 192.

27. Reynolds Farley, "Racial Progress in the Last Two Decades: What Can We Determine About Who Benefitted and Why," Unpublished paper presented at the 1979 meeting of American Sociological Association, p. 31.

28. *Ibid.*, p. 31.

29. *Ibid.*, p. 31–32.

30. *Ibid.*, p. 32.

NOTES FOR CHAPTER X

Conclusion

1. Charles Keil, *Urban Blues*, (Chicago: University of Chicago Press, 1966), pp. 185–186.

2. *Ibid.*, p. 191.

3. *Ibid.*, p. 193.

4. Wade W. Nobles, "African Root and American Fruit: The Black Family," *Journal of Social and Behavioral Sciences*, (Spring, 1974), p. 61.

5. Gil Scott-Heron, Brian Jackson and The Midnight Band, *The First Minutes of a New Day*, Arista Records, Catalog No. 4030, New York. The song/poem was written by Bro. Bilal Sunni Ali, saxophonist.

INDEX